Bright Beginnings for BOYS

Engaging Young Boys in Active Literacy

INTERNATIONAL
Reading Association
800 BARKSDALE ROAD, PO BOX 8139
NEWARK, DE 19714-8139, USA
www.reading.org

Debby Zambo • **William G. Brozo**

Executive Editor, Books   Corinne M. Mooney
Developmental Editor   Charlene M. Nichols
Developmental Editor   Tori Mello Bachman
Developmental Editor   Stacey L. Reid
Editorial Production Manager   Shannon T. Fortner
Design and Composition Manager   Anette Schuetz

Project Editors   Tori Mello Bachman and Rebecca A. Stewart

Cover   Design and illustration by Monotype

Illustrations: On p. 44, detail from illustration in *David Goes to School* by David Shannon. Scholastic Inc./Blue Sky Press. © 1999 by David Shannon. On p. 79, © 2008 JupiterImages Corporation. On p. 129, © 2008 JupiterImages Corporation.

Library of Congress Cataloging-in-Publication Data
Zambo, Debby.
  Bright beginnings for boys : engaging young boys in active literacy / Debby Zambo, Bill Brozo.
      p. cm.
  Includes bibliographical references and index.
  ISBN 978-0-87207-683-9 (alk. paper)
  1. Reading (Early childhood) 2. Boys--Education (Early childhood) I. Brozo, William G. II. Title.
  LB1139.5.R43Z36 2008
  372.4081--dc22

                                                                                      2008043196

CONTENTS

Debby Zambo teaches courses in educational psychology in the College of Teacher Education and Leadership at Arizona State University (ASU) in Phoenix, USA. She has also taught graduate reading courses in best practices, essential elements, and differentiated instruction.

Before coming to ASU, Debby taught in public schools for 8½ years and at a private school for adolescents with learning needs for 1 year. Most of Debby's public school experience has been working with primary-grade children (grades K–3) with learning and emotional challenges. Her year working with adolescents broadened her perspective and allowed her to gain insight on the continued struggles that readers with disabilities face. Debby's PhD is in educational psychology in learning and instruction. Her dissertation was a qualitative study of the academic and emotional problems that adolescents with reading disabilities face.

Debby has one daughter, Nikki, who is a speech and language therapist. Debby's son-in-law, Perry, is so much a part of her family that she considers him her son; he sells computer software and plays in a rock band. Debby's husband, Ron, is an associate dean at ASU, and before taking that position Ron was a math educator.

When not teaching or writing, Debby enjoys the outdoors. She finds solitude in the desert and in watching birds and other wildlife.

If you would like to contact Debby, her e-mail address is debby.zambo @asu.edu.

William G. Brozo (Bill) is a Professor of Literacy in the Graduate School of Education at George Mason University in Fairfax, Virginia, USA. He earned his bachelor's degree from the University of North Carolina in Chapel Hill, USA, and his master's and doctorate from the University of South Carolina in Columbia, USA. He has taught reading and language arts in the Carolinas.

Bill is the author of numerous articles on literacy development for children and young adults. His research on literacy and masculinity has been ongoing for more than 10 years and has resulted in a previous International Reading Association (IRA) book titled *To Be a Boy, To Be a*

Reader: Engaging Teen and Preteen Boys in Active Literacy (2002). His other books include *Content Literacy for Today's Adolescents: Honoring Diversity and Building Competence* (with Michele L. Simpson, 2006, Merrill/Prentice Hall); *Principled Practices for Adolescent Literacy: A Framework for Instruction and Policy* (with Elizabeth G. Sturtevant, Fenice B. Boyd, Kathleen A. Hinchman, David W. Moore, and Donna E. Alvermann, 2005, Erlbaum); *50 Content Area Strategies for Adolescent Literacy* (with Douglas Fisher, Nancy Frey, and Gay Ivey, 2006, Merrill/Prentice Hall); *Supporting Content Area Literacy With Technology: Meeting the Needs of Diverse Learners* (with Kathleen Puckett, 2008, Allyn & Bacon); *Setting the Pace: A Speed, Comprehension, and Study Skills Program* (with Ronald V. Schmelzer and Deborah A. Andrews, 1984, Merrill); and *The Adolescent Literacy Inventory* (with Peter Afflerbach, 2009, Allyn & Bacon).

Bill serves on the editorial review board of the *Journal of Adolescent & Adult Literacy*, coauthors the "Content Literacy" column for *The Reading Teacher* with E. Sutton Flynt, and writes a regular column for *Thinking Classroom* titled "Strategic Moves." He is also a past member of IRA's Commission on Adolescent Literacy, current member of IRA's Adolescent Literacy Committee, and member of the PISA/PIRLS Task Force.

When not working, Bill and his wife, Carol, enjoy international travel, making music, and spending time outdoors with their standard poodle, Ted.

If you would like to contact Bill, his e-mail address is wbrozo@gmu.edu.

A while back, I called my 90-year-old aunt to ask about her experiences in one-room schools during the Depression. She said that teachers were often not well-trained, explaining, "I was in high school before I knew what a vowel was."

"But did kids learn to read," I persisted.

After a pause, "Yeah, the girls."

Teachers have known for years about boys' struggles with reading, their placement in various programs for extra help, their ingenious evasions, and the fake reading that for many becomes the norm. Reading, one of my college students explained, was a "girl thing." In an insidious way, this failure has been tolerated as natural. Boys are just too (pick your adjective) active, social, inattentive, nonverbal, media-obsessed to become serious readers of books. It's just the way things are.

In this thoughtful and hopeful book, Debby Zambo and William Brozo try to turn this ship around. They argue that the pleasure and moral guidance of literature should be open to everyone. At the same time they carefully lay out the developmental and physiological constraints that frequently cause boys to start slowly and experience difficulty early. This early experience of failure and frustration often turns a *difficulty* into an *identity* as boys decide they are just "not good at reading." As the reading expectations increase, a page of print can look like a minefield to an unsure reader. Rather than exposing weakness, boys can develop resistant attitudes ("this is stupid," "this is boring") and develop positive identities around the activities they do well. Some of these non-readers find a way, much later, to books they love. But some have abandoned reading for good. The less they read the farther they fall behind, and the farther behind they are, the less they want to expose their deficiencies. Increasingly, they are overmatched by the books they are expected to read.

This book is filled with teaching strategies, book suggestions—and insight. Two points stand out for me. The first concerns attention. When I was in school, this always seemed a moral category, a form of manners or respect—the failure to "pay attention" was a personal failing. The authors complicate this issue. They show that the inattentiveness of boys has developmental roots, and that teachers need strategies to capture and develop the attention of boys. These strategies might involve movement and performance, but most powerfully, they involve connecting to issues and interests that engage boys (see particularly the Motivation to Read Profile in Chapter 5). Readers of this book will be primed with ideas for attracting and developing the attention of boys to reading.

The second major idea is development. Boys often start more slowly. In a recent study of international achievement in reading, boys were behind girls at fourth grade in *every country surveyed*. But slow starts are not a predictor of long-term failure, so long as we can keep boys engaged in reading. No boy that I have ever met would not prefer to be a reader (though he might bluster that it doesn't matter). But by the same token none will voluntarily and regularly display a lack of competence—and be exposed as failing. How, then, can we help boys feel engaged and successful as they work through a developmental period where they may experience difficulty? That, I think, is a major educational question for our time. This book is a powerful and useful response to this question.

Thomas Newkirk
University of New Hampshire
Durham, USA

I t seems reasonable that a book about the power of literacy should begin with our own stories. Through our stories we introduce ourselves, explain our experiences with boys and literacy, and reveal our beliefs. Our stories begin in different locations, at different times, and with boys of different ages.

Bill's story is about adolescent boys and their literacy futures, and Debby's story is about young boys and their literacy beginnings. But despite these differences, our personal stories focus on boys and literacy and converge in the writing of this book. Bill's story, published in *To Be a Boy, To Be a Reader* (Brozo, 2002), begins with his experience as an inchoate English teacher in an all-black high school in rural South Carolina. As a new teacher, Bill faced a challenging situation. He was hit head-on with students who could not read the required anthology because they were below grade level in their reading skills. Bill's students knew they were failing and had given up on school, themselves, and on literacy. As a teacher of struggling readers, many of whom were boys, Bill realized he had to do something to make literacy accessible and meaningful to his students.

His solution was to throw out the required anthology and use Alice Childress's (1973) *A Hero Ain't Nothin' but a Sandwich*. Bill chose Childress's book because it was decodable by many of his students and he thought many of them would identify with 13-year-old Benjie, its main character, who was growing up in Harlem and facing many challenges. Choosing this story was a good idea, because it captured the attention of Bill's students and connected to their lives—and it began a transformation in Bill's class. It reacquainted many adolescent boys with the power and insight that literacy could bring to them. Behavior problems dropped, and students who had been disengaged and disinterested in reading began to ask for similar books. Using material at their level, and which appealed to their interests and needs, transformed many of Bill's students and made their literacy futures brighter.

This experience and countless others over the past 25 years convinced Bill that more must be done to reach struggling and detached adolescent male readers. Bill believes the way to accomplish this goal is to use literature with positive male characters, or archetypes. All cultures have stories with male characters, and these stories have been used for centuries to help boys face challenges and understand the honorable men they can become. Literature with positive male archetypes speaks to boys' interests and needs, and as Bill's experiences have shown, they can lead boys to become engaged readers.

Debby's story parallels Bill's in many ways, but instead of starting her career confronting the challenges of transforming the literacy futures of adolescents, she had to find ways to support the literacy beginnings of boys in kindergarten through grade 3. As a new teacher in the southern United States, Debby was hired to teach students with emotional and learning disabilities in a self-contained classroom. Just as Bill was hit head-on with disengaged adolescent male readers, Debby was hit head-on with young boys who were struggling with learning and with fitting their active bodies into classroom life. Just as Bill encountered adolescent boys who could not read the required anthology, Debby encountered young boys who were delayed in their oral language, phonemic awareness, and vocabulary.

Even though they were just starting their school careers, most of the boys in Debby's class were already behind. Debby knew that social and emotional skills are just as important to classroom success as are literacy skills. Each of Debby's students had already been labeled as a behavior problem. They all had learning difficulties and low self-esteem. Debby knew that once young boys get labeled, a self-fulfilling negative cycle often begins and they are unlikely ever to be successful in school. The boys in Debby's classroom easily could have become the adolescents in Bill's class. They could have continued to struggle with reading and remain distant to the many life-affirming and transformative experiences literacy could provide. Fortunately Debby, like Bill, saw the importance of positive male characters for young boys.

Debby used picture books with positive male characters to engage her students. Each male character spoke to the spirits of the young boys in Debby's class: Justin, an oppositional boy, loved *Willy the Wimp* (Browne, 1995); Peter, the optimist, begged to hear *Ronald Morgan Goes to Bat* (Giff, 1990); and Robert, the latchkey boy, adored the larger-than-life *Mike Fink* (Kellogg, 1992).

In 2007, Debby wrote an article for *The Reading Teacher* (Zambo, 2007) applying Bill's ideas from *To Be a Boy, To Be a Reader* to young boys. Before this, Bill, living in Virginia, and Debby, living in Arizona, had never met. By coincidence, one of Debby's colleagues knew Bill and had his e-mail address. Debby wanted to get his approval and insight on her work and sent the article to him. From this simple introduction we have come to write *Bright Beginnings for Boys: Engaging Young Boys in Active Literacy*. Our work with boys now adds up to more than 30 years of experience. We have worked with boys with different abilities, ethnicities, classes, and cultures, in varied settings. Our stories bring us together in a shared commitment to do more to reach struggling and unengaged boy readers—and this must start early, when boys are first beginning to understand what it means to be a boy and to be a reader. With this goal in mind, we have written this book to encourage positive literacy beginnings for young boys. Within these pages are the stories of many boys with whom we have worked as teachers, mentors, and friends. (All student and adult names in this book are pseudonyms.)

How This Book Is Organized

Teachers are the primary audience of this book—teachers in general education, teachers of students with special needs, and literacy coaches. We open with a foundational chapter that discusses our views about the state of boys and literacy today. Then we look at the developmental needs of young boys and continue on to explain how to create a literacy classroom to nurture those needs.

Because we recognize that not all reading occurs within school walls, we have taken care to include information and suggestions specifically for parents, caregivers, librarians, community workers, and anyone interested in the literacy beginnings and futures of boys. The final chapter of this book is dedicated specifically to helping teachers reach all these influential people in boy students' lives. A detailed description of each chapter is presented in the following paragraphs.

Chapter 1, "Nurturing Young Male Readers," addresses the many educational challenges boys face. When it comes to boys and literacy, a pattern of aliteracy or underachievement prevails, which is taking its toll on many boys even when they are just beginning to read. Although we recognize that they struggle because of a complex mixture of factors, we believe that helping boys become lifelong readers and good men is an imperative educational challenge. We pose that the way to do this is with entry-point texts that contain positive male role models. Boys intuitively want to understand the qualities of good men, and in Chapter 1 we introduce the eight positive values that we suggest using to frame boys' interests and needs.

Chapter 2, "Understanding the Physical and Cognitive Development of Young Boys," addresses developmental issues and explains the impact that they have on young boys' success in literacy and in school. Chapter 2 begins with an exploration of biological influences and how they set boys on a unique developmental trajectory, one that is different from that of girls. It also addresses gender differences from a social and cultural standpoint, for a deeper understanding of the complex interplay between biology and environment. In Chapter 2 we address one big difference in particular—attention—and what this means to boys' early literacy development. Understanding these differences can help you design the responsive instruction so many young boys need.

Chapter 3, "Understanding the Social and Emotional Development of Young Boys," opens with a look at boys' early school experiences and builds the case for why emphasis on academics in earlier grades contributes to young boys' struggling and getting turned off to school. But it does not have to be this way, and to help boys get off to a bright beginning we explain how using developmentally appropriate learning activities and understanding how boys feel about reading are key.

Chapter 4, "Creating a Classroom Climate That Meets the Special Needs of Young Boys," transforms research into practice by explaining how to differentiate instruction for boys. In this chapter, you will learn how to take the best practices and recommendations from IRA and make them boy-friendly. Phonemic awareness activities, sound cards, and Readers Theatre are introduced with a boy-friendly twist and with an eye on helping boys develop emotionally, morally, and socially. You also will learn strategies to use with boys who encounter difficulty focusing and sustaining their attention.

Chapter 5, "Matching Literacy Activities to Boys' Interests: Real-World Examples," provides strategies and practices you can use to help young boys have a bright start and become motivated to read. In order for instruction to be motivating to boys, you must first uncover all you can about their burgeoning identities and what they find interesting. With this information, you can craft learning experiences that boys will enjoy—and these segue to academic literacy and learning both in and out of school. Chapter 5 supplies several sound strategies to capture boys' interests and engage them with texts.

Chapter 6, "Making School–Home–Community Connections to Enhance the Literacy Development of Young Boys," extends ideas out of the classroom, because the literacy lives of young boys extend into the family and community. Chapter 6 begins with ideas for helping families to strengthen literacy, especially using fathers and brothers as role models. We extend this discussion to neighborhoods, focusing on the challenges that poverty brings and the ways community members can be actively involved in boys' literacy learning and success.

This book is rich in resources that help you to transform ideas in your classroom. Some features to help you do this include About a Boy vignettes, which contain stories of real boys in real literacy learning situations, and Learning From a Character boxes, which provide a picture book with a male character, the positive qualities he displays, and questions to spark your thinking about how to use the book to help boys develop positive traits. To make your search for good books for boys easier, the Appendix contains a lengthy annotated bibliography organized around the eight positive male values described in the Learning From a Character boxes throughout each chapter.

Bright Beginnings for Boys is written to help you assist boys in their journeys to lifelong literacy. It is written for boys who struggle and for boys who become victorious at cracking literacy's code. It is written to demonstrate the transformational effects responsive practices and good stories have on boys' engagement in reading and perceptions of who they are as young men. We have written this book to provide teachers, parents, mentors, librarians, coaches—and anyone interested in boys' literacy development—with the information and resources needed to ensure that every young boy has a successful literacy beginning and an increased chance to have a bright and healthy future.

ACKNOWLEDGMENTS

Debby thanks her husband, Ron, for the love, support, and encouragement he consistently provided as she worked on this book. She is also grateful to her children, Nikki and Perry, and to Michael Kelley and Debra Fisher, whose support came at crucial times. She also wishes to acknowledge the inspiration and guidance of her coauthor, Bill Brozo, whose book *To Be a Boy, To Be a Reader* brought them together for this project. Bill's guidance and support in writing this manuscript never wavered at any step along the way.

Bill expresses his warmest gratitude to his wife, Carol, and daughter, Hannah, who continue to give him the space to follow his bliss. And he wants to remember in this acknowledgment his late father, John Nelson Brozo, the best example he knows of a thoughtful reader and an honorable man.

Together, we want to express our deepest gratitude to Tori Bachman and Corinne Mooney of the International Reading Association, who believed in this project and supported it with their hard work and insight. We also want to recognize the IRA production staff, namely Rebecca Stewart, Shannon Fortner, Anette Schuetz, Lisa Kochel, and R. Lynn Swanson, whose attention to detail and aesthetic touch have made this book an inviting resource for teachers and parents alike.

Above all, we would like to thank all the young boys we have worked with over the years. Each one of them helped us understand the strength that boys have inside and the importance of literacy in their lives.

CHAPTER 1

Nurturing Young Male Readers

Here we begin to make the case for including special literacy supports for boys in the primary-level classroom. Boys will have great potential as active readers when they

- Are viewed as a resource with unique imaginations, abundant curiosity, and the capacity for self-regulation and sustained attention

- Become engaged readers because of responsive instruction that is sensitive to the achievement and motivational challenges they face

- Have, upon entering school, print encounters that capture their unique and burgeoning male imaginations and build strong literate identities

- Are exposed to books with positive male characters that serve as both entry points to reading and templates of honorable masculinity

We view boys optimistically. We believe that boys are creative, energetic, interested in learning, and interested in learning to read. We also believe in the resiliency of boys—but we recognize that only adults who take time to know and communicate with boys can foster resiliency. We believe that boys come to school with motivation, dreams, and desires, including the desire to read. Unfortunately, many boys enter school excited but soon lose their passion because they perceive the reading they are asked to complete as boring. They fail to connect with their literary interests and needs. Although it is true that many boys love school and become avid readers, it is too often the case that boys leave our schools feeling empty, burned out, and uninspired to read. Success motivates boys to try harder, and failure squelches motivation and drive. To understand the value of literacy in adolescents' lives, we must understand adolescents' lives. We must look back to the young boys they once were and to the education, culture, and society that either nurtured them or turned them away from literacy.

Why are so many boys indifferent—indeed, hostile—to the printed word? Throughout this book we examine reasons for boys' disaffection with and underachievement in reading, and we propose strategies and practices to engage young boys' unique imaginations and set them on the road to lifelong literacy. From our experience working with boys at various levels, we know we can make literacy better for boys and that understanding boys is key to doing that.

Boys' Underachievement in Literacy

The notion that girls read better than boys has become embedded in the popular consciousness. But it's not a myth. Indeed, it is indisputable that boys read less well than their female peers. For nearly a century, research in North America has confirmed a pattern of gender differences in reading achievement favoring females (Hedges & Nowell, 1995; Herman, 1975; Samuels, 1943).

Gates's (1961) landmark study of 13,000 U.S. elementary students produced the first hard evidence to buttress the popular idea of female reading superiority. Gates found that girls significantly outscored boys on tests of reading comprehension and vocabulary. Boys in elementary school through high school continue to score significantly lower than girls on standardized measures of reading achievement (Grigg, Daane, Jin, & Campbell, 2003) and writing achievement (Applebee, Langer, & Mullis, 1990; Fletcher, 2006). These same patterns favoring girls over boys in verbal ability have been documented in the United Kingdom (Skidmore, 2008), Canada (Canadian Council on Learning, 2007), Australia (Alloway, Freebody, Gilbert, & Muspratt, 2002), and more than 40 other countries around the globe (Mullis, Martin, Kennedy, & Foy, 2007; Organisation for Economic Co-operation and Development, 2001).

Since at least the early 1930s, there has been increasing evidence of boys far outnumbering girls in remedial reading classes (Holbrook, 1988). Today, we know that boys of all ages fail in reading more often than girls, dominating the rolls in corrective and remedial reading programs (Gambell & Hunter, 1999; Rutter et al., 2004). This same gender distribution holds true in programs for the learning disabled, emotionally impaired, and speech and language impaired (Shaywitz, 2003; Shaywitz, Shaywitz, Fletcher, & Escobar, 1990). Furthermore, boys are far more likely to be retained (Jimerson, 2001).

What is of particular concern is that the gender disparity in reading in favor of girls shows up right away in children's language development. By first grade, girls are already ahead of boys in reading and they continue to make greater progress in reading throughout the elementary years (National Center for Education Statistics [NCES], 2000). What is more, this pattern of superior female achievement on verbal tasks appears to be universal and worldwide. In reading, 9-year-old boys score an average of 5 points lower than girls, and this gap widens to 14 points by age 17 (U.S. Department of Education, 1994; NCES, 2001). When a boy fails in the early elementary grades, it is unlikely he will ever catch up (Gurian & Ballew, 2003). Test scores in reading and writing have implications for school success, but in classrooms across the United States many boys are not faring well, as the following facts reveal:

- In elementary school, boys receive more Ds and Fs than girls ("Boys and Books," 2006).

- Between the ages of 5 and 12, boys are 60% more likely to have been retained ("Boys and Books," 2006).

- Boys are referred to special education 4 to 1 over girls (NCES, 2000).

- Boys make up the majority of students in remedial classes (NCES, 2000).

- About 2% to 5% of American children between the ages of 6 and 16 are diagnosed with attention-deficit hyperactivity disorder (ADHD), and of these, 80% are boys (Rothenberger & Banaschewski, 2004).

- Of the estimated 500,000 to 1,000,000 students who annually drop out of U.S. schools, more than 55% are boys (NCES, 2000).

These statistics reveal the urgency to saving the educational, social, and emotional lives of boys. Kipnis (1999) notes that failure in reading tops the list of esteem-busting events in the lives of boys. From our experience with boys we know it does not have to be this way. Boys can be motivated to read and write when they encounter literature and assignments that pique interests and affirm their needs.

Many ask why we are concerned now about boys' underachievement in reading, because they have been underperforming relative to girls for decades. Some feel the timing of the current boy-advocacy climate in the United States comes as a response to several years of attention paid to girls' academic and social development, which most would agree has significantly increased educational opportunity and advancement for females (Sommers, 2000). In other words, many feel it's just "the boys' turn" (Weaver-Hightower, 2003). Furthermore, some wonder if the so-called "boy crisis" isn't media sensationalism rather than fact, designed to sell newspapers, magazines, and air time. After all, males continue to dominate corporate, institutional, and political life in the United States (Young & Brozo, 2001). So, what's the problem?

Throughout this book we argue that failing to meet the literacy needs of all young boys isn't so much a crisis as it is an imperative educational challenge. And it is also a challenge to address a glaring social justice issue, because those who struggle most to learn how to read—who dominate remedial reading classes and programs, and who will suffer disproportionately as adults if they fail to become competent readers—are boys of color.

Furthermore, concerns about boys' reading attitudes and achievement should not be framed exclusively by gender. Comparing boys and girls may direct our attention away from what must surely be the central reason for our advocacy—more responsive literacy instruction and interactions for *all* children. Boys need to be engaged and capable readers not solely to be as good as or better than girls, but to increase their educational, occupational, and civic opportunities, and above all, to become thoughtful and resourceful men.

Why All Boys Need to Become Active Readers

Standing in line recently to purchase movie tickets, Bill couldn't help notice a mom and her young son in front of him wrangling over the film the boy's mother had chosen for them. The boy squirmed and balked, importuning his mother to take him to see another movie, until she leaned down, grabbed his shoulders firmly, and looked him directly in the face, angrily uttering the following injunction that left Bill stunned: "You're going to see this with me so that later when your teachers ask you to read the book you won't have to because you already saw the movie!"

After the shock of these words wore off, Bill realized how reflexively we enable aliteracy for children, especially young boys who may already be reluctant readers. Aliteracy is choosing not to read, and we enable this proclivity among boys by filling their lives with visual and digital media, by allowing television to drone on throughout the after school and evening hours, and by taking boys to soccer and baseball practice but not to the library or bookstore. Far too many boys typify what it means to be aliterate. They avoid reading at all costs, doing only what's required of them for school (Ready, LoGerfo, Burkham, & Lee, 2005).

We assert that aliteracy in boys is a legacy of aliterate habits among the adults in their worlds. Boys will not be readers if their parents and guardians tell them to read but are not themselves models of active reading. Boys will not be readers if popular culture and media communicate in many direct and subtle ways that reading is not compatible with maleness and masculinity. And boys will not be readers if the adult men around them are not readers.

Failure to become an engaged and capable reader could deny a boy the opportunity for expanded selfhood, but it will surely limit additional educational and future employment options. This may be especially true for boys of color (Sum, Khatiwada, McLaughlin, & Tobar, 2007). In light of the ever-increasing demands placed on students to develop high levels of academic literacy needed to succeed in school and the workplace, the single most important tool boys will need is skillful reading ability. Skilled readers are effective problem solvers, flexible decision makers, and critical thinkers.

Sadly, too many boys in the elementary years are failing to develop adequate skills and strategies for comprehending academic text and communicating effectively using academic language. Although most elementary and middle school boys can read and comprehend text at basic levels, far fewer have demonstrated competencies on more challenging comprehension tasks (Donahue, Daane, & Grigg, 2003). These students are at risk of entering middle and high school with literacy levels too low to ensure success. Every day it is estimated that between three and seven thousand students drop out of U.S. schools—and it is not surprising that most are boys (Hammond, Linton, Smink, & Drew, 2007; Kids Count, 2004). Male youth who drop out are often doomed to grinding cycles of poverty, unemployment, and other economic, social, and personal setbacks (Sum et al., 2007; U.S. Chamber of Commerce, Center for Workforce Preparation, 2004). In a world driven by information and knowledge, boys' skill deficiencies will limit access to the full range of opportunities enjoyed by their more literate peers (Hofstetter, Sticht, & Hofstetter, 1999). Thus, the quality of literacy competence that boys develop as children will have a great impact on their competence in personal, occupational, and community life as adults (Brozo & Simpson, 2007).

Finally, the importance of helping boys in the first few years of school to develop self-regulation skills as readers cannot be overemphasized. Biological explanations of male underachievement in reading focus on differences in brain structure, hormone production, and maturation rates, which place young boys at greater risk of failure in school-related tasks (Kindlon & Thompson, 2000). Research has shown that the parts of the brain responsible for processing verbal information and permitting the exchange of information between hemispheres may not be as highly developed in young boys as it is in young girls (Kimura, 1992). Young boys also exhibit less development in regions of the brain responsible for impulse control, and in general, mature later than girls (Jacklin & Martin, 1999; Viadero, 2006).

These biological differences may manifest themselves in behavioral differences that make it difficult for boys to attend to text for extended periods of time and to sustain effort on literacy related tasks. The implications for teaching are clear—strategies and practices that build boys' self-awareness and self-regulation need to be woven into the daily curriculum and all phases of instruction, because reading skills and habits are formed early and lay the foundation for success academically, socially, morally, and psychologically. From our experience we have seen that when boys value reading they read more, achieve academically, do better on standardized tests, and have a richer, more meaningful life.

ABOUT A BOY

Recently, Bill was asked by a local school principal to observe a young man, Joshua, who was being referred by his teacher for special education placement. An average-size kindergartner with wide brown eyes, Joshua had become "increasingly difficult to control," according to his teacher, Ms. Thompson. His behavior was further characterized as impulsive, babyish, and aggressive. Joshua was also described as being unable to pay attention or stay on task. His report card for the first grading period was dismal, especially in the area of language and writing skills. With these concerns from Ms. Thompson—an intelligent and earnest teacher—firmly in mind, Bill spent the next week in her classroom watching Joshua and getting to know this young boy who seemed destined for a special learning environment.

What Bill saw during that week was startling and revelatory—and in no small way eerily reminiscent of his own experience in school. Plainly put, he saw a *boy*. He saw a boy filled with exuberance, often frustrated by having to sit still for extended periods of time, and constantly ready for gross motor activity. He saw a boy filled with curiosity but entirely lacking in classroom etiquette. He saw a boy quick to react to the stories read by Ms. Thompson, often blurting out feelings and opinions about characters and events without waiting to be called on. For instance, Joshua made it quite clear on several occasions which books he thought were for "sissies" or "girls" and asked repeatedly for books about baseball, karate, and trucks. Bill saw a boy who managed only crude approximations of people and scenery when asked to draw with a marker or crayon and who resented the finely fashioned dogs and children sketched in detail by his table partner, Kyley. And in Joshua, Bill saw himself as he must have been nearly half a century ago, before special education, before remedial reading, before decades of social upheaval leading to dramatic shifts in popular cultural perspectives of gender identity.

Bill's professional opinion of Joshua was asked as a favor. It would not have much to do with the ultimate decision about his future placement, which would be made by a diagnostician, a special education coordinator, Ms. Thompson, a counselor, and Joshua's parents. Before Bill wrote his report on his observations of Joshua, he talked with the special education teacher who would likely be receiving him. Not surprisingly, Joshua, if placed in her classroom, would be joining 18 other boys out of a total of 22 kindergarten, first-, and second-grade students on the special education teacher's caseload. And although there may be several benefits for Joshua in special education, such as a smaller class, more teacher attention, and individualized learning goals, there could also be the stigma that labels bring. Many boys, especially boys of color and boys who come from a lower socioeconomic class, get labeled early and never move outside of special education's grip.

On your own or with colleagues, brainstorm answers to the following questions about Joshua:

- Why are impulsive, exuberant young boys like Joshua so often destined for disappointment in school?
- What role could books with positive male values play in helping improve Joshua's ability to self-regulate his behavior?
- What could Joshua's teacher do to make instruction more responsive to his reading and learning needs that might eliminate the need for a special education placement for him?

Capturing Boys' Reading Imaginations

Because our culture sustains the myth that boys are not capable of high levels of reading engagement and achievement, reversing stereotypes of boys as weak readers and addressing the complex problems facing those who have been turned off by reading is, perhaps, our biggest challenge (Brozo, 2007). However, we who see potential in our male students discover ways of teaching and reaching them that are personally meaningful, culturally responsive, and capitalize on the resources they bring to the classroom (Alloway et al., 2002; Coles & Hall, 2002).

Viewing boys as a resource in the classroom holds great promise for helping them overcome a lack of motivation to read as well as literacy and learning difficulties (Martin, 2003). Young boys care about many things and have passions, hobbies, aspirations, and experiences rife with opportunities for genuine curricular links (Brozo, 2002). Exploring these links and inviting young boys to find connections between their lifeworlds and books and literacy practices in school may be the key to helping them find entry points to lifelong reading while reducing achievement disparities with their female peers (Brozo, 2004).

To capture boys' reading imaginations, teachers and parents need to discover their entry-point texts. This is the material that boys will find immediately gratifying and that will propel them to seek and read more. Once we have helped a young boy find an entry point, the chances improve that he will continue on a literate journey of lifelong reading. All of our literate journeys have humble beginnings. Yet these simple entry-point texts can possess big ideas and have profound influences on the direction and duration of the journey. That's why it is so important for all adults who interact with boys to support them in their search for a point of entry to reading. We assert in this book that the right kind of books—books with characters and themes that promote positive male values—will not only serve admirably as entry-point material for boys but also give them identity-affirming and even life-altering print experiences.

Living Vicariously Through Books

Introducing boys to picture books with positive male characters can be one way to accomplish this important goal because, when carefully selected, these books do three things. First, when boys step into a story they step inside others' lives. Rosenblatt (1978) expresses this idea nicely when she writes, "As the student shares through literacy the emotions and aspirations of other human beings he can gain heightened sensitivity to the needs and problems of those remote from him in temperament, in space, or in social environment" (p. 261). Learning about others shows boys the emotional value of texts, and when this happens, boys experience Rosenblatt's aesthetic response. They read for personal insight and enjoyment and respond to text in very personal ways. When boys do this they read more, get better at reading, and reap the many benefits literacy brings.

Second, feeling happy or sad about a character's behavior encourages boys to become aware of their feelings and learn to label how they feel. Emotional awareness helps boys realize when they are feeling anxious or sad. Self-awareness leads to self-control.

Third, stories help boys learn how to deal with strong emotions by letting them feel these emotions vicariously, a little at a time. Experiencing feelings in small doses helps boys get a bit of experience yet not be overwhelmed. This prepares boys to deal with similar complex emotions when they encounter them later.

Thinking about how characters feel allows boys to step outside themselves into someone else, to understand that others have feelings and perspectives that may differ from theirs. Piaget and Inhelder (2000) describe young children as egocentric because they often lack this ability. Instead of understanding the views of others, young children believe that everyone has the same viewpoint. The ability to understand various viewpoints is an individual ability that some boys are better at than others and is an important cognitive and emotional step. When children are able to think about others' thinking—when they recognize that other views exist—they begin to understand that friends and adults have other views and feelings. Coming to recognize the feelings of others leads to moral reasoning. Fortunately, there can be a reciprocal relationship between reading and emotional development. But too many boys never reach this transformational state. They learn how to decode text and read words out loud, but they never internalize meaning or become transformed by a good book or character.

ABOUT
A BOY

Many of the young boys in Sally Richardson's first-grade classroom own action figures like Spider-Man, GI Joe Extreme, and Captain Jack Sparrow. The boys know the characters' attributes and traits from the books they have read and the movies and cartoons they have seen. At recess, the boys often pretend they are these characters. Some sail on pirate ships, others drive fast cars, and others become embroiled in fierce battles. These boys often must be reprimanded for their rough-and-tumble play.

The boys' love for action and play goes beyond the outside world into their classroom. Many of the boys have expressed that they would rather play than read because "reading is for girls." However, their tone and actions change when they become interested in a book. The action and superhero books in the classroom library make them change their tone.

When the boys read these they do not think reading is "girly." They love to read and talk about these books. Sally feels a bit exasperated because the boys seem interested in nothing else.

- Are the boys in Sally's class similar to the boys in your classroom?
- What should Sally do about the boys' choices?
- Do you feel that superheroes are poor role models?
- How could you use boys' love for action and superheroes to enhance boys' literacy skills?
- Would it be possible to use superheroes to help boys discover positive images of who they are and who they can become?

Choosing Books of Interest

One misconception that may affect book choice for boys is that they only like to read nonfiction books and do not like storybooks. Although there is no doubt that informative books about machines, animals, and sports are often high on boys' reading lists, the research of Chapman, Filipenko, McTavish, and Shapiro (2007), conducted in first-grade classrooms in Canada, indicates that boys like storybooks as much as they like information texts. However, something interesting occurred when these researchers asked boys to tell them the type of books their peers preferred. Even though they themselves preferred storybooks, they said that other boys would prefer information books and girls would prefer storybooks. Chapman et al. believe that the discrepancy between boys' own preferences and their perceptions of what other children would enjoy indicates that beliefs are socially constructed. The boys in this study said they were drawn to books for their visual appeal, humor, and merit. These findings align with those of Smith and Wilhelm (2002, 2006), who observe that it is not the text type that engages boys but its features. Beautiful illustrations and interesting topics appeal to boys and encourage them to read.

Learning From Positive Models

Books that appeal to boys for their interesting features can also be selected because they promote values worth imitating and characters worth modeling. The idea of using models to teach is not new. It comes from the work of Bandura, Ross, and Ross (1963), who, more than 40 years ago, discovered that children learn aggression from models. In their experiments these researchers beat and spoke harshly to a doll, and when children saw this they did the same. Children picked up aggressive behaviors simply by watching someone being aggressive, and they transferred this behavior to new situations. In a later experiment, Bandura (1965) also found children imitate aggression not only from live models but also from models they see on television. When children see television characters being rewarded for aggression they are more likely to act this way. Bandura and his colleagues (1963, 1965) discovered that simple observation, either from a live or televised model, is a powerful way to learn. We can use these ideas by carefully choosing models and using them effectively.

For boys to learn and retain information from a model, the model must capture the boys' attention. The model must be attractive, colorful, and dramatic; be doing something interesting; and have a certain prestige or level of competency. In other words, if a model is engaging and doing something of interest, it is more likely that boys will pay attention to it and learn.

Since Bandura et al.'s (1963) time the battle over models in the media has raged on. Many authors, researchers, psychologists, psychiatrists, and doctors believe that during the past 50 years cultures around the world have begun legitimatizing narcissism and promoting an unrealistic image of manhood. These include the American gangster culture, He-Man dolls, violent video games, and television shows that depict men killing for pleasure and without care. Boys learn core values from models. Unfortunately, close bonding and attachment with positive male models is often weak or nonexistent for many boys today. For far too many boys, opportunities to participate in positive rituals and rites of passage have been replaced by negative ones like bullying and joining gangs.

Identifying With Characters

Boys must be able to identify with characters in order to engage with texts. Boys want stories with grit and glory. Comprehending the rules of masculinity and trying to live up to them is part of every boy's search for self. Using literature that contains positive male characters can help boys gain this insight (Brozo & Schmelzer, 1997), and we offer more on this idea later in this chapter and throughout the book.

Sipe (2001) notes that boys resist reading if they fail to find characters like themselves in the stories they read. Resistance can take many forms, from outright refusal to read to passively sitting and doing nothing during reading time. Boys who resist reading invest little time in it and lose many opportunities to develop important literacy skills (Martin & Halverson, 1987; Stanovich, 1986; Stanovich & Cunningham, 1992). When boys resist reading they miss out on the identity-affirming experiences that books have to offer (Brozo, 2002). In other words, although literacy is related to academic success and academic success offers boys more career and life options (Tyre, 2006), literacy also can offer positive images of who boys are and who they can become.

Furthermore, being able to form an image of what one is reading is an important comprehension skill. The unique thing about picture books is that they help the mind dually code information, and this increases the likelihood of story recall (Sadoski & Paivio, 2000). Sipe (2001) calls the text–picture relationship synergistic, because it is neither the text nor the illustration that creates understanding. It is a combination of the two.

When boys see boys like themselves in illustrations and can identify with a character's story they come to see reading as insightful and captivating. Stipek and Seal (2001) note that children put forth more effort when they find learning to be captivating and exciting. Brozo (2002) relates that when students read interesting and enjoyable material they recall more facts and remember them for longer periods of time. Reading books with positive male characters helps young boys hear a good story and see what positive character traits look like within the context of a character's life.

The Power of Children's Books With Positive Male Values

It's difficult for those of us who have made reading an integral part of our identities to explain the pleasures and benefits to disaffected boys. We could impress upon them that reading competence can translate into economic and professional advantage, but there's more to it than that. Regular print encounters can also enlarge a boy's sense of self. Reading can allow young men to transcend time and place, to take flights of imagination, to meet and interact with other people and cultures, and to confront new challenges. And when the book ends and a boy returns from his journey of imagination, he will find himself a changed person with new ideas, sympathies, and understandings. As boys become better, more thoughtful readers they may become better and more thoughtful men.

Children's books of all genres can imbue young boys with images and models of positive male values while simultaneously capturing their imaginations with print and engaging them as readers. Books with positive male values can help boys envision ways of being male that are different from the stereotypical images of masculinity saturating popular media and culture (Kipnis, 1999; Renold, 2004). Regular exposure to these books can also help boys incorporate thoughtful and competent reading into their burgeoning male identities (Brozo, 2002; Zambo, 2007).

From the lengthy list of positive values young boys need to read about and engage in learning experiences around (cf. Farrer, 2000), we distilled eight for consideration in this book. These eight represent a range of values and behaviors that are important and worthy of emulation (Boylan & Donohue, 2003; Kidder, 1994; Porpora, 2001). Books representing all eight positive male values are showcased in Learning From a Character boxes throughout the book. The books described in these boxes do not necessarily refer to specific ideas and strategies in the chapters. Instead, they are meant to serve as reminders of the kinds of texts that will capture boys' imaginations because of their lively prose, interesting stories and topics, and above all their good male characters. All the books featured in the Learning From a Character boxes are also included in the Appendix, Books That Demonstrate Positive Values for Boys, which lists numerous books with positive male characters, organized by the values they showcase. In the following pages, we describe each value and demonstrate how it is given expression in a children's book admirably suited for showing young boys positive images of boyhood and masculinity.

Cooperation

All young boys can relate to the pleasurable feelings that have resulted when they wanted or needed cooperation and someone cooperated with them. Young boys should be brought to see that cooperation is not a zero-sum game in which one person's success is at the expense or exclusion of others. Instead, boys need to recognize that the aim of cooperation is a mutually beneficial result—that by working together everyone's situations and lives improve, and that cooperation is everyone's responsibility.

When boys work together with other children and adults toward a common goal, they are cooperating. To do so effectively requires a boy to value everyone's contribution and to have respect for his collaborators. Young boys should also be helped to play both the leader and the follower in cooperative situations.

LEARNING ABOUT COOPERATION FROM A PICTURE BOOK CHARACTER

Elephant on My Roof (Harris, 2006)
Lani has a problem—there's an elephant on his roof. Once he realizes he can't get the elephant off on his own, he turns to the people in his village for help. With the cooperation of the villagers, Lani is successful in dislodging the elephant. In gratitude, he and the elephant reciprocate by lending a hand to the fisherman, some children, and an old woman. The villagers show their appreciation for their new friend by throwing a surprise party. The narrative concludes with Lani and the elephant back on the roof, but Lani now knows he can count on his fellow villagers to lend a helping hand.

Courage

Movies and television can fill boys' heads with visions of courage that involve daring feats of agility and demonstrations of physical prowess. To counter these stereotypes, boys need to recognize that to act courageously means doing the right thing when it's easier to do otherwise, even if it means being ridiculed. For example, boys who are shy should understand that to be courageous they do not have to be louder or more assertive. Quiet courage—the courage to say no to something that is wrong, the courage to say hello to a child who has no friends—is as important a form of courage as any other. For young boys, usually all acts of courage involve overcoming a thumping heart and a mind full of uncertainty. This is especially true of moral courage, which requires taking a stand against others who are doing something wrong, telling the truth when a lie is easier, and championing an unpopular but worthy cause.

LEARNING ABOUT COURAGE FROM A PICTURE BOOK CHARACTER

More Than Anything Else (Bradby, 1995)

In this fictionalized story about the life of young Booker T. Washington we see the true embodiment of courage. From his home in a West Virginia settlement after emancipation, 9-year-old Booker travels by lantern light to the salt works, where he labors from dawn till dusk. In town, the young Booker sees a man reading aloud from a newspaper, and his imagination is captured by the magic of print. In a time when few former slaves could read, Booker's overwhelming desire is to possess this wonderful knowledge and pass it on to others. With dedication Booker does his back-breaking job every day, and although he's hungry and sore he musters the courage to pursue his dream to become a reader. When other children are playing he studies the letters in the alphabet book his mother has given him as a present. Booker seeks the help of the newspaper man when he is feeling frustrated. The story concludes with an excited Booker using the alphabet book to learn how to write his name.

Generosity

Generosity is a marvelous trait to see in boys and men, and it comes in many forms. Some men who are exceedingly privileged, such as George Soros and Bill Gates, give great sums to worthy causes around the globe. But small gestures of giving that occur day-to-day are no less significant, such as volunteering time at a senior citizens' center or day care, donating clothing and food to homeless shelters, or giving a classmate lunch money because he forgot his.

Boys in the United States grow up in a capitalistic society that too often teaches that what they can acquire and own is more important than what they have to offer. Boys need to find ways of incorporating the habit of generosity into their developing masculine identities. The goal is to give boys a sense of joy in the act of giving, rather than giving only so they might get something in return.

LEARNING ABOUT GENEROSITY FROM A PICTURE BOOK CHARACTER

Sam and the Lucky Money (Chinn, 1997)

As part of the traditional Chinese New Year celebration, Sam receives four bright red envelopes decorated with shiny gold emblems, each containing a dollar. On his way to Chinatown with his mother, he has big ideas about how to spend the money. His mood changes, however, when he realizes that the "lucky money" won't buy as much as he had hoped. Then Sam stumbles upon a homeless man in the street and realizes there is something more important he could do with his four dollars than buying things for himself. In an act of pure generosity, Sam gives his money to the barefoot stranger. Sam's thoughtful manner demonstrates the important message that it is better to give than to receive.

Honesty

A boy who is honest is true to himself and to others. A young man can be said to be honest when there are no contradictions in what he thinks, says, and does. This means that honesty requires a boy to know what is right and appropriate when he is acting alone and when he interacts with others. With honesty, there is no hypocrisy or artificiality to create mistrust in the minds and lives of others. Above all, boys should come to understand that to be honest makes for a life of integrity.

LEARNING ABOUT HONESTY FROM A PICTURE BOOK CHARACTER

The Empty Pot (Demi, 1996)

Ping loves flowers and has a green thumb. So when the Chinese emperor announces that he will be succeeded by the child who can grow the most beautiful flowers from the seeds the emperor distributes, Ping is thrilled. Ping's joy turns to sadness, though, when after months of attention, the emperor's seed will not grow. Instead of replacing the seeds with his own so as to grow beautiful blossoms that might entitle him to the crown, Ping—in the ultimate expression of honesty—appears before the emperor holding only an empty pot. Although the emperor has received many pretty flowers from other children, he chooses Ping, revealing that the seeds he gave him had been cooked and could not grow. Thus, Ping shows himself to be a person whose honest values make him a worthy heir to the emperor.

Perseverance

Perseverance is challenging for young boys. It often seems easier to give up when the going gets tough. A culture of instant gratification reinforces the idea that if something doesn't come quickly and easily, it's OK to move on to something else that will. And yet, boys who excel on the basketball court or the soccer, baseball, or football field, who become skillful at computer games, or who master a musical instrument well enough to join a band have needed to learn perseverance. Boys should recognize that perseverance is needed to deal with most of life's challenges, from learning a difficult concept in science to making new friends. Boys can also be brought to see that perseverance can help them overcome barriers to achieving their goals.

LEARNING ABOUT PERSEVERANCE FROM A PICTURE BOOK CHARACTER

Leonardo's Dream (de Beer, 2004)
Leonardo the penguin has a dream that one day he will fly, much like his namesake from the 1500s. Despite the doubts of his fellow penguins, Leonardo is determined to make his dream a reality. Eventually, an albatross friend agrees to serve as a model of successful flight and allows Leonardo to create large, strap-on wings in the shape of albatross wings. Although his maiden flight results in a crash, lucky Leonardo falls into a snow bank where he finds a biplane. The wise penguin studies the plane's instruction manual, and with the albatross as copilot takes his fellow penguins for a ride. Leonardo finally discovers the joy of "flying." Leonardo's perseverance pays off as he also learns to experience flying underwater with his own wings.

Respectfulness

A respectful boy is considerate of, among other things, the rights, needs, feelings, beliefs, and opinions of other people. When teaching boys to be respectful, it is important that they understand that other people's qualities are not necessarily better or worse than their own, just different. We should not assume that young boys understand what it means to be respectful in general, and certainly they need opportunities to learn about what it means to be respectful in specific situations. A focus on being respectful requires us to think carefully about resources and learning experiences that will engage boys and teach them good lessons about behavior.

LEARNING ABOUT RESPECTFULNESS FROM A PICTURE BOOK CHARACTER

Alley Oops (Levy, 2005)

J.J., the main character in *Alley Oops*, has been bullying an overweight boy named Patrick, calling him Pig-Pen and Porky. Patrick's father has asked J.J.'s father, Mr. Jax, to speak to his son because Patrick is having nightmares and is afraid to come to school. J.J.'s dad insists that they sit down for a talk. When J.J. says he is just having fun, Mr. Jax relates a story of his own bullying when he was J.J.'s age. He tells J.J. how recently he met that same boy, who had now become a police officer. Mr. Jax regretted his bullying when the officer told him of the long-lasting effects his taunting words had had on him. Mr. Jax's discussion influences J.J. to change his behavior, and he begins a friendship with Patrick.

Responsibility

When a boy chooses to behave responsibly, he does the following three things:

1. Makes sure he is aware of consequences that accompany each choice or action

2. Considers the impact the choice or action will have on others

3. Accepts the consequences as part of making the choice or taking the action

Furthermore, the responsibility to do something often means that a boy is obliged to make a certain choice or to take a certain action. For example, schools make rules that endorse specific behaviors, such as wearing clothing that does not display gang insignia. In addition, an individual boy may have personal obligations, such as choosing to recycle his lunch wrappers and packaging. No young boy—or any person for that matter—acts or chooses responsibly in every situation; we teachers can help boys envision responsibility and behave responsibly with books and lessons that help them make good choices not induced by threat of punishment.

LEARNING ABOUT RESPONSIBILITY FROM A PICTURE BOOK CHARACTER

Just a Dream (Van Allsburg, 2002)
Walter is a boy who imagines the future as a time of wonderful inventions like tiny personal airplanes and robots that do all of your work for you. In his everyday world, however, Walter is a litterbug who refuses to sort the trash for recycling and thinks it's silly that the girl next door receives a small tree for her birthday. Everything changes when Walter has a dream of a polluted and overcrowded future. Instead of fun, effort-saving contraptions, Walter sees only endless streets covered in mounds of trash, including his own street. He sees forests that have been reduced to stumps and an industrial wasteland with spewing smokestacks. Walter's nightmare helps him understand the importance of taking the responsibility to care for the environment. He begins sorting trash for recycling and plants a tree like his neighbor does.

Tolerance

Young boys should be helped to appreciate that tolerance does not mean conceding or being indifferent, but is a form of respect that comes from understanding. Although young boys may find it difficult to be patient, they are not inherently intolerant. Nonetheless, intolerance can be imprinted on a young boy's psyche if he is surrounded by adults who have fear and ignorance of individuals different from themselves. We need to provide boys with a vision of what the world would be like if everyone was tolerant, if everyone tried to understand and respect one another. Boys can be shown how to maintain self-respect while extending dignity and respect to others. They can learn to see each individual as unique, detached from stereotypes of nationality, religion, race, and culture. Teaching tolerance to boys as children will better prepare them for honorable adulthood in our increasingly complex, pluralistic, and global society.

LEARNING ABOUT TOLERANCE FROM A PICTURE BOOK CHARACTER

Teammates (Golenback, 1992)

When Jackie Robinson first broke into baseball's major league in 1947, racist epithets were hurled at him on and off the field, he was forced to endure the indignity of segregated hotels and restaurants, and he regularly faced death threats for simply taking his position on the field. In the midst of it all, his teammate "Pee Wee" Reese did something that remains one of the bright moments of that historic season: Between plays, he walked over to Jackie and put his arm around him, saying, "Don't let them get to you. It's going to be all right." With that simple yet powerful act, Jackie's teammate set an example for the other players and the fans. And while the racial slurs and death threats didn't end, Pee Wee demonstrated to all that intolerance toward Jackie was no longer acceptable—and that Jackie would henceforth be considered a full member of the Dodgers baseball family.

In her book on the brain and reading, Wolf (2007) notes that reading is more than fluency, more than saying the words on a page. We agree, and believe that even though young boys are just developing their reading skills they need to go beyond decoding and remembering from a given text. Boys must identify with characters, feel what they feel, and in the process learn more about life and themselves. If the reading we ask boys to do does not provide this transcendent leap it is just another skill learned in school. Wolf captures this nicely by stating the following:

> The end of reading development doesn't exist; the unending story of reading moves ever forward, leaving the eye, the tongue, the word, the author for a new place from which the truth breaks forth, fresh and green, changing the brain and the reader every time. (p. 162)

We believe reading can lead boys to a positive vision of manhood—a vision that embraces empathy, tolerance, and being a good friend. Characters who reveal these traits lead boys to understand themselves. But just as important as self-awareness is the fact that books with positive male characters can lead boys to the power and many benefits reading brings to one's life.

QUESTIONS FOR DISCUSSION

- Do the facts about boys' underachievement in reading match your own and your colleagues' experiences with boys?

- What factors in your school and community may be contributing to boys' depressed literacy achievement? How might you and your colleagues learn more about these factors?

- What was your entry point to literacy? Have you been fortunate enough to help young male readers find their own entry points to active literacy? Which books or reading material made the difference?

- Reflect on the boys you teach. Which positive values do the boys exhibit? Which values would you like to see the boys exhibit to a greater extent? How might this be achieved through picture books?

- Think about a picture book or other reading material you use in your classroom. Are there identifiable positive male values in the material? Which ones? How can these values be given more prominence in your instruction?

CHAPTER 2

Understanding the Physical and Cognitive Development of Young Boys

I n this chapter we focus on the influences that physical and cognitive development have on the learning and literacy of young boys. Boys develop as readers when their

- Biological variations in language, vision, and hearing are understood
- Love for play and movement are incorporated into their learning of literacy
- Attention differences and needs are honored as part of who they are
- Status as "digital natives" and 21st-century learners is built upon

Sex Differences in Language Development and Literacy Learning

Language is the foundation of reading and the way we communicate and connect with others. Language consists of words that can be written, signed, or spoken, and the rules people use to vary and combine these words (Santrock, 2008). In order to communicate effectively, children must understand how sounds are combined into words, the meaning of words, and the conventions for carrying on a conversation in a socially acceptable way. The following speech abilities need to be learned and practiced (American Speech-Language-Hearing Association, 1993):

- Receptive language—one aspect of which is phonology, or the ability to distinguish among the smallest sound units in a word
- Fluency—smooth oral speech or typical speech rhythm problems (such as stuttering)
- Syntax—the ability to produce correct word order
- Semantics—the interpretation of words with multiple meanings and consistent use of the precise meanings of words

- Pragmatics—the rules of language, like knowing when to stop talking to give another child a turn

Between the ages of 2 and 6 children make rapid advances in acquiring new words, understanding syntax, and constructing narratives (Thompson, McKerchar, & Dancho, 2004), yet they often overregularize language rules (*foots* instead of *feet*), mix up word order (*me went with*), and sometimes have difficulty pronouncing phonemes and blends (*r, th, sl, dr*). Reading is built on language and developing expressive language is extremely important for reading and getting one's needs met. Young boys who have difficulty expressing themselves often become frustrated and lose their self-respect when others make fun of them. The story of Rodney Rat in the following Learning From a Character box is a good way to introduce your students to speech differences and to respectfulness.

LEARNING ABOUT RESPECTFULNESS FROM A PICTURE BOOK CHARACTER

Hooway for Wodney Wat (Lester, 1999)

In the story *Hooway for Wodney Wat*, a rat named Rodney has a difficult time articulating the letter *r*, which causes all sorts of trouble for a rodent boy. His classmates taunt him so mercilessly that Rodney becomes the shyest rodent in his class. Things only get worse for Rodney when a bully named Camilla Capybara moves in. Camilla is bigger, bossier, and meaner than any of the other children. Rodney is terrified to speak in front of her, but he has to face his fears when selected to lead a game of Simon Says. In the end, Rodney gains the respect of his classmates when he rids the school of Camilla.

- What might you do if a boy in your classroom consistently omits phonemes, stutters, or lacks the pragmatics of speech?

- What might you do to enhance the literacy skills of boys with oral language difficulties?

- When you teach about differences, do you go beyond the surface?

- How do you help all the boys in your classroom gain the respect they deserve?

Language difficulties are different from language differences, but they both can cause embarrassment and shame. Helping boys respect others whose native language is not English, or who have oral language problems like Rodney, provides them with insight that will last a lifetime. Boys show respect when they consider the needs, rights, feelings, and beliefs of others. Boys learn respect by interacting with others, including children who are different, and they learn respect from the models in their world.

- What do you as a teacher do to bring individuals with differences into your classroom?

- How might an adult who has learned to overcome a speech barrier become a role model for the boys in your classroom? Envision how you can get this started and then take the first steps.

- If you teach children with disabilities, do you bring in role models who can speak directly about their experiences and talk about how they have gained respect?

Rodney Rat's story (Lester, 1999) reveals how difficult school can be for boys with expressive language problems. Not only do the boys' classmates ridicule them, but also it is likely that they will develop reading problems without intervention and support. If a boy cannot articulate sounds, it is unlikely that he will be able to connect the beginning sound of /r/ to the letter *r*. Therefore, boys with articulation problems have a difficult time making the speech-to-print connection, which has implications for early literacy acquisition and future reading progress (Tallal, 2003).

Articulation difficulties and dysfluent speech, or stuttering, are the two most common speech problems found in schools today, and it is often in preschool where these problems are revealed (James, 2007). Speech problems affect boys six times more often than girls, and because reading is based on oral language, speech problems often cause boys to fall behind in reading and subsequently get labeled with a learning disability more often than girls (The National Assessment of Educational Progress, 2004). Two thirds of all students in special education are boys (Shaywitz, 2003). If a boy has trouble getting words out, is difficult to understand, or omits sounds, he may need to be screened by the school nurse or a speech therapist. Recent advances in treatments are helping children who stutter to make great strides (Dodd & Bradford, 2000), and early intervention that is targeted, structured, and persistent can help boys with language difficulties.

Teachers of students with special needs are often called on to make observations of children before they get referred, and Debby did this as part of her job. One particular observation of José, a special little boy with big brown eyes and long dark hair, stands out in her mind. Debby found the following information in José's file: José, age 6, lived in a bilingual family. His parents immigrated to the United States from Mexico four years prior (when José was 2). José had two siblings, and his father and mother both worked at a local fast food restaurant. The family did not qualify for public assistance and there was little extra money for health care, but José had chronic ear infections. Throughout his preschool experience there were notes of ear infections that were so bad José's teacher had to call his parents to pick him up because he was in so much pain. Now that he was in first grade, several academic challenges were becoming evident. José's speech was not clear. He deleted phonemes from the beginning of words or substituted wrong sounds (e.g., *fig* for *pig*). Furthermore, José could not yet recite the alphabet, and he was having a difficult time making the speech-to-print connection. José's teacher believed he was very immature and did not have the attention, memory, or motivation needed to succeed in second grade. José was not achieving early childhood standards or benchmarks.

During the observation, Debby saw José sitting with his classmates trying to participate but having difficulty expressing his ideas. When the class recited chants and poems José chimed in, but his contributions were difficult to understand. However, a most curious thing occurred when Mrs. Smithwik, his teacher, read *Smash! Crash!* (Scieszka, Shannon, Long, & Gordon, 2008) to the class—José really came alive! He knew all about Hook, Ladder Lucy, and Pumper Pa and made text-to-world connections as he spoke about the fire truck he sees speeding by his house.

On your own or with colleagues, brainstorm answers to the following questions about José:

- What is going on with José?
- Does he have a language disability? Or might a hearing problem be hampering his literacy learning?
- What role might being a learner of English play?
- What role is this particular book playing in José's literacy development?
- What strategies could José's teacher use to help him make academic gains?

New Insights From Neuroscience

Physical development includes development of the body along with that all-important organ boys use when they read, dream, and communicate—the brain. Researchers are beginning to understand the chemistry and biology of brain development, and with new imaging techniques they are beginning to get a clearer picture of the brain's smallest parts—neurons, or brain cells. Researchers are now able to see the structures neurons form, track the physical and functional changes of these structures, and observe how these structures are used when a task, like reading, is performed. This information has added to our understanding of language and literacy, especially when sciences converge. Researchers from neuroscience, genetics, biology, and other fields are working together to reveal many new and exciting findings that we can use, especially when it comes to language and literacy (James, 2007). We are beginning to understand how the brain processes and organizes information as it reads and what happens when things go wrong.

Many teachers are turning to brain research for insight on language and reading development. We, too, are excited about these findings and have included many in this section. But we also want to make our readers aware that we take a cautious view, because some findings have been taken out of context and used to make broad generalities. No matter how enthusiastic we get about new findings from neuroscience we, as educators, must remember that these results are correlational and not causal. This means that even though research finds a relationship there is no clear or 100% indication that one causes the other. When it comes to a complex organ like the brain and complex issues like reading and gender, there are no definitive answers but there are useful advances. For example, science now tells us that hormonal influences during gestation may be the reason for boys' and girls' varied cognitive, social, emotional, and behavioral styles (Brizendine, 2006). In other words, girls and boys play differently, learn differently, and have different language and literacy needs because of brain structure and body chemistry.

Another example of new insight comes from electroencephalograms (EEGs). EEGs conducted on 3- and 4-year-old children show a dramatic upsurge of connectivity in language areas. Thanks to neuroscience, we now know that young children make rapid advances in acquiring new words, understanding syntax, and constructing narratives because neurons in Broca's area, a brain structure responsible for expressive language, and Wernicke's area, an area responsible for understanding speech, increase in both connectivity and activity at this time. This is why caregivers witness a vocabulary explosion in their children around the age of 2 (Cole, Martin, Peeke, Seroczynski, & Fier, 1999).

Children who spoke approximately 900 words when they were 2 increase the number of words they use to 2,500–3,000 words by the time they are 5. When children enter school and learn to read, they learn even more words because reading is a major source of vocabulary development in the early years. By the time children are 6, they typically know 8,000–14,000 words because of brain development (Clark, 1993). Vocabularies and language abilities typically increase as children develop, and these vary between boys and girls. Some boys do not express themselves in long sentences, but rely instead on body language and a few chosen words, like the boys in *Yo! Yes?* (Raschka, 1993) in the following Learning From a Character box. There are distinct ways that boys speak and communicate and sometimes those ways can help teach boys about cooperation.

LEARNING ABOUT COOPERATION FROM A PICTURE BOOK CHARACTER

Yo! Yes? (Raschka, 1993)

In the Book *Yo! Yes?* two boys become friends with very few words between them. Yet from their short sentences, subtle punctuation hints, and body posture the boys manage to understand each other.

- What are the verbal abilities of the boys in your classroom?
- How do they communicate with each other?
- How do they express their ideas and needs? How tolerant and encouraging are you to these ways of expression?

Yo! Yes? helps us understand boys' speech patterns, and it can also be used to help boys learn about cooperation. The story begins with two boys standing on opposite sides of the page. Their greeting is, "Yo! Yes?" and their body language may be interpreted as either threatening or inviting. On pages 2–3 they continue their questions with "Who, me?" and this breaks the ice. One boy asks, "What's up?" and the other reveals he has no friends. This begins a line of communication with few words, ending with the idea that they should cooperate and become friends. Agreement is reached, and they walk off together.

In many schools and classrooms competition is the norm. Children compete against one another on standardized tests, teacher-made assessments, and through other means. Although boys enjoy mild competition, it can be carried to an extreme. If boys are always trying to outdo others, little will be gained. Learning merely to compete promotes temporary recall and simple rote skills. It does not lead to a lifetime of remembering and the joy of co-constructing information with friends. Young boys need to recognize that cooperation leads to a win–win situation—that by working together, everyone's recall of information and life improves.

- How do you promote cooperation among the boys and girls in your classroom?

- Do you allow children to cooperate, work together, and co-construct knowledge?

- Do you allow diverse opinions, positions, and feelings to be expressed without fear of being put down?

- What strategies and books do you use to help boys learn how to cooperate with their peers?

- What activities do you ask children to do that require cooperation and community support?

Boys use fewer words to get their message across, and neuroscience is providing some insight as to why. Functional magnetic resonance imaging (fMRI) scans show girls have 11% more neurons in brain areas devoted to language than do boys (Brizendine, 2006; Harasty, Double, Halliday, Kril, & McRitchie, 1997). Teachers of young children attest that, even as toddlers, girls often have larger vocabularies than boys. Sax (2007) has noted that the language areas in the brains of many 5-year-old boys look like the language areas of the average 3½-year-old girl. Having more neural density in key language areas provides an explanation as to why—even when they are young—girls, on average, tend to be more verbal than boys. This can have implications for classroom expectations, especially when it comes to oral response and writing.

Another neural difference that has consequences for language and literacy comes from myelination. Myelin is a fatty coating wrapped around the axons of neurons that allows neurons to transmit information quicker and with less interference. Reading happens when groups of brain structures work in concert, and research has found that critical cortical regions—areas responsible for integrating information and performing tasks with automaticity—get myelinated more slowly in boys than they do in girls. When asked to produce words beginning with a certain letter or to generate synonyms, girls are able to produce more and do it quicker (Morisset, Barnard, & Booth, 1995). According to Geschwind (1965), boys seem slower at language and slower to develop reading fluency because of how their brains get myelinated. Although we do not often consider the development of neurons or myelination when they plan lessons, there may be educational implications. If the brains of boys develop differently, expecting young boys to keep pace with girls may not be realistic. This is not to say that all boys will not be fluent with language or that some boys will not soar ahead of girls in literacy. It just adds to our understanding of the importance of differentiated instruction.

There is even more evidence of language variation between boys and girls when it comes to hemispheric differences, because girls as young as 3 and 6 months old have a higher response to stimuli in their left hemisphere—the hemisphere where language is processed—than do boys, whose right hemisphere shows greater activity (Shucard & Shucard, 1990). Although boys' left hemispheres do develop, they tend to develop a bit slower and this is why girls tend to speak approximately one month earlier than boys, speak more clearly, acquire words faster, form longer sentences, and have vocabularies two times larger than boys (Maccoby, 1998). From the beginning, girls tend to outperform boys on tests of reading, writing, spelling, and verbal ability. Girls' early facility with language and reading comes from the way their brains develop, process, and use language. This has implications for boys, because if they see girls outperforming them on verbal tasks boys might believe they are not good at these tasks (Smith & Wilhelm, 2002). If this way of thinking gets combined with uninteresting and difficult tasks, boys will avoid them, and as a result, fall behind. This shows up in retention rates and in the high number of boys placed in special education. In 1999, 8.3% of boys ages 5–12 were held back at least one grade, compared with 5.2% of girls (NCES, 2000). Far more boys are identified with language difficulties and far more are diagnosed with dyslexia, a severe reading problem (Halpern, 2000; James, 2007; Shaywitz et al., 1990).

If we ignore neurological differences and expect boys and girls to develop language abilities and skills at the same rate, we may place undue pressure on boys. When boys are not good readers, boys get placed in the low reading group and they come to dislike reading and avoid it at all costs. The work of Stipek (2002) reveals that when boys as young as 5 years old fail at literacy, they are very aware of their shortcomings and conscious of their lower status among their peers. Five-year-old boys who witness peers soaring ahead in language and literacy as they struggle to succeed often give up on themselves. They feel they will never be successful and try to get out of uncomfortable situations by acting out. When boys resist reading and writing, for whatever reason, they give up on learning and miss out on a world full of personal and educational opportunities.

Combining Neuroscience and Environmental Views

Advances in neuroscience are forging new ideas about the biological origins of language and literacy. However, some researchers question just how much behavior is really predetermined, immutable, or "hard-wired" in the brain. Instead of focusing on specific brain structures involved in a task like reading, these researchers are looking at the brain's plasticity, or its capacity to change in response to the environment (Kolb, Gibb, & Robinson, 2003). As the brain develops, synapses—the gaps between neurons where communication and learning occurs—form and get stabilized. Maintaining synapses takes energy, and those that are not used get pruned away. This is an important idea for teachers because it helps us understand the importance of experience and practice. Synapses that get used fire more rapidly and are maintained. When boys read often, their synapses fire quickly and their dendrites reach out to make connections. Halpern (2004) presents these ideas in her psychobiosocial view of gender and learning. From her standpoint, variability between the sexes occurs because nature and nurture alter each other in sequentially interacting ways. What boys learn influences the structure (branching and size) of their neurons and the architecture of their brains. These, in turn, support certain skills and abilities, which lead boys to select additional experiences. From this standpoint, environments shape and foster the development of a reading brain. In other words, reading is both a biological and environmental variable; biology and context are an inseparable pair.

Another environmental factor that influences reading development is socioeconomic status. Numerous studies have shown there are differences in language acquisition and proficiency between children in lower and middle class homes (see, for instance, Hart & Risley, 1995; Morisset et al., 1995). Children from low-income homes, especially boys, tend to be slower to use expressive language than children from middle class homes. In their work with young children, Hart and Risley (1995) found that children from professional homes hear a cumulative total of approximately 50 million words, whereas children from poor families hear only 13 million words. So children in a language-rich environment typically speak earlier and know more words because they hear more words. Children who sing songs and play word games with their caregivers also increase their language and vocabulary skills.

Reading with caregivers and other adults is another way to learn language and acquire new words. By kindergarten, books become a major source of words for children (Cipielewski & Stanovich, 1992). Gambrell, Morrow, and Pressley (2007) note that one of the most important activities for building language and literacy is reading aloud to children every day. One reason for this is that books contain a very different, and often richer, language than is typically found in everyday speech. When adults read stories to boys and explain the meaning of new words, boys begin to match these words to the pictures in the book. Reading builds language within context in a rich and transformative way. Books allow boys to experience ideas from other places and other times. Idioms, metaphors, and analogies enrich language and conceptions of the world (Booth, 2006). These environmental contributions matter to literacy development.

Physical Development and Literacy Learning

Physical development refers to biological growth of the body and brain and is important to learning and reading. Functioning eyes and ears help boys make sense of print, and if ears and eyes are not functioning properly boys may have problems early on. Major vision, hearing, speech, and communication disorders are often revealed in the preschool years when what is normal within a home environment proves to be inadequate for learning in a classroom. Variations in health and sensory systems cause learning differences and can cause boys to feel self-conscious and to give up on themselves as readers. This is especially true if peers make fun of them. For example, in the Learning From a Character box that follows, Freddy helps us understand how difficult a vision problem can be to a boy striving to achieve his dream. Freddy's story reveals how self-conscious boys can feel when they are perceived to be different and how important tolerance for individual differences can be.

LEARNING ABOUT TOLERANCE FROM A PICTURE BOOK CHARACTER

Why Do I Have to Wear Glasses? (Williamson, 2005)
In the book *Why Do I Have to Wear Glasses?* a young boy named Freddy wants to be a football star like his hero, Touchdown Joe. Unfortunately, Freddy has difficulty seeing things clearly. He just cannot see those long passes flying through the air. Freddy gets glasses and discovers that, although they solve his vision problems, they make him self-conscious. In the end, it is Touchdown Joe who helps Freddy learn how to cope with his vision difficulties and be comfortable with himself. Vision is important to young boys not only to catch long passes, but also to become a reader.

- What do you do if you notice a boy in your classroom squinting, or doing other odd things, to see print on the page?

- What strategies do you use to enhance the literacy skills of boys with visual impairments? What do you do to help them feel good about themselves?

Now consider the other meaning of vision, one that goes beyond the physical to mean seeing others in a clear and sensitive light. Intolerance for differences because of gender, ethnicity, culture, or physical traits can be imprinted on a young boy's psyche if adults display narrow-minded views. Across a boy's lifespan he will come in contact with many different people, and as a result, will need to learn how to listen, negotiate, and compromise. As educators we need to recognize this and provide young boys with a clear vision of what it means to be tolerant and kind to everyone. Tolerance begins with self-acceptance, and books like *Why Do I Have to Wear Glasses?* can help boys learn how to like themselves even if they are different. Books also can help boys learn to be empathetic—to walk in another's shoes and understand what that person feels when someone makes fun of the way that person looks, sounds, or behaves. Boys like Freddy and men like Touchdown Joe can do this, along with caring teachers who help boys come to see differences as unique qualities. This may be difficult for some boys, who may have been taught incomplete or stereotypical views.

- What do you do to help the boys in your classroom develop tolerance and respect for differences in their peers?

- How do you help the girls in your classroom to understand the differences of their male peers?

- How can the story of Freddy and Touchdown Joe be used to help your students develop empathetic relationships?

The Importance of Vision

Boys who have vision problems in the form of acuity, binocularity, or tracking will have difficulty clearly and accurately seeing print on a page. Discriminating one letter from another, seeing tiny punctuation marks, or tracking print left-to-right will be difficult and will get worse in upper grades as print gets smaller and denser on a page, and words get longer (Tompkins & McGee, 1986). If a boy lacks the ability to identify visual stimuli quickly, he will not make automatic connections between printed words and their meanings (Stanovich, 2000).

Boys with visual problems find reading to be a difficult and tiring chore. If a young boy has difficulty with perception or complains of tired eyes, ask the school nurse to conduct a screening. This is especially important for boys who live in poverty because they often do not get early screenings because of a lack of health care. Early diagnosis and intervention of vision problems are important to prevent unnecessary frustration and discouragement in young boys. Having the ability to clearly see letters on a page is unquestionably one of the basic elements of early literacy.

Gender Differences in Vision

It is important to recognize that, even without vision difficulties, the eyes of boys register information differently than the eyes of girls. Sax (2005) nicely summarizes these visual differences, and in this section we rely on his insight but extend it to young boys and literacy.

Because of variations in thickness and layering of the retina—the part of the eye composed of rods and cones—boys and girls see differently. The female retina is thinner than the male retina because it contains more of the smaller P ganglion cells—cells responsive to textures and longer light waves—which register bright colors like red, orange, beige, green, and pink. The male retina, on the other hand, has more of the larger M ganglion cells, which are responsive to the shorter light waves that produce black, green, blue, and silver (Alexander, 2003). Walk into any toy store, and you'll observe a distinct marketing tactic based on biological visual differences. Toys marketed to girls are typically sparkly, textured, and packaged in bright pink boxes, whereas toys marketed to boys are often dark green, black, or silver, and packaged in brown or black. Manufacturers do this intentionally because they know that perception precedes attention and if they can capture a child's eye, that child may want the toy.

The biological difference in eye structure has implications for selling toys, and we suggest that this idea can be used to "sell" books to boys. Because boys do not perceive textures or subtle colors as well as girls, it makes sense that the books they like to read would be subtle and not full of bright colors. Young boys are often drawn to books with plain illustrations, and young boys prefer comic books with male characters in exciting scenes more than books with sparkly illustrations. The popularity of Spider-Man and other superheroes illustrates this point. We should make sure that in our classrooms there are books that catch boys' visual attention. Remember that visual input has the ability to capture attention, and that attention is a prerequisite to learning.

A biological difference in vision not only influences what captures boys' attention but also influences the emotions that come to be associated with early written expression. Boys and girls enjoy drawing equally, but the subjects and colors they choose often are influenced by the visual pleasure they receive (Gurian & Stevens, 2005). When girls draw, the P ganglion cells in their eyes are attuned to subtle color variations, so girls want the crayon pack that contains the entire color spectrum. When boys draw, however, they choose fewer crayons. Boys stick to black, gray, silver, and blue to get their ideas across because they see these colors best (Iijima, Arisaka, Minamoto, & Arai, 2001). Unfortunately, female teachers often perceive the brown and black drawings that boys produce to be inadequate, especially when compared with the colorful ones girls produce. We believe this may be one of the earliest contributing factors to some boys' distaste of writing. If drawing, which many children enjoy and use to express their ideas, is associated with bad feelings because of negative feedback, it is unlikely that a boy will enjoy drawing or writing as modes of expression.

The eyes of boys and girls also are wired to perceive location and movement of objects differently because connections from the retina to the cerebral cortex are different (Horvath & Wikler, 1999). Girls have more P ganglion cells, which send information to the thalamus, a brain structure specialized to detect color and texture, and this helps girls perceive subtle differences and distinguish what things are. Boys have more M ganglion cells, which send their visual input to the cerebral cortex or the brain region specialized for analyzing motion and spatial relationships. Tuman (1999) shows that being adept at perceiving things in the environment causes girls to draw more objects or nouns. In contrast, the eyes of boys are wired to detect location, direction, and speed so boys are more likely to draw more active pictures or verbs. Walk into any classroom and it is likely you will see girls drawing rainbows, houses, and families, and boys drawing spaceships flying through the air. Although social and cultural influences likely play a part, boys' eyes focus on movement. We often hear teachers say that it is typically the boys in a classroom who get in trouble for throwing things. Pencils, crayons, and wads of paper become projectiles that boys toss around, simply to determine where they will land or how fast and far they can go.

These physical actions based on biological differences have implications for literacy learning and can be used for literacy development. For example, if boys enjoy drawing verbs in the form of action-packed scenes, it is important that we encourage this passion just as much as we encourage children to draw colorful pictures with central themes. Furthermore, the enjoyment boys receive from tossing objects and watching them sail through the air may be used, if it is used carefully. Incorporating soft objects to toss and movement into literacy can enhance the literacy skills of boys, from learning letter sounds to developing fluency. We explain how this can be accomplished in any classroom in Chapter 4. Because boys enjoy motion and spatial relationships, books that focus on these concepts are likely to appeal to them. Books about large machines like trucks, bulldozers, and cranes were always favorites of the young boys in Debby's classroom. Boys also enjoy books that use maps or spatial directions to solve a mystery or find a treasure, because these books cause boys to visualize and use their spatial sense. Books that explain how to do or make something are often welcome because they use boys' visual skills, lead to physical action, and provide insight on something boys can use or do.

The Importance of Hearing

The research of Gopnik, Meltzoff, and Kuhl (2001) reveals that from birth through about 6 months of age babies are "citizens of the world" (p. 108). Babies are born with the ability to hear all the phonemes spoken in the world, and they recognize when spoken sounds change most of the time, no matter what language is used. But over time the auditory perception of infants becomes more refined. It becomes tuned only to the sounds they hear.

Being able to hear the sounds of language is an important skill and is one of the earliest challenges children face. Young children must become attuned to the sounds of their language and learn how to distinguish words from a nonstop stream of speech. But this is not easy, because adult native speakers speak quickly. We do not pause between each word. Being able to distinguish sounds and words from an endless stream of speech is an auditory challenge that has an impact on language and literacy (Jusczyk, 2000).

According to Kuhl et al. (2006) children are natural linguists; they want to communicate with others and are interested in the things and people around them. Unfortunately, important auditory input can be compromised by physical abnormalities like prolonged ear infections, injury, or a lack of environmental stimulation. Any one of these factors—or a combination—can cause neurological problems that interfere with speech interpretation, language development, and ultimately reading acquisition and progress.

Early diagnosis and intervention for hearing problems, including ear infections, are important to prevent unnecessary frustration and discouragement in young boys. One common ailment among young children is otitis media with effusion. If a boy has this type of ear infection for an extended period of time it is unlikely that he will be able to distinguish words from a stream of speech, hear beginning or ending sounds, or be able to pick out individual phonemes in words. These auditory abilities should sound familiar to us because these abilities influence phonological awareness, which is a literacy skill that develops during the preschool and early elementary years (Goswami, 1999). Hearing disorders that affect the acquisition of phonological awareness disrupt a foundational literacy skill and could affect reading over one's lifetime. Awareness of this is especially important for teachers of boys who live in poverty, because they often have untreated ear infections and do not get early screenings because of a lack of health care (Brooks-Gunn, Duncan, & Aber, 1997).

But even when a boy has adequately functioning hearing, he may still experience problems in school because of physiological differences in the way he hears. The research of Cone-Wesson and Ramirez (1997) discovered that the average baby girl has an 80% greater acoustic brain response to tones within the range of human speech than the average baby boy. Likewise fMRI scans show that girls have more neurons, or brain cells, devoted to hearing than do boys (Brizendine, 2006; Harasty et al., 1997). From the moment they are born, girls hear better than boys, and girls' hearing continues to be more acute as they grow. Boys do not hear in the same way as girls, either. The hearing of boys is more attuned to low, loud sounds as opposed to high-pitched, soft sounds (Cone-Wesson & Ramirez, 1997; Sininger, Cone-Wesson, & Abdala, 1998). Furthermore, boys are better at noting the location of sounds. Because boys' cochlea—the ear structures where sound energy gets converted into neural energy—are longer than those of girls, it takes boys a fraction of a second longer to hear sounds. So when we ask a question, boys need a little more processing or wait time (McFadden, 1998).

Sax (2005) has noted that these hearing differences have implications for the classroom and perhaps even contribute to some boys' diagnoses with attention problems. For instance, boys who ignore their female teacher are often believed to be defiant and to have trouble focusing. When it comes to schoolwork, boys rush through their assignments, do not read or follow directions, and get many answers incorrect. When this happens repeatedly, we feel that a boy is being naughty or has an attention disability, when in reality he may just have missed the oral directions supplied by his female teacher who has a soft, high-pitched voice. Before referring a boy for attention problems, Sax suggests that we talk slowly, clearly, and loudly to him and move him to the front of the room. Be sure young boys sit near you during read-alouds, and if you have many boys in your class, read a bit louder. Another idea may be to build on boys' strength of sound location by moving around as you talk. Also be patient with noisy boys because they have a higher tolerance for noise, which is evident when one considers how often boys use an outside voice inside the classroom and when they play. In Readers Theatre it is often the boys who loudly perform their lines. Be patient with noise and help boys learn how to use a quieter voice when the situation demands. Also, according to Rowe (1987), we typically wait a second or even less before we answer a question ourselves or call on someone else. This sends a message that quick thinking and short answers are valued more than slower, well-considered ideas. When you ask a boy a question, give him a few minutes to think, process what you have asked, get his ideas together, and get them into verbal form. Being patient and allowing think time should be part of every classroom's culture and routine. In Chapter 4 we explain how to bring these ideas into the classroom.

Motor Development and Literacy Learning

Walk into any preschool or elementary playground and it will become evident that boys love to play. When it is time for recess, boys run to tricycles, sand boxes, and jungle gyms with glee. A lot of happy talk, fantasy, and sheer joy accompany play. As boys develop, their play becomes more sophisticated because of advances in gross and fine motor skills. Gross motor skills employ the larger muscles used in locomotion, and their continual development during the early years allows boys to become skilled in gross motor acts (Owens, 2005). When compared with girls, boys show some slight advantage in gross motor skills related to throwing and kicking. Young boys enjoy being physical and are very proud of their motor accomplishments (Poest, Williams, Witt, &

Atwood, 1989). It is not uncommon to hear young boys say things like, "Watch me, watch me!" or "See what I can do!"

We contend that this joy and pride in movement can be positive for young boys' literacy development when it is understood and incorporated with their classroom experiences. Combining movement and the learning of academic skills can provide the bodily response and energy release that many young boys need. However, despite current knowledge of child development that maintains that 5-year-olds learn from active and concrete experiences, in many classrooms children are being given fewer opportunities to learn in a hands-on, active way (Sax, 2007). The push down of academics into the early grades is forcing children to learn passively from verbal instruction. We believe in taking a developmental approach to literacy, and we recommend incorporating movement with literacy learning. Chapter 4 provides ways to bring movement into literacy and literacy into the movement young boys need and love.

The Importance of Play

The ages from 2 to 6 are often referred to as the "play years" because they are magical, carefree times (Owens, 2005). In many ways boys are built to play, and they are genetically programmed to play in certain ways. A study by Ann Campbell (as cited by Sax, 2005) found that 9-month-old boys prefer to play with boy toys such as balls, trains, and cars, because these toys appeal to boys' innate abilities and interests. This connects to what we discussed earlier, as well: Boys are attuned to motion and movement because their eyes have more M ganglion cells that are specialized for analyzing motion, location, direction, and speed. Therefore, boys enjoy toys that fit together spatially, move, or can be thrown because they catch boys' eyes.

Boys love to play, and experts on young children consider the preschool and early elementary years the golden age of symbolic play. Make-believe play peaks at 4 or 5 years of age and strengthens a wide variety of cognitive and social skills including attention, memory, language, and the ability to cooperate and understand another's point of view (Bergen & Mauer, 2000; Berk, 2005; Fein, 1986). When children enter kindergarten and first grade, play helps ease their tensions and anxieties as they make the transition from the world of home to the world of school. Playing tag at recess releases pent-up stress, and fending off monsters in make-believe play helps a boy face his fears and develop courage. It is in play that young boys begin to face their anxieties, problem solve, and envision who they can become.

Around the age of 3, children begin to show a preference for same-sex playmates. From 4 to 12 years of age this preference increases, and during the elementary school years boys spend a large majority of their time with other boys in play. One of their favorite forms of play is rough-and-tumble, which consists of running, chasing, and wrestling, and is one of the major ways young boys interact with one another and learn social conventions (Garvey, 1990). Rough-and-tumble play allows boys to display their developing physical prowess and learn restraint. Play is especially fun when it becomes entwined with fantasy. In play, boys become bigger than they are in real life. They become superheroes who fly through the air, wrestlers who roll around on mats, and pirates who set sail for foreign lands. Boys love to engage in chase play, where they run after other children and pretend to be predators (Steen & Owens, 2000). In play, restrictions and inhibitions are cast aside and learning happens easily. Given play's ability to make learning fun, it seems reasonable that play should be used to enhance boys' literacy development, and one type of play we often use in the classroom is games. Boys like to participate in organized group games, interact in large groups, and work toward group goals (Benenson, Apostoleris, & Parnass, 1997).

Boys' natural propensity for competition and challenge can, and should, be used to encourage boys' literacy development. Author and reading specialist Booth (2006) suggests that, "Games belong at the heart of childhood, and help us remember the child in each of us" (p. 133). He suggests using games as a medium to alter attitudes and abilities. We believe that playing games is good for boys because games require boys to focus their attention, plan strategically, and recognize patterns. Games teach boys how to get along, to follow directions for a goal, and to work cooperatively. Playing games can be an important way of learning for young boys, and in Chapter 4 we bring these ideas into the learning of literacy.

Young boys love to play, and play is good for their literacy and social development. Boys love to imagine and pretend as they play with others, and they love to hear about male characters that do the same. Little boy characters who fight evil and save their friends motivate boys to read and at the same time teach them positive character traits. Nowhere is this more evident than in books with the loveable character of Skippyjon Jones. The following Learning From a Character box shows how to capture boys' playful needs with the positive character trait of courage, which boys can build as they imagine themselves in a bigger-than-life scenario.

LEARNING ABOUT COURAGE
FROM A PICTURE BOOK CHARACTER

Skippyjon Jones (Schachner, 2003)
Skippyjon Jones is the story of a rambunctious boy kitty with a very active imagination. Skippyjon Jones loves to sleep with the birds—something no respectable kitty should ever do—and this upsets his mother, Junebug

Jones. She sends him to his room to think, but in reality Skippyjon Jones is doing anything but thinking. He has become Skippito Friskito, the sword-fighting Chihuahua who battles a humongous "bumble beeto" and saves a roving band of Mexican Chihuahuas. Skippyjon Jones makes so much noise that his mother and sisters go to his room and find his birthday piñata on his head! Skippyjon Jones has quite an imagination, an imagination that catches him up in his role-play.

- How do the boys in your classroom play? What types of games and imaginative adventures do the boys create?

- Now think about literacy and the type of activities you typically ask the boys in your room to do. Do these activities incorporate elements of imagination and fun? Are they play-like and active? Do they allow boys to get up and move?

In addition to stressing the importance of play, this book also can be used to teach boys about courage. When Alfredo Buzzito flies straight for Skippito Friskito, he pokes the humongous bumblebeeto with his sword and this reveals the courage in this small kitty boy. For young boys, acts of courage involve overcoming a thumping heart and a mind full of uncertainty. This is true of moral courage, as well, which requires standing tall against others who are doing something wrong, telling the truth when it is easier to tell a lie, and championing an unpopular but worthy cause.

- Do you allow and encourage the boys in your classroom to display a full range of emotions?

- Do you help the boys understand that even brave men get fearful sometimes?

- When young boys in your class take on a literacy challenge and master it, do you remind them of how courageous they were?

The Importance of Fine Motor Skills

During the preschool years young children make great strides in their fine motor development, and this is important because fine motor skills are essential to success in school (Cole & Cole, 1993). Fine motor skills involve small muscles that are used in manipulation and coordination of small objects such as pencils, buttons, and beads. There are many individual differences in fine motor skills. Some young boys struggle to learn how to tie their shoes and get their jackets zipped just right. Furthermore, some evidence indicates that some fine motor activities, like cursive writing, are more difficult for boys than for girls (Cohen, 1997). Many young boys are not good at writing small letters or drawing fine details and would rather exercise their gross motor skills instead (Poest et al., 1989). Given this preference, it is no wonder that when it comes to writing, teachers in the early elementary grades often note a lack of enthusiasm from boys. When boys are required to write in the classroom, they do it quickly so they can go out to play. In his book on boy writers Fletcher (2006) notes that, even in the elementary grades, many boys think of writing as a boring subject that must be endured. Therefore, it is no wonder that boys are struggling.

Dominant Discourses and Gender Stereotypes in Classrooms

Individuals that look at gender through a poststructural feminist discourse lens pose that gender is constructed from one's world. From this perspective, ideals of masculinity and femininity develop in various cultural, social, and historical contexts, change over time, and hold notions of power and privilege (Davies, 1997). In poststructural discourse, being male or female offers membership and access to knowledge and this can cause one gender to be treated differently and become marginalized (Young & Brozo, 2001).

Gee (1992, 1996) points out that there is a dominant Discourse—or recognizable coordination of people, objects, places, and tools—and ways of speaking, listening, reading, and writing in schools, and that these create insiders and outsiders. We believe this is true. In many classrooms today, female teachers control and lead this Discourse and this can—often unintentionally—oppress and disadvantage young boys. For example, boys enjoy writing about bloody battles and they like to add graphic illustrations to provide a visual of their exciting tales. Fletcher (2006) notes that anyone who works with boys knows that their writing will be heavy on action and conflict and light on introspection and character analysis. Unfortunately, many female teachers find this disturbing and unacceptable because they believe it shows too much violence. When the dominant Discourse for writing is dictated by female teachers who do not understand the passions and interests of boys, writing assignments become oppressive. When topics boys enjoy talking and writing about are forbidden, their voices become silenced (Hyde, 2004).

Oppression can occur early when the dominant Discourse does not consider boys' interests when providing reading choices. Collins-Standley, Gan, Yu, and Zillmann (1996) discovered that by the time boys are 2, they already have a strong and growing preference for violent and scary fairy tales. Likewise, Millard (1997) has found that boys enjoy action over personal relationships, excitement over the unfolding of character, and humor over all other elements. But because motivation to read for children depends on children's preferences—what they know and what they want to learn—asking boys to read stories that are not connected to their interests, or stories with long drawn-out plots, is likely to discourage them (Gurian & Ballew, 2003; Sax, 2005). The research of Millard has shown an imbalance in many classroom selections, with titles catering more to girls' interests than to those of boys. In Millard's work, she postulates that these imbalances arise from the following:

- A focus on narratives with a linear structure
- Discouragement of certain kinds of texts boys enjoy, such as comic strips
- A mismatch between boys' reading in school and reading outside of school

It's unfortunate that the stirring tales of mystery and adventure that boys want to read about are often missing from library shelves. For example, in one classroom Debby frequents there are ample books for each child but only one tattered copy of a Spider-Man book that the boys in this class adore. On any given day, it is not unusual to see two or three boys sitting on the rug pretending to read this book. The boys bond together and talk about this book. They jump like Spider-Man when they see pictures of him leaping into the air, and they make noises when he hangs precariously from a rope. Even though the boys seem content with this one tattered book, the fact that there is only one sends a message that has implications for their literacy development. Without books that appeal to boys, boys come to believe that topics of interest to them cannot be found in books. It is important that female teachers remember boys' interests and needs.

Equally as important as honoring young boys' interests is helping them gain a broader perspective of manhood. Television and other social messages can fool young boys into thinking men behave in stereotypical ways. Television often portrays men in general to be brutes and men with dark skin to be robbers and criminals (Eisenberg, 1996). Research shows that as early as 18 months of age, some children already use adjectives like *rough* and *hard* to describe men and adjectives like *round* and *soft* to describe women (Eichstedt, Serbin, Poulin-Dubois, & Sen, 2002). Young boys are impressionable and can easily develop misconceptions about gender and particular groups (Huston & Wright, 1998). Given their potential to think in this way, it is important that boys see strong, powerful men of all ethnicities interacting in positive ways and doing honorable things.

We do not mean to insinuate that there is only one way of doing boyhood or that all boys will like what are considered to be typical boy books. There are many ways to manhood, but when boys follow paths that look different from traditional ones, they are often harshly sanctioned. Millard (1997) notes,

If there are to be genuine opportunities within society for both boys and girls to express aspects of their personality freely, it is the controlling mechanisms of masculinity that require deconstructing, for currently too many paths are barred to young men simply because the option deemed to be effeminate, whereas a girl with an enthusiastic interest in male pursuits may find barriers to overcome but these will not usually include the disabling of her own sex. (p. 159)

As educators we have the opportunity to influence children's perceptions of gender stereotypes. Unfortunately, gender is not a clear-cut issue, and there are no simple solutions to the various choices and conflicting messages that boys receive. But we can confront our own biases and stereotypes and choose stories that appeal to boys, portray male characters in both traditional and nontraditional roles, and demonstrate that not all men fit the stereotypes. We must become reflective about our choices and tolerant of young boys who do not act in stereotypical ways. The following Learning From a Character box presents Elmer's story to help you reflect on your tolerance of young boys who stretch gender stereotypes. (Find more books that contain characters who learn about tolerance in the Appendix.)

LEARNING ABOUT TOLERANCE FROM A PICTURE BOOK CHARACTER

The Sissy Duckling (Fierstein, 2002)
Elmer—the protagonist in *The Sissy Duckling*—stretches traditional gender boundaries, and his behaviors make the other ducks, and his own father, very uncomfortable. As a result, Elmer is labeled a sissy and gets banished from his home. Forced to go it alone, Elmer finds comfort and pride in who he is. Elmer has a chance to prove he is brave when he saves his father from hunters. In the end, Elmer's father learns to be tolerant of his unique son.

Elmer challenges ideas of gender because he does not act like a "typical" boy. The lives of boys in Elmer's situation are often filled with conflict, both within themselves and with others in their world. Young boys should be helped to appreciate that tolerance is a form of mutual respect that comes from mutual understanding. We need to provide young boys with a vision of tolerance and respect.

- How does Elmer's story make you feel about gender stereotypes?

- How do you help the boys in your classroom see each of their classmates as unique, detached from stereotypes of gender, nationality, religion, race, and culture?

Cognitive Development and Literacy Learning

Whether one believes that boys and girls think differently because their brains are different or because of societal expectations, it is undeniable that children act and think differently from adults. These differences are real, and we must cope with them every day.

As with girls, boys become better thinkers as their brains develop and change. Myelination, neural growth and connections, and hormones all affect a growing mind and brain, as do interactions with the physical, emotional, and social aspects of one's world. However, even though young children are learning through their experiences and moving toward logical thinking they cannot yet think abstractly or metaphorically. Children really do know a lot about their world, yet they sometimes use faulty reasoning. Piaget and Inhelder (2000) found young children to have animistic thinking, believing that inanimate objects like the sun and wind have lifelike qualities. To them natural phenomena think, have wishes and intentions, and can feel emotions. Berk (2005) expands on these ideas and notes early childhood to be a mix of "puzzling contradictions" (p. 315). Given this way of reasoning, it is no wonder that young children sometimes believe the stories they read and hear are true.

Young children think as novices, and this influences how they interact with others and what they believe others know. Piaget and Inhelder (2000) describe the thinking of young children as egocentric because of their inability to take others' viewpoints into consideration. In other words, young children believe everyone thinks like they do and that the world revolves around them. This way of thinking has implications for teaching, especially for teaching young boys. It is important to help boys discover their misconceptions, question what they see, and understand that not everyone shares their viewpoint. If the thinking of boys is not challenged they will let others do their thinking for them, and they will become followers instead of leaders.

Boys learn from the adults in their world, so when we give up easily, lack commitment, or fail to focus our sights on goals we do not model perseverance for them. Setting goals and monitoring them is one way to show boys that focus and persistence pays off. It is also important to recognize that not all goals children set are the same. Children with performance goals focus on learning, not out of genuine interest, but only to put on a show. When challenges arise, these students choose the easy option because they want to appear competent. In contrast, children with learning or mastery goals *want* to know and learn. They are interested in the subject matter and do not care if they are not the best at the task. They focus on what they want and work persistently toward their goals, because they have a genuine interest and believe they will succeed if they work hard enough (Pintrich & Schunk, 2002). It is important for us to recognize the cognitive abilities of young boys and to teach them in developmentally appropriate ways, setting reasonable, achievable goals. Providing hands-on experiences; presenting puzzles, brain-teasers, and riddles; and asking open-ended questions and listening to varying perspectives encourage boys' novice thinking to move toward more open, reasoned, and logical thought.

Literacy activities, especially using stories that contain male characters puzzling over important issues, can help boys advance their thinking. The following Learning From a Character box provides a perfect example because it contains a lovable pigeon that tries to sway the reader's thinking. This book can be used to help young boys consider their thinking, weigh decisions they make, and learn how to make responsible decisions when peers or other influences try to convince them to do something they know they should not do. There are more books about responsibility in the Appendix at the end of this book.

LEARNING ABOUT RESPONSIBILITY FROM A PICTURE BOOK CHARACTER

Don't Let the Pigeon Drive the Bus! (Willems, 2003)
In this story, a bus driver leaves his bus in the reader's care with the plea that he or she not let the pigeon drive the bus. Many pages that follow focus on the persistent pigeon pleading, conniving, and trying to convince the reader to let him drive. At the end, the bus driver returns and drives the bus away, so the pigeon never gets to drive the bus—but when he sees a big, red truck, we can only imagine what he is thinking and who he will try to persuade next.

- Do classmates ever try to fool the young boys in your classroom?

- How might you use picture books with positive male characters to help boys understand they are being fooled?

- Consider the type of thinking the young boys in your classroom typically perform. Do they ever display egocentric thinking?

- If so, how might you use literacy experiences to understand others' points of view?

In addition to helping us learn about boys' thinking, this book can be used to help boys learn about responsibility. The driver leaves the care and safety of his bus to the reader. Given this big responsibility, the reader must keep the driver's wishes in mind even as the pigeon tries to sway the reader into forsaking this duty. Having such a big responsibility is not always easy for young boys. They must stand up to temptation and be firm in their resolve. Being responsible means using self-control, considering consequences, and being accountable for the choices that you make.

- In what ways do you promote responsibility in the young boys in your classroom?

- Do you entrust the boys with manageable and important chores and encourage and reward them when they act responsibly?

- Do you read stories to the boys that show men thinking about issues of importance and acting responsibly?

- Do you use your boys' interests, strengths, and needs to help them set developmentally appropriate learning goals?

- Do you communicate—and expect—that with work, focused effort, and persistence the boys' goals will be achieved?

The Importance of Attention

Attention is more than a behavior, it is a cognitive resource children use as they learn and as they comprehend. To hear sounds in words a boy must focus his attention carefully and listen for subtle differences, like the difference between /p/ and /b/. Coming to a read-aloud when a boy's teacher calls him in from the playground and paying attention to the story demands a focus shift. Understanding the plot of a story requires inhibiting other thoughts. Each of these is an example of the important role attention plays, both in reading and in school.

Eighty percent of the children diagnosed with ADHD are boys, and boys with attention problems are more likely than girls to be placed on medication (Rothenberger & Banaschewski, 2004; Sax, 2007). These facts have major implications for boys' literacy futures. We also know that as teachers of young children, you are often the first to notice if there is an attention problem and the first to refer the boy for testing. Attention problems are often first noticed when a boy comes to school, because school activities can be very different from those in which he normally engages. Boys who are active do fine playing outside, but they have difficulty when they must sit still and concentrate. David, highlighted in the following Learning From a Character box, has a hard time focusing his attention and adjusting to the expectations of school culture.

LEARNING ABOUT PERSEVERANCE
FROM A PICTURE BOOK CHARACTER

David Goes to School (Shannon, 2001)

In the picture book *David Goes to School* a young boy encounters much difficulty regulating his behavior and focusing on his schoolwork. He is late for class, has difficulty being quiet in the library, and gets in trouble waiting in the cafeteria line. His teacher is at her wits' end as she constantly reminds David to raise his hand and keep his hands to himself. In the end, the teacher enforces a punishment, and David knows he must try harder tomorrow to be a good boy at school.

Think about the boys in your classroom who are like David, active and distracted by other things. Look at David's use of the book as a drum in the illustration, and ask yourself if you have boys in your classroom who might do the same.

- What words do you use to describe these boys? Do you ever get impatient with them and say they have ADHD?

- What are these boys' literacy needs and passions?

- Do boys who have attention difficulties relate to characters in stories who are active like themselves?

- What might be the reasons that so many young boys are being diagnosed with ADHD and being placed in remedial and special education classes?

Biological Aspects of Attention. As teachers, we must realize that inhibiting one's desires and focusing on a task depends on the brain's frontal lobes, and that these brain parts are slower to develop in boys than they are in girls. The importance of having a brain that can suppress or inhibit impulses is far greater than anyone ever realized. Attention is a system that involves the coordinated effort of several different parts of the body and brain, and is a valuable resource a boy must draw upon to learn, to read, and to comprehend. This is lived out every day in the classroom when we ask young boys to focus their attention on a read-aloud or to gain meaning from print on a page. One thing we must remember is that the curriculum being used in many classrooms is demanding more than what the brains of boys are designed to handle. The focus in classrooms has shifted, and learning more, quicker, and earlier is becoming the norm. Kindergartners now do first-grade–level work, and first graders now do what second graders once did. This is causing problems for boys in all aspects of their learning, including literacy, simply because boys are not biologically ready to perform these tasks (Sax, 2007). When it comes to persevering at tasks that are above boys' abilities, they are likely to tune out, give up, or act out (Stipek, 2002). Reading demands focus, and as a boy moves up in grades his attention must be maintained on longer passages for longer periods of time. When a boy gets off-task or frequently forgets what he has just read, even when reading at his independent level, attention may be the culprit.

Many years ago Atkinson and Shiffrin (1968) developed a model of how information gets from the outside world into our memory. This model can help us understand where attention fits in the reading process. The first step in processing information is to sense that something is there. When a boy looks at print, the lines, colors, and shapes enter his sensory register, and his brain begins to interpret these sensations. To get the information into conscious thought (working memory), he must be able to perceive it or recognize the pattern that is there. For example, his brain must tell him that the lines /-\ put together form the letter A. When you think about this early stage of processing, it becomes clear that the visual, perceptual, and auditory difficulties mentioned at the beginning of this chapter can be devastating to the reading process. Boys who do not easily perceive letters on a page or hear phonemes in words have processing difficulties that cause learning to break down early on. Very little information enters into their consciousness and gets processed (encoded) into boys' long-term memory store. Little gets connected to what is already there.

Another breakdown may happen if the flow of information is not smooth or quick, when one's attention fails. Attention is a limited mental resource and boys can only pay attention to one cognitively demanding task at a time (Anderson, 2005). Developing a skill to the point of automaticity—being able to perform a task with little effort—is important, and this applies to reading. When a boy decodes fluently, when he does not have to focus his attention on sounding out each word, his brain is free to move that information to working memory where it can be processed and connected to what he already knows. When a boy has difficulty focusing, maintaining, and sustaining his attention, information never sticks in his mind.

An Environmental View of Attention. Processing resides in one's mind, and breakdown is caused by a problem with internal flow. But another important feature of learning is the environment in which it is embedded. Reading resides in the context of a young boy's world. It takes up a large part of his school life. Thinking about the processing of print within the context of one's world allows us to understand how important the environment is in creating readers or nonreaders. The environment provides the experiences a boy needs to build a solid long-term memory store, full of ideas and strategies he can use to comprehend print. Paying attention to print on a page is a behavior boys learn from those around them.

Unfortunately, many boys are entering school without knowing how to focus and sustain their attention. (Remember David in the Learning From a Character box on page 44?) Many boys do not have physiological attention problems. Instead, the people in their environments have never taught them where or how to focus their mental resources. When a boy's attention has been developed by stimuli in entertainment that comes in quick sound bites, or when a boy lives in a home where there is a lot of stimulation and little quiet time, it is unlikely that he will have developed the focus he needs to be successful in literacy and in school (Stamm, 2007). Sitting still long enough to read a book or regulating one's self in a classroom demands a high level of both behavior and attention control. Posner and Petersen (1990) suggest that attention is a complex process, and to attend a boy must do the following things:

- Become alert or aware of something that captures his attention

- Shift or change what he was previously focusing on and orient to something new

- Maintain or sustain his focus as long as necessary and tune out (inhibit or suppress) other distracting stimuli that come from the outside world or from his own inner thoughts

All normally developing children are born with the first component, the ability to become alert and aware of things happening in their world. The second component of attention, shifting, also begins early, usually during the first two years and can be influenced by what is found in a child's world (Stamm, 2007). There are different types of attention, like auditory attention—the ability to maintain a focus on verbal information—and visual attention—the ability to maintain a focus on what is seen. As humans, we are visual creatures and visual attention improves significantly during the preschool years. Formerly distractible preschoolers become captivated by television and often sit and watch it for 15 minutes or more. Unfortunately, this attention-grabbing commodity has negative effects on attention. For instance, watching a lot of television causes the brain to become accustomed to short attention span use. The research of Christakis, Zimmerman, DiGiuseppe, and McCarty (2004) shows that for every hour children between the ages of 1 and 3 spend watching television each day they are 10% more likely to show symptoms of ADHD, and neuroscience is confirming this potential damage to attention control. When young boys watch a lot of television or play quick-moving video games, their brains become used to shifting and scanning instead of sustaining focus.

The impact of television on children under the age of 2 is so potent that the American Academy of Pediatrics (2001) recommends that those children watch no television at all and that children over the age of 2 watch no more than two hours of television per day. The work of Woodard and Gridina (2000), however, shows that a majority of U.S. families with children ages 2 to 17 years have a television, basic cable, a computer with Internet access, and several video games in their homes. The work of Rideout, Vandewater, and Wartella (2003) has shown that this electronic media gets used even by young children. Children younger than 6 years of age spend an average of two hours daily with screen media, and many children between the ages of 2 and 4 spend more than four hours per day exposed to media, primarily television (Rideout et al., 2003). Two out of three children 6 years old and younger live in homes in which a television is left on at least half the time. In homes where the television is left on almost all or most of the time, children appear to read less than other children and are slower to learn to read. More than one third (36%) of all children have a television in their bedrooms, and 43% of children ages 4 to 6 years old have access to a VCR or DVD player (Rideout et al., 2003).

Children from all economic groups are watching television, but for boys in poverty much of this viewing time is being performed alone without adult guidance or interaction and this screen time is affecting language and literacy development (Roberts, Foehr, Rideout, & Brodic, 1999). The language a boy hears on television is different from his caregiver's words. Words on television are spoken quickly, decontextualized from the here and now, and not interactive. Television language is not about what is around the child or shared with another person who can extend ideas (Stamm, 2007). Boys growing up in homes in which a lot of television is viewed are less likely to develop a rich vocabulary, and they are also less likely to read at night. The number of words a boy is exposed to through reading before he enters school and the number of words he gets exposed to during the elementary years makes a huge difference to his language and reading later on. West (2000) reports that when parents read to their children for just five minutes per night, three nights a week, reading achievement is increased. So even though television exposes boys to words, they are not the same as words read to a boy by his teachers and caregivers or spoken in real life.

The third component of attention, sustaining it, develops more slowly. Being able to keep one's attention on one thing while ignoring other things requires inhibition or the ability to suppress an impulse. To maintain and sustain attention a boy must damp down his response to other incoming information, including his own internal thoughts. He must suppress the urge to get up and move. This is especially important in tasks such as reading because it demands a lot of mental energy. David's story (Shannon, 2001), described in the previous Learning From a Character box on page 44, reveals the importance of inhibiting one's impulses—especially in terms of focusing one's attention—in school and as one reads. But this is difficult for boys because their frontal lobes mature more slowly than do those of girls. By age 2, inhibitory skill development is underway, but for most boys the ability to inhibit impulses and focus for long periods of time does not fully develop until age 7 or older. Given all this information, it is easy to understand the important role attention plays in learning how to read. In Chapter 4 we supply strategies that you can use to help young boys learn how to attend.

Harnessing New Literacies

Although throughout this book we write negatively about the effects of television, video games, and other electronic media, we do not mean to imply that *all* media is bad for boys. We accept, welcome, and honor the positive aspects of media as a new form of literacy. New literacies have become and will continue to be a part of the literacy lives of boys. Prensky (2001a, 2001b) calls today's children "digital natives" because they are the first generation to grow up with technology. People of older generations are "digital immigrants" because we learned to use technology later in our lives. Today's students are native users of the digital language of computers, video games, and electronic books, and boys are major consumers of these. The question for us as educators is, How can we use these new forms of input in productive ways to lead boys to reading and prepare them for the 21st-century skills they will need?

Perry and Szalavitz (2007) and Jensen (2006) state that the brain is use dependent. Different experiences lead to the construction of different brain structures and different processing styles. Because of the brain's malleability, it is continually changing in response to the input it receives. What we must realize is that today, much of this input is technology driven. An analogy to understand this idea can be drawn from the research conducted on different cultures. We all recognize culture's influence on what children know, the strategies they use, and what they want and need to learn. Children who grow up in different cultures not only see things differently, but also experience and think about things differently. Forward thinkers like Prensky (2001a, 2001b) believe that children who grow up with technology are part of a new culture. The brains of digital natives process information in a different way and at a different rate. For example, when boys play video games for 100 minutes a day, five days a week (which is not a far-off estimate of typical game play for boys) their brains get used to quick processing and accustomed to quick challenges and immediate rewards. This is not a new phenomenon. Since the game Pong was invented in 1974, boys have been reprogramming their brains to be faster and more interactive. Boys raised in today's technological world think differently, and they want mental challenges.

This relates to issues of attention, self-regulation, and engagement because when one thinks about boys as digital natives, it is easy to understand why they display short attention spans for old ways of learning (e.g., workbooks and drills) yet have very long attention spans for video games and other activities of interest to them. As teachers, we must realize this is happening to younger and younger boys. As a solution, Prensky (2001a, 2001b) poses the idea of "game-based learning" (p. 5), or using appropriate video games and technology to make learning more game-like. Prensky is quick to point out the difference between true learning with technology games and "eye candy," noting the latter to be an insufficient condition. Game-based learning is not based on flashy gimmicks. Instead it uses technology to provoke deep thought and build problem-solving skills. Good video games challenge boys physically, intellectually, and emotionally. It is the continual challenge, at the right time and in the right context, that motivates boys to set goals and learn.

Young boys growing up in the 21st century are digital natives who face an exciting and information-filled world. Yet we must still remember they are young boys with young minds and limited reasoned logic. No matter how great the technology or how fascinating the games, boys still need us at their side teaching, nurturing, and helping them construct visions of manhood. In her book on the science of the reading brain, Wolf (2007) points this out and notes that adult guidance is necessary to guard against immediacy, high amounts of input, and questionable information. Wolf asks some very tough questions, such as,

- Will the amount of information spark curiosity, or will children become complacent and accepting of what they read?

- Will children be able to problem solve effectively and think critically if brains become habituated for partial attention and multitasking?

- If information is able to be stored electronically and virtually, will memory become a forgotten art?

- If children become exposed to too much information, will they lose their inner dialogue and ability to reflect on what they do?

- If children interact more with video games and computer screens, will they lose the ability to converse and interact with others in productive ways?

- Will children be given all their thoughts and lose creativity and imagination?

- As images become clearer and more colorful, will children be able to distinguish reality and truth?

These are important questions we must ask ourselves, because in many ways the answers will dictate how the young boys in our classrooms learn and develop. No matter how great the information or what form it comes in, we, their teachers, must sit beside boys and help them navigate and understand what they find. In the following chapters you will learn more about boys and strategies to use with them to give them bright beginnings in literacy.

QUESTIONS FOR DISCUSSION

■ How can problems with vision or hearing affect literacy acquisition and motivation?

■ How can biological differences in vision and hearing between boys and girls affect the literacy learning of boys?

■ Who are young boys as readers?

■ How does the interaction of biology and the environment influence young boys' reading and sense of who they are?

■ How do young boys think and what does this type of thinking mean to their literacy needs?

■ What do boys living in the 21st century need to become both readers and good men?

CHAPTER 3

Understanding the Social and Emotional Development of Young Boys

I n many ways, we continue to gain insight on young boys' literacy and educational needs. We know content, genre, and the way we teach matter to boys' motivation to read. Young boys get off to a bright start when they

- Experience positive environments and developmentally appropriate practices based on their strengths and needs

- Develop self-regulation because it is the foundation for good behavior and literacy development

- Learn ways to understand and regulate their emotions and the range of emotions they feel

- Discover positive male characters who show them how real men think and act

Foundations for Literacy Learning

In today's world, many children live far from their extended families. Grandparents, aunts, and uncles who once took part in the care and teaching of children are seen only occasionally. It is also a fact that in many families both father and mother work outside the home. As a result of these and other factors, early and extensive enrollment in child care and preschools has become the norm. The percentage of children enrolled in extended child care in the United States rose from 25% to 80% in just one generation (Berk, 2005).

Research provides ample evidence that high-quality preschools can jumpstart cognitive abilities, close achievement gaps, and reduce rates of retention and placement in special education, and that these benefits can be sustained with quality teaching in the elementary years and beyond (Ramey & Ramey, 1998). Studies also show only a small percentage of 3- and 4-year-olds—those living in higher socioeconomic neighborhoods—have access to quality care (Brooks-Gunn, 2003).

Preschools are the place where many boys begin their journey into the wider world away from their family, and it is in preschool where many boys encounter their first social and academic challenges. If these are not handled with sensitivity, boys may come to believe preschool is not for them. Expulsion is the complete removal of educational services without any alternatives, and it is the most severe disciplinary response a school can impose. Across the United States increasing numbers of 3- and 4-year-olds—mostly boys—are being expelled from preschool for being disobedient and disrespectful. Consider these facts gleaned from the research of Gilliam and Shahar (2006), who surveyed 3,898 prekindergarten teachers about their experiences with expulsion:

- Ten percent of teachers reported they had expelled at least one preschooler within the past 12 months.

- Boys are being expelled from preschools 4½ times more often than girls.

- The likelihood of expulsion rises 9½ times if a boy is African American.

- Expulsion from preschool rises for boys as they age; 4-year-olds are being expelled 50% more often than 2- or 3-year-olds. Five-year-olds are twice as likely to be expelled as their 4-year-old classmates.

Foundations for literacy are built in preschool and continue to form in kindergarten and the early grades. But just as in preschool, many boys in early elementary grades are not doing well, and as you learned in Chapter 2, one reason for this is a curriculum shift. The curriculum in kindergarten and the early elementary grades has changed from play and exploration to academics and standardized demands, and this is causing stress for young boys who are not developmentally ready to master what is being asked of them (Sax, 2007). The following Learning From a Character box explains the story of such a character. Leo was a later bloomer, much to his father's dismay.

LEARNING ABOUT PERSEVERANCE FROM A PICTURE BOOK CHARACTER

Leo the Late Bloomer (Kraus, 1971)
Leo, a young lion, lagged behind his peers. He just could not do anything right! He could not draw, read, or write as well as any of his peers. And he never spoke a word. As one can imagine, this caused Leo's father some distress. He watched and compared Leo with the other young lions.

On the other hand, Leo's mother never made comparisons or watched him with a critical eye. She had faith that Leo would bloom even if he may be a bit later than the rest. She reminded her husband that if he continued to watch Leo he would not bloom.

So Leo's father stopped watching, and when he did, Leo bloomed. He began to read, write, and speak! His first full sentence, appropriately, was, "I made it!"

- Are there any boys in your class like Leo?

- What do you do for them to help them feel successful in reading and writing?

- What analogy can you draw between Leo and young boys in our schools today?

Leo the Late Bloomer is a book you can use to help young boys who may not be blooming to persevere. Leo is asked to do things above his ability, but he keeps trying until he blooms. Leo displays the positive character trait of perseverance and helps even the smallest boys understand that when things get difficult it is important to never give up. Use Leo's story as a starting point.

- Is your classroom developmentally appropriate for young boys?

- Do you focus on the many things young boys can do and help them develop skills they need?

- Do you talk to boys about their achievements and help them set realistic goals?

We need to consider young boys' language and literacy development in terms of differences instead of delays. Biologically, boys and girls differ. Their bodies and brains develop in a different sequence and at a different pace, and these differences play out in how each gender thinks and what boys and girls are able to do. Differences have implications for learning, especially when it comes to expectations and needs.

Researchers and classroom teachers have embraced differentiated instruction yet, for some reason, they have overlooked gender as a legitimate reason to differentiate. Each child deserves to have his or her developmental pace honored with appropriate activities and materials because these influence his or her learning and esteem. If boys need extra time to develop their reading skills, they should not be made to feel that there is something wrong with them.

The Importance of Self-Regulation

Self-regulation is the ability to control one's behaviors, emotions, and cognition (McDevitt & Ormrod, 2007), and the lack of self-regulation is causing boys to experience difficulties from the moment they enter school. Boys are arriving at schools without the ability to focus their attention and regulate their behavior well enough to get along (Rubin, Bukowski, & Parker, 1998). Self-regulation can be challenging for young boys because it requires capabilities that are only beginning to emerge. Girls, on the other hand, tend to develop regulation earlier. They adjust easier to schedules and are able to regulate their emotions and their attention earlier than boys because of the way their brains develop (Brizendine, 2006; Sax, 2007). When the behavior of young boys is compared with that of girls, boys seem out of sync and difficult to control. Boys who cannot regulate themselves in a classroom have trouble in school because peers reject them, teachers find them hard to manage, and they get expelled (Gilliam & Shahar, 2006). Self-regulation matters when it comes to reading and learning in any domain (Bronson, 2000).

Although it is difficult to pinpoint the exact cause of regulation difficulties, we believe that caring adults can do much to help boys learn to regulate themselves. In general, young children develop regulation by being attuned to their caregivers, and we can take on that role if it has been missed or is lacking in the home. To develop self-regulation, boys need caring teachers who will do the following (McDevitt & Ormrod, 2007):

- Create an orderly, predictable environment
- Provide age-appropriate opportunities allowing for choice and independence
- Provide specific guidance, support, and scaffolding

We, as teachers, can create classrooms that incorporate these factors by establishing routines for reading, providing materials boys are able to decode, and using picture books with positive male characters to help boys learn how self-regulation looks, sounds, and feels. We believe this is important because even though self-regulation may seem far from learning phonemes it is an important component of learning how to read. For instance, coming to storytime when the teacher calls demands that a boy self-regulates to a classroom schedule; sitting next to someone during storytime requires a boy to keep his hands and feet still.

When boys get older, early abilities to adjust to routines and demonstrate self-control lead to self-regulated learning. Self-regulated learners set schedules to complete assignments, monitor their comprehension as the read, and use strategies they have been taught. Being a self-regulated learner helps a boy fit into a classroom and gain respect from his teachers and peers. Boys with self-regulation difficulties have the greatest needs, because they are the ones being expelled from our classrooms and missing the early literacy instruction they need (Gilliam & Shahar, 2006). This is unfortunate, because preschool and the early grades should be the place where these boys become acquainted with literacy. They should be the place where stories of positive male characters are used to teach boys about restraint and control. The following Learning From a Character box contains a positive male character that you can use to help young boys learn about self-regulation and the respect they will receive when they self-regulate. The Appendix contains more books that you can use to help young boys learn about respectfulness, as well.

LEARNING ABOUT RESPECTFULNESS FROM A PICTURE BOOK CHARACTER

Ronald Morgan Goes to Bat (Giff, 1990)

The main character in *Ronald Morgan Goes to Bat* is a good model for self-regulation and the respect one receives when one controls oneself. Ronald is an eternal optimist and quite regulated when it comes to baseball. He practices every day, despite the fact that he shuts his eyes every time he is at bat. But Ronald's positive attitude changes when he realizes that he is the worst hitter on the team and receives no respect from his teammates. Ronald is ready to give up baseball, but his father intervenes and tells Ronald how he, too, once was a poor batter. Instead of letting Ronald give up, his father scaffolds his learning. He helps him control his fears, focus his attention, and regulate his body to be still enough to hit the ball. With the help of his father, Ronald is able to gain self-respect and the respect of his teammates. Thinking about your classroom,

- What do you do to promote respectfulness in your classroom?
- What do you do to promote self-regulation in your classroom?
- Is your literacy routine orderly and predictable?
- When boys need assistance, are you patient and respectful of their needs?
- When boys have difficulty regulating themselves, do you offer guidance, support, and scaffolding?

The Importance of Age-Appropriate Learning Activities

Young children are typically optimistic about their ability to learn. No matter what the task or domain, they believe they can learn it and are headed for success (Stipek, 1993). Unfortunately, optimism can be changed to pessimism, or learned helplessness, if children are asked to engage in developmentally inappropriate tasks (Cain & Dweck, 1995). When unreasonable tasks are required of them children are likely to display a negative affect, avoid what is being asked, and set low goals for themselves. Neuroscience shows that high stress, boredom, and anxiety all interfere with motivation and learning (Wolf, 2007). Unfortunately, in many early elementary classrooms boys are feeling stressed because of the curriculum shift from play and exploration to academics and standardized demands. As noted previously, students in kindergarten and the early elementary years are expected to master skills once considered appropriate in much higher grades (Sax, 2007). Although the intent of this shift is to help children gain skills they need to be successful in the elementary years, there can also be a dark and unintended side. Children who are not developmentally ready to master a task may develop negative perceptions of themselves and of learning, including learning literacy. When considering the developmental progression of young boys, it is important to provide them with differential instruction, scaffolding, and time to develop.

Developmentally appropriate challenges that are fun, active, interesting, and performed in a supportive environment can make a big difference for boys' motivation to read. Young boys need to learn literacy skills. They need to develop phonemic awareness, fluency, and vocabulary, and in Chapter 4 you will discover ways to develop each of these in age-appropriate and boy-friendly ways. But learning is a two-way street; boys need to do their part. When tasks are reasonable, boys need to find inner strength, persevere, and try their best. The following Learning From a Character box contains a male character who displays perseverance and shows how important this quality is to boys. There are more books that demonstrate perseverance listed in the Appendix.

LEARNING ABOUT PERSEVERANCE FROM A PICTURE BOOK CHARACTER

Today Was a Terrible Day (Giff, 1980)
The picture book *Today Was a Terrible Day* stars the lovable character Ronald Morgan once again. But this time, instead of being an optimistic baseball player, Ronald is struggling in school, especially in reading. In Ronald's classroom there is the Satellite group that is stellar, the Mariners who get the teacher's attention, and then there is his group, the Rockets, whose focus is on workbook pages. In Ronald's words he is in the "dumb group"—and in his mind he is at the bottom of that group.

One day Ronald gets a note to take home and he is encouraged by his teacher to try to read it himself. On the way home Ronald perseveres until he is able to read the note—and the note is positive. It is at this instant Ronald discovers that he really can read! Striving to read the note helps Ronald understand that if he has an authentic reason to read, if he perseveres, and if he is not under stress, he is capable.

Today Was a Terrible Day teaches us the importance of authentic reading for young boys. This book can also be used to help young boys understand perseverance. Ronald Morgan struggles with every aspect of literacy, but he perseveres.

- How can you use Ronald Morgan's story to help boys understand that when it comes to literacy they need to persevere?

- How can you use this story to help boys who struggle with reading to boost their self-esteem?

- How can you use both of Ronald Morgan's stories to help the boys in your classroom learn about what good and honorable boys do?

Social Development and Literacy Learning

When it comes to reading and overall school achievement, many boys are not faring well, which affects their self-esteem. When boys lose confidence in themselves, they lose sight of their inner goodness and either isolate themselves from others or get swayed by anyone who makes them feel good. Too often this turns out to be popular cultural messages that promote less-than-desirable ideals.

In his book *Misreading Masculinity: Boys, Literacy, and Popular Culture*, Newkirk (2002) speaks against the notion of boys as passive absorbers of media messages, and we certainly agree. We do not want to promote the idea that boys are incapable of resistance. Boys are active agents. They shape their environment just as much as it shapes them. But as you learned in Chapter 2 the thinking of young boys can be swayed, which is why the needs of young boys should be considered through a developmental lens. In other words, we adults need to consider the potential impact of media messages, especially if boys watch television alone. Young boys do not think abstractly or logically; they view images in a more literal way. Realistic images are captivating and persuasive to everyone and have a greater impact on young children if no one tells them otherwise. If boys interpret what they see as real they may develop a distorted view. This is more likely to happen if a boy lives in a violent household or has few personal connections.

Socially, boys want to fit in. They want be part of the "in crowd" and are often led to believe the way to do this is to own things and act in certain ways. Advertisers take advantage of this all the time. They cultivate a desire for toys and products with the promise they will make boys popular. Images of a basketball player wearing expensive sneakers are designed to sell shoes by making boys believe that if they buy this brand they will achieve the abilities of their hero, be adored, and have friends. If we do not do some selling of literacy, boys may never understand that it, and not external things, can help them gain insight and develop friendships.

Boys learn social ways from the models they see on television and in their lives, and this applies to reading. In their work, Pottorff, Phelps-Zientarski, and Skovera (1996) gathered survey data on the types of genres students at various grade levels see their parents read. The results of this survey indicate 56% of students see their mothers read books more often than their fathers. Fathers, most students indicated, read the newspaper more. Because reading books is the typical form of reading performed in most classrooms, we must ask ourselves if boys are seeing this type of reading being modeled in their home. If boys see their mothers reading books they will believe book reading is for mothers, or girls, and that reading is not for them unless it is in newspaper form. In their book *Reading Don't Fix No Chevys* Smith and Wilhelm (2002) make this point for adolescents, and we extend this idea to young boys. We must show boys that men also choose to read books when they appeal to them, and we must honor reading newspapers because all forms of reading are important.

Newkirk (2002) provides a good example in his book when he explains his son's reading of a table of National Basketball Association standings. As teachers we think of tables as static and fact driven, far from our vision of literacy. Yet the way Newkirk's son read it was informative and emotional. Boys read tables for information about a favorite player, and tables capture moments of a player's success and failure. It is not the reading of this information that makes it important, but the emotional and personal connection it forms for boys. When boys share and discuss what they have read with others in a social context, they bond together and make friends. In her work with successful young male readers Smith (2006) finds that when boys read material on topics of interest and are allowed to share this with other boys, they gain status and power among their peers. The boys in Smith's study used their literacy abilities to build relationships with other boys and to make themselves popular. No matter what form literacy comes in, the insight it brings and the networks it allows boys to form play an important role.

Stories have been used to teach socialization skills for a very long time. All cultures have stories they use to pass down wisdom, teach the way of the tribe, and guide boys along the path to manhood (Schank, 1995). For example, stories of the "big man" of New Guinea, the "muy hombre" of Spain, and the "worthy man" of the Samburu people each show boys how real men act with honor to protect the ones they love, show the emotions they feel, and care for the Earth. Boys become attached to certain characters and know them well (Brozo, 2002; Zambo, 2007). Boys learn vicariously through characters, and stories can offer boys positive images of who they are and who they can become. When boys identify with a character, they love to read about his adventures—promoting all aspects of literacy development.

In Chapters 1 and 2 you learned that boys acquire pleasure from stories that appeal to their active bodies and their imaginative minds. They do not enjoy books with flowery language or books with long, complicated plots (Gurian & Ballew, 2003; Millard, 1997). Therefore, it is important that books used with young boys have a simple story and contain an interesting character. When choosing books to use with young boys, one thing to keep in mind is their desire to understand themselves and their roles as men (Kindlon & Thompson, 2000; Pollack, 2000). Comprehending the rules of masculinity is part of every boy's search for self and using literature with positive male characters can encourage this insight (Brozo, 2002; Brozo & Schmelzer, 1997).

You will notice two types of positive male characters in picture books. There are traditional positive male characters, or grown men facing challenges and doing noble deeds. And there are young characters becoming good because they face an important challenge and make an honorable choice. You can use either older or younger positive male characters to teach young boys.

Do not forget the added benefit the illustrations in picture books provide. Illustrations can motivate boys to read and can teach social skills. Illustrations capture boys' attention and scaffold their early literacy attempts to make sense of what they read. Pictures offer context clues that allow boys to decode texts they might not be able to read on their own. Furthermore, illustrations contain messages and some illustrations teach as much as print. The reading of images is called visual literacy, and it is as important as any decoding skill because it helps boys' social development (Evans, 1998). Chapter 2 discussed the egocentric thinking of young boys, how they tend to believe everyone sees the world through their eyes and how this does little to help them make or become good friends. We have found that encouraging the development of visual literacy helps boys understand that others see the world through different eyes and have different points of view. Encouraging young boys to look carefully at a character's facial expressions and body language helps boys see that we often express how we feel outwardly (Falk, 2005). The following Learning From a Character box provides a good example; this book's illustrations show a mature male character demonstrating generosity. The illustrations also show delight on the faces of those he helps. More books that teach about generosity can be found in the Appendix.

LEARNING ABOUT GENEROSITY
FROM A PICTURE BOOK CHARACTER

Oscar Wilde's The Happy Prince (Grodin, 2006)

Oscar Wilde's The Happy Prince is the story about a swallow that comes to rest on the base of the Prince's statue. The swallow notices the Prince's tears. The Prince reveals that when he was young he lived his life at the palace and never ventured out, but now that he is a statue perched high above the town he is able to see all the suffering of the people below. The Prince asks the swallow to help give away his material treasures. The Prince gives the ruby from his crown, the gold leaf from his clothing, and the emeralds in his eyes to the needy townspeople.

The Prince gives of himself until has no more and the little swallow, once so eager to leave, becomes reluctant to leave his friend even though winter is approaching. On a cold night at the stroke of midnight the swallow freezes to death, and the Prince's heart breaks. Bare and no longer beautiful, the statue is melted down. The men at the furnace save his broken heart and place the dead bird with it in a place of honor to remind everyone of the kindness and compassion this pair gave.

This is a powerful story, one that helps boys understand how generosity is part of being a friend. The story gives voice to the concept of generosity through the Prince's brave and caring words as he gave parts of himself away. The illustrations in this book are also powerful. They show what courage, generosity, and caring for others looks like on the character's face.

- How can you use this story and the illustrations in this book to help young boys understand generosity and how friends are generous?

- How do you encourage young boys to show generosity in your classroom?

- How can you use this story and the illustrations in this book to help the young boys in your classroom learn how real men act and feel?

ABOUT
A BOY

It is time for the daily read-aloud in Mr. Brooks's kindergarten classroom, and the children have gathered around. John is sitting next to his best friend Pablo, excitedly waiting for the story to begin. John enjoys hearing his teacher read, but when he is in a large group he often has trouble managing how he feels, which becomes evident as soon as Mr. Brooks begins. John gets mad at Pablo and blurts out angry words because he touched John with his elbow. Mr. Brooks cautions the boys about this behavior and with this reprimand they settle enough to let the story continue. Within a few minutes, however, John and Pablo are at it again; this time Mr. Brooks asks them to leave the group. The instant Mr. Brooks does this John stands up and says, "I don't care about hearing a stupid book" and storms away. He begins to cry. Several of his classmates comment that he is a baby and should go back to preschool, which makes John even angrier. Because of his outburst John was excluded from the remainder of the story reading and the literacy experience that followed.

- How did John's emotions interfere with his learning and the learning of his classmates?
- What proactive steps might Mr. Brooks have taken to help John learn to cope with how he feels?
- How might picture books with positive role models be useful for John?

Emotional Development and Literacy Learning

Young boys like John want to fit into their social world and learning how to cope with their emotions plays an important part. Emotions are the psychological and physiological feelings we have in response to events that are relevant to our needs (Campos, Frankel, & Camras, 2004). A large part of the brain is devoted to emotional processing, so emotions can energize thinking or they can make thinking shut down (LeDoux, 1996; Zambo & Brem, 2004). Emotions drive thinking and learning to regulate them develops over time as a boy interacts with others. Simple emotions like fear and anger appear in infancy and self-conscious emotions, such as shame, embarrassment, and pride (Lewis, 1993), emerge in early childhood. These affective states reflect awareness of social standards as well as the concerns and standards others have, and young boys learning how to read definitely feel these emotions. Young boys feel pride when they are successful, and they feel shame and embarrassment when they are asked to read in front of others and are not prepared (Stipek, 1993; 2002).

Emotional development varies between boys and girls. Boys in preschool show more anger than girls, and boys in the early elementary grades put on confident airs even when they feel self-doubt (Eisenberg, 1996). It is also common for a gender difference to be evident in the outward expression of emotions. Many boys believe it is not OK for them to cry or show they are weak. Caregivers often unknowingly reinforce this emotional suppression, and at school we often prefer the passive emotions girls display (Pollack, 2000).

As boys develop, they try to cope with their feelings and learn strategies by observing others (Campos et al., 2004; Hoffman, 1991). They watch how the adults around them handle anger, happiness, and fear. Boys may adopt the negative coping strategies they see, but if they have friends who help them understand their emotions, as does Little Rabbit in the Learning From a Character box that follows, they will learn that everyone experiences sad emotions and that it is OK to cry.

LEARNING ABOUT COURAGE FROM A PICTURE BOOK CHARACTER

Why Do You Cry? Not a Sob Story (Klise, 2006)

This is the story of a 5-year-old boy rabbit who decides he is done with crying because crying is for babies. He also decides that no one who cries will be asked to his birthday party, but he finds this a difficult requirement. His friend the squirrel cries when people do not ask him to play. His friend the cat cries when he is alone and it is dark. Even his big friend the horse cries when a bee stings him. Little Rabbit is resolved that no one can come to his party except his mother and is ready to accept this until she breaks the news that she too cries at sad movies, when she gets a toothache, and when she looks at him because he is growing up so fast. She teaches Little Rabbit that anyone can cry for any reason, even when they are happy. Little Rabbit is amazed at this and asks Mother Rabbit if she will mind if he cries; she hugs him and says of course not. In the end Little Rabbit has his party with all his friends and not a single tear is shed. This book teaches boys that it is OK for everyone to cry sometimes.

- Do you allow the boys in your classroom to display a full range of emotions?

- Do you help them understand that even brave men and brave boys cry sometimes?

- Do you help boys understand that emotional courage is a true form of courage, and that courage and empathy can be real sources of strength?

- Do you help boys develop an emotional vocabulary so they will better understand themselves and communicate more effectively with others?

- Do you bring positive male role models in to the classroom or read aloud picture books with male characters who model emotional attachment?

Uncovering Boys' Emotions About Reading

Identifying how boys perceive themselves as readers and how they feel about reading is as important as identifying any cognitive skill or deficit. Unfortunately, uncovering how boys think and feel about reading is not always easy. Many boys bury how they feel beneath a tough exterior. This is true in reading, especially when a boy struggles with print. Boys who have trouble with reading will do anything they can to avoid showing their vulnerability, which might disrupt a classroom (Zambo & Brem, 2004).

One method we have used to get at boys' perceptions and feelings about reading is drawing. We have used drawings because there is robust evidence suggesting they are reliable indicators of cognitive development (see the Goodenough–Harris Drawing Test, 1963, which is used to understand children's experiences and what they know about body parts). We use drawings with young boys because they are fun and not as threatening as a survey or interview. One particular type of drawing we have used is thought bubble pictures. Thought bubbles are the little thinking bubbles one sees above a character's head in a cartoon. They allow an observer to understand what a character is thinking or feeling but not expressing in words.

Figure 1 shows a thought bubble picture to use with the boys in your class. To use it, distribute the picture, read the directions, and allow time and space

---

FIGURE 1
Thought Bubble Picture

Note. Figure reproduced from Zambo, D. (2006). Using thought bubble pictures to assess students' feelings about reading. *The Reading Teacher, 59*(8), 798–803. Used with permission.

for your boys to complete their drawings. Say, "This child is reading. Draw what his face looks like as he reads, and draw in the bubble what he is thinking." To analyze the drawings, use a coding system that scores the face, the bubble, and the drawing overall. First look at the faces boys draw for any physical features or emotional clues. Rank each face +1 for positive/happy, 0 for neutral, and –1 for negative/sad. To determine these scores look carefully at facial features such as eyes and their focus, gaze, and brow angle, and mouth curvature and shape. Then look for clues that these drawings contain—features like tears or smiles. Table 1 provides the facial features (eyes, eyebrows, and mouths) that we have found to be helpful in interpreting drawings. In the table are ideas for +1 and –1 scores. Assign a neutral score of 0 if you are unable to determine what emotion is being portrayed or if the face does not fit either extreme. For example, a mouth drawn as a straight line does not indicate happiness or sadness, and eyes with no expression or slant should be considered neutral and assigned a score of 0.

After you have analyzed the faces, analyze the thought bubbles in the same way. To determine the boy's score, carefully examine the symbols (e.g., question marks), signs (e.g., a crumpled book), and words (negative or positive) the thought bubble contains. Table 2 provides key symbols, signs, and words

TABLE 1
Facial Drawing Ratings, Features, and Clues

Rating	Physical Feature	Feature Clues
Positive (+1)	Eyes/eyebrows	• wide open • upward slant • open with interest • have a spark to them
	Mouth	• full smile (some with teeth showing, others without)
Neutral (0)	Eyes/eyebrows	• typical with no expression • no slant
	Mouth	• drawn as a straight line • expression not clear or intriguing
Negative (–1)	Eyes/eyebrows	• downward slant, droopy lids • closed • dark circles underneath • drawn as spirals • slanted inward or down
	Mouth	• contains a frown • open in a scream • drawn as a jagged line
	Extra elements drawn on face	• tears • tongues stuck out and upward in frustration • teeth in a growl

Note. Adapted from Zambo (2006).

Rating	Features	Feature Clues
TABLE 2		
Thought Bubble Ratings, Features, and Clues		
Positive (+1)	Symbols	• peace signs
	Signs	• smiley face • thumbs up • characters they are reading about
	Words	• easy • good • fun • cool • I do well • really interesting • I like • very happy • feels good
Neutral (0)	Symbols, signs, and words	• no expression (e.g., a book title) • cannot discern emotion
Negative (−1)	Symbols	• question mark • zzzz's to indicate sleep/boredom • dark scribbles
	Signs	• child with a sword battling a book • hand holding a crumpled book
	Words	• dang boring • blah, blah • confused, hard, bad, • never get done, no point • daydreaming • I don't want to read right now • hate • sad • can't • too hard • this stinks • I want to burn it

Note. Adapted from Zambo (2006).

prevalent on drawings we have gathered over time. There are also ideas for +1 and −1 scorings based on thought bubble features and clues. Assign a neutral score of 0 if the thought bubble does not fit either extreme. For example, vertical lines or designs are difficult to interpret, as are titles of books. If you cannot tell what the symbols, signs, or words indicate, or if it is clearly a neutral sign (e.g., a book title, character name), assign it a neutral score of 0.

Children's drawings reveal their cognitive abilities and their inner thoughts. Altered lines, erasures, unusual signs, and shapes have all been used to understand children's creativity and their perceptions of the world (Greig, Taylor, & MacKay, 2007). However, we also want to make it clear that drawings, including thought bubbles, should always be interpreted with caution because they are mediated by fine motor abilities and susceptible to false impressions. To establish reliability for thought bubbles, score each drawing, and then have two other raters score a randomly selected sample of them. Doing this will estimate inter-rater reliability. Always discuss ratings with the other scorers and reach consensus. Doing this helps with rating consistency.

Validity is making sure that your data accurately measure what they purport to measure (Greig et al., 2007). To establish the validity of thought bubbles we always use them in conjunction with other data sources. We have used thought bubbles to enrich our understanding of interviews and observations we conduct. You can triangulate thought bubbles with what boys write in journals and what they do on assignments and tests to help ensure conclusions are valid. You should also validate findings with prolonged engagement. Work with the boys until no new information is gained. When used with other measures and interpreted cautiously, thought bubbles are an easy and simple way to gain an initial insight on boys' perspectives of themselves as readers and how they feel about reading.

We are learning much about young boys and their development and social and emotional needs. Understanding the influence of self-regulation on learning and how emotional development influences learning and the learning of literacy makes us more empathetic and understanding of boys' needs. In some ways this learning is helping boys who are different, active, or troubled emotionally to gain the respect they need. The next Learning From a Character box contains a Native American tale of a great chief who in some ways is a lot like boys in our classrooms. He is a strong and good male character who is connected to others just as the boys in our classrooms are connected to us and to their peers in the webs of learning we form. Young boys deserve our respect, and they need to learn how to respect those in their world who help them understand their emotions, offer them friendship, and show them what a gift reading can be.

LEARNING ABOUT RESPECTFULNESS FROM A PICTURE BOOK CHARACTER

Brother Eagle, Sister Sky (Jeffers, 1991)
Chief Seattle tells his story about the heartaches Native Americans faced as they saw their land disrespected and destroyed. The book begins with a young boy hearing his father's explanation for why he cannot own the Earth, the eagles, or bears because these are his brothers. From his father the boy learns that streams hold the blood of his grandfather's grandfather, and he learns he must respect the rivers as his own brother. But Chief Seattle points out the destruction being done to the Earth and asks, what

will happen when the buffalo are all slaughtered, when the horses are tame, and when the hills, eagles, and ponies are gone?

Brother Eagle, Sister Sky teaches boys about respect for animals, the Earth, and its people. Reading this story helps us, as teachers, to understand the care young boys need to become literate. Too many young boys see literacy as something disposable, a task only useful in the classroom with little connection to real life. If we listen to the words of Chief Seattle, who said, "all things are connected like the blood that unites us" (unpaged), we might see that losing even one boy to aliteracy is a tragic waste. All boys deserve the right to be brought into the web of literacy and to hear great stories like *Brother Eagle, Sister Sky*.

- Do you read stories with positive male characters in your classroom?

- Do your classroom structure and the activities offered help boys develop social and emotional coping skills?

- How do you help young boys gain the respect they need?

QUESTIONS FOR DISCUSSION

■ What is school like for boys in preschool and the early grades?

■ What are young boys like socially and emotionally, and what can we do to contribute to the development of each of these?

■ How can we uncover boys' perceptions and emotions about themselves and reading?

CHAPTER 4

Creating a Classroom Climate That Meets the Special Needs of Young Boys

n this chapter we transform ideas presented in Chapters 1, 2, and 3 into specific strategies you can use to make your classroom more conducive to boys' language, cognitive, emotional, and social needs. You play an important role, and the boys in your classroom will get off to a bright start when you

- Focus instruction on best practices and recommendations from IRA, especially with regard to oral language, phonemic awareness, and fluency
- Vary skill instruction so it is captivating and enticing
- Develop a learning community in which boys' voices and contributions are honored and respected
- Provide literacy experiences that capture and focus boys' attention

Although we have narrowed the main discussion of this chapter to oral language, phonemic awareness, fluency, and attention, we recognize that the learning of literacy is not broken into bits. We take a holistic view of learning. However, because of space limitations we focus on particular skills and abilities because we feel that they are most important to young boys when they are beginning to learn how to read. We want you to remember that even if a component such as comprehension or vocabulary is not mentioned we do not mean it is any less important. We encourage you to seek other sources to better understand how to teach each of these.

Building Learning Communities

Learning communities are places where teachers and students work together collaboratively and purposefully to construct meaning and enhance learning. These skills are important in the world today. Borders are not the barriers they used to be, and students in the 21st century need to learn how to cooperate with a diverse population and co-construct knowledge as a team (Prensky, 2001a, 2001b; Wenger, 1998).

Shared learning, partnerships, and a sense of family are forged in learning communities, and this can be especially important for the social and emotional development of boys. Early friendships can last a lifetime, and young boys learn much about emotions from other boys. When young boys see other boys displaying empathy they learn a valuable lesson in care and responsibility. Just as in any family there is a head, as teachers we need to take this lead but in a facilitative way. The following list is adapted from the work of Tompkins (2005), who explains ways to build learning communities within the context of reading. We build on and extend Tompkins's ideas to address the unique qualities and needs of boys, and the instructional ideas presented in this chapter will help you build a constructive, nurturing learning community in your classroom.

- Responsibility—Boys must be responsible for their learning, behavior, and the contributions they make to the classroom. To build responsibility, boys must have goals and the means to meet them. No matter what their reading level, boys must feel that their contributions matter and that they are respected and valued members of the group.

- Opportunities—Boys must have the opportunity to read and write for authentic purposes. They should be given the opportunity to read for authentic purposes and write for real audiences.

- Engagement—Boys are motivated to learn, but they need to be actively involved in the learning process. When possible and appropriate, boys must be free to engage actively, to choose the books they want to read, to decide how they want to respond, and to pick which projects they wish to pursue.

- Demonstration—We need to demonstrate literacy skills and strategies, and boys need to observe. Boys need to see, hear, and feel what capable readers do as they read. We also need to allow boys to demonstrate what they learn to their peers.

- Risk taking—Boys need to work on puzzles and challenges, and they need to be encouraged to explore topics, make guesses, and take risks without being put down. Taking risks in a safe environment builds self-esteem, and when boys work together they build friendships. Being someone's friend demands a moral sense, and boys who work together advance their emotional, social, and moral reasoning.

- Instruction—We serve as the experts, and through minilessons on reading processes, skills, and strategies boys become versed in what they need to know.

- Response—Boys make personal connections to stories when they relate to their interests and needs. Boys need to connect and respond to literature in authentic ways, such as by developing scripts for Readers Theatre and participating in grand conversations. No matter how small responses are they should be honored and celebrated. Young boys enjoy having their accomplishments acknowledged and sharing their success with others.

- Choice—Boys need to be given choices, within parameters we set. They need choices that honor their learning experience and have meaning to them.

- Time—Boys need time to read. Two or three hours of uninterrupted reading time per week is recommended. This time needs to be free of distractions and interruptions, especially in the primary grades.

- Assessment—Boys need to work together with us to establish guidelines for assessment, and this should always entail self-monitoring of their own progress and expand beyond simple skills. Boys should be assessed for their achievement, participation, cooperation, and responsibility.

The brains and bodies of young children are often under stress, both in school and at home. Friendship and a sense of belonging are important to young boys, and they feel stressed if they believe that no one cares about them or values their thinking. When boys feel uncared for, their learning often shuts down. However, when classroom structures encourage friendship, cooperation, and communities, boys feel a sense of belonging and begin to learn. Wenger (1998) believes that learning communities, or communities of practice, are places in which knowledge is constructed in a useful and practical way. Throughout this chapter, we explain how these ideas can be implemented in the classroom.

ABOUT
A BOY

There is a buzz of excitement in Ms. Anderson's second-grade class today because it is Readers Theatre day. Students are doing an author study of Kevin Henkes and have developed performances from his work. They visited Henkes's website (www.kevinhenkes.com), read an interview with him, and learned how he became an author. Ms. Anderson has provided access to Henkes's books and from these students have chosen two of their favorites, *Lilly's Purple Plastic Purse* (1996) and *Owen* (1993), to develop into Readers Theatre scripts. Ms. Anderson divided her students into two groups. One group, of mostly girls, will perform *Lilly's Purple Plastic Purse* and the other group, made up of mostly boys, will perform *Owen*. Ms. Anderson helps each group develop their scripts. All students are able to contribute—especially exciting because several boys with attention deficits are staying engaged and some of the quieter girls have found their voices and have demonstrated their leadership qualities. Writing and performing the scripts contributes to students' literacy development but the building of learning communities seems to enhance all students' feelings of responsibility, accountability, and inclusion.

On your own or with colleagues, brainstorm answers to the following questions:

- How did Readers Theatre foster a learning community and create a positive learning experience for both boys and girls in Ms. Anderson's classroom?

- What role did the author study and choice of books play in encouraging the boys in Ms. Anderson's class to become actively engaged in literacy activities?

- How might you replicate this experience in your own classroom?

Developing Oral Language

Oral language is the ability to speak and listen and is the basis of reading. Good readers draw on oral language to interpret and understand print. There are three components of oral language that boys need to develop:

1. Form   Boys need to understand the physical aspects of language. They need to be able to hear the sounds in words (phonemes), speak at an appropriate pace with a good tone (fluency), understand meaningful word parts (morphology), and understand the order of words (syntax). Syntax is often a stumbling block for boys who are learning English as a second language.

2. Content—To be successful readers, boys need to have a rich vocabulary and understand the meaning of the words they use (semantics). Pronoun referents are also important to comprehend characters and text. Boys who struggle with reading often have difficulty with these referents.

3. Function—Boys need to know how and when to use language to convey their thoughts, wants, and needs (pragmatics). They need to learn how to interact appropriately in conversations. They need to recognize when they must wait their turn and how to ask questions.

Talk With Boys: The Form of Language

To help boys develop their oral language they need to talk, talk, talk. Boys need to talk to adults and they need to talk with their peers. Vygotsky (1978) has noted that all learning occurs twice, once on a social level and once inside the mind. When young boys work on challenges with others they talk out loud, and this external talk moves them toward self-regulation. In other words, parents and teachers say things to boys as they work to help them regulate their actions (Do not touch that candle!), then as boys develop they begin to use the same form and functions of the language they hear to manage others (Do not take my toy!). Eventually this language becomes internalized and the boy uses it to regulate himself (I had better not do that!). This is what Vygotsky (1978) calls private inner speech.

It is not easy in busy classrooms to take time to talk with boys each day about their experiences, interests, and needs or to allow boys to talk to each other, but it is imperative. Boys need to hear stories read to them and they need to talk about stories' content and illustrations. Teachers also need to talk to boys about the electronic media they use. For instance, if you know a boy likes a certain video game, talk to him about it and ask him to explain the strategies he uses. Imagine the pride and positive feelings he will gain when you show you are interested in the same things.

There are a number of ways to get conversations going in your classroom. Watch a movie with your students and talk to them about it. Listen to a song and sing along, then investigate the artist and talk about the meaning behind the lyrics. Take a walk around the school and talk to boys about what they see, hear, and feel. Point out things that you see, give them labels, and discuss them in words appropriate to their maturity. Model the pragmatics and functions of real-world conversations and be sure to listen more and talk less. Listening should account for as much as 80% of your conversation time. Do not monopolize the conversation or say things you think boys mean. Ask questions, but not too many, and when you do ask questions make sure they are open-ended and require more than a yes-or-no answer: How did you..., Why did you..., Tell me what happened...?

Don't be surprised if the boys you talk with say few words. Remember the characters in *Yo! Yes?* (Raschka, 1993) that you read about in Chapter 2? When responding to a boy's simple utterances, elaborate what he says with a longer sentence and extended vocabulary. If a boy says, "I see," extend his idea with, "You see the books stacked in the corner. I wonder how tall they are? How could we measure their height?" Remember the goal for doing this is to help boys think in longer sentences, build vocabulary, and express themselves more readily.

Young boys learning English as a second language need to be immersed in the language and supplied with opportunities to talk. Talk is critical to helping these boys acquire the structures and vocabulary they need. Young boys learning English need caring individuals who are patient and who have respect for their dialects and dialogues. They need models that let them know when their message is not clear or when it is incomplete. To do this, be patient and ask those boys to provide clarification as needed.

Read Aloud, Discuss Books, and Ask Questions: The Content of Language

No matter how old boys are, they need to hear stories read aloud every day (Cooper, Chard, & Kiger, 2006), even if boys can read to themselves. Hearing stories read aloud develops language, builds fluency, and improves vocabulary by introducing bigger and more complex words. Reading with expression will help boys understand how elements of speech supply information, so as you read use stress, pitch, and tone to help boys comprehend what they hear. When you read with expression, boys come to understand that they need to do the same.

As you read, watch boys' facial expressions for indications that they do not understand a word or concept. Use words from read-alouds often throughout the day to reinforce their meaning. Words become familiar with frequent use and connection to the world.

Encourage boys to talk about stories, illustrations, and points of interest in the books you read. Keene and Zimmermann (1997) note that children make varied text connections. They make connections to texts they have heard before (text-to-text), relate texts to themselves (text-to-self), and connect texts to the broader world (text-to-world). Each of these is important, so when you read to boys encourage them to make such connections. Also be sure to allow time and space where boys can get together, read side-by-side, and talk to one another about what they read, hear, and see. This will enhance their reading as well as their social and emotional development.

Play With Words: The Function of Language

Good games challenge boys physically, intellectually, and emotionally, and word play fits right in. Games encourage boys to talk and negotiate, and games extend vocabulary and social skills. Talk is fun and exciting when it centers on a game. In his book on boys, literacy, and popular culture Newkirk (2002) notes how important oral and physical humor is to boys. Boys love to act silly, and bodily humor is often part of this. Unfortunately, most of us do not appreciate this trait and boys' love of humor often goes underground, which could lead to boys becoming discouraged or resistant to reading. As you read or talk to boys, encourage them to play with words they find interesting. Teach familiar poems and songs to help boys gain pleasure in language (Cooper et al., 2006). Have boys create new lines or verses for favorite songs. Choose boy-friendly songs and topics with predictable, repetitive patterns. Write the patterns on chart paper leaving blank lines for words. For example, the well-known song "The Wheels on the Bus" may look like this:

The wheels on the _____ go _____ and _____.

Encourage boys to echo read the results of such exercises to build syntax and prosody, which is especially important for boys learning English as a second language. Rhythm and rhyme aid memory and offer an opportunity to discuss how words and music combine. Boys like to be active in their leaning, so encourage them to make up motions to go along with songs. Many young boys have a difficult time sitting for long periods, so get them out of their seats to perform. As you sing, let boys move to the beat or keep the beat by clapping or tapping their feet. Also remember to write down stories, songs, and rhymes as you work on oral language so they can be read or sung later. This will help boys make the speech-to-print connection.

In Chapter 2 you learned about how boys' eyes are built to detect motion, location, and speed, so it is now easier to understand why many boys love to toss objects. Tossing things wakes up their brains and if used with caution and supervision it can be an active and motivating way for boys to use and practice their language skills. Provide boys with a word and have them toss a beanbag as they call out its rhyme, antonym, or synonym.

And don't forget board games and card games. Digital natives (Prensky, 2001a, 2001b) may have short attention spans for old ways of learning yet have very long attention spans for games that pose a challenge. Take a tip from game developers and choose, develop, and use games that are easy to learn, difficult to master, thought provoking, and allow short-term goals to be met.

Developing Phonemic Awareness

Phonemic awareness is the ability to hear and isolate individual sounds that make up words (Cooper et al., 2006). It is an essential skill for decoding, or sounding out unknown words, and encoding, or putting sounds back together to spell. It is important to understand that phonemic awareness is not phonics. There are no printed letters or words involved. Phonemic awareness is an auditory skill that is taught without pencil or paper. As researcher Cory Hansen notes, "You can teach phonemic awareness in the dark" (personal communication, July 10, 2007). Phonemic awareness develops naturally in environments where language play occurs. Songs, poems, traditional rhymes, and books like *The Cat in the Hat* by Dr. Seuss help build awareness skills in an interesting, enjoyable manner.

Phonemic awareness is a powerful predictor for early reading success (Adams, 1990). A lack of phonemic awareness may stem from faulty brain connections, little experience with stories and nursery rhymes, status as an English-language learner, a lack of exposure to standard English pronunciation, or persistent ear infections as a young child. To hear phonemes in words, boys need healthy auditory systems and input. Ninety percent of students identified as having learning disabilities lack phonemic awareness, and many children placed in special education might have caught up if their problems had been identified early (Shaywitz, 2003). Because boys make up the majority of children placed in remedial classrooms and special education, it is important to provide explicit and systematic instruction in this important language and reading skill to boys who need it.

The Importance of Repetition

Many boys learn by experience (by doing and moving) but today's push of academics into earlier grades leaves little time for this type of learning. The more a boy uses a skill the easier it becomes. Neuroscience shows that the more synapses get activated the faster and easier they fire (Freberg, 2005; Stamm, 2007). Over time, repetition causes the level of neurotransmitters needed to fire a neuron to be reduced. Practice and repetition lead to physical changes in the structure of the brain, which leads to the conservation of mental energy.

Also remember that from an information-processing perspective, working memory has limited space. So it is important to repeat letter sounds until they become automatic. When a boy can manipulate sounds in words he is ready to make the speech-to-print connection. When word recognition becomes automatic, areas in the brain used for attention, working memory, and cognitive control become free to focus on making meaning from print. This is the greatest gift we can give boys because it is the beginning of comprehension.

A Good Sequence for Teaching Phonemic Awareness

You can nurture phonemic awareness with songs, nursery rhymes, read-alouds, and games. According to Yopp and Yopp (2000), phonemic awareness activities should be the following:

- Age appropriate, engaging, and encouraging of children's experimentation with oral language

- Planned and purposeful, not incidental

- Part of a balanced literacy program that includes comprehension, decoding, vocabulary, spelling, and written expression

The key is to help boys hear sounds in speech then transfer this skill to print.

As the criteria above demonstrate, phonemic awareness should not be taught in isolation. Instruction in phonemic awareness should be set in a larger context (i.e., with books for support) and be explicit, systematic, and active. The following sequence for teaching phonemic awareness, adapted from Cooper et al. (2006), is provided as a sample:

- Segment sentences into words—*The boy can run.* = *The / boy / can / run*
- Blend words into a sentence—*The / boy / can / run = The boy can run.*
- Segment compound words into separate words—*baseball = base + ball*
- Blend separate words into a compound word—*base + ball = baseball*
- Segment two-syllable words that are not compounds into syllables—*transformer = trans + form + er*
- Blend syllables into words—*trans + form + er = transformer*
- Segment words with multiple syllables—*brotherhood = /bro/ + /ther/ + /hood/*
- Blend syllables into words—*/bro/ + /ther/ + /hood/ = brotherhood*
- Segment words (or syllables) into onsets and rimes—*dad = /d/ + /ad/*
- Blend segmented onsets and rimes into words—*/d/ + /ad/ = dad*
- Segment words into individual phonemes—*ball = /b/ + /a/ + /ll/*
- Blend individual phonemes into words—*/b/ + /a/ + /ll/ = ball*

Books with favorite male characters can also be used for important phonemic awareness activities. Troia, Roth, and Graham (1998) offer seven ways to provide practice in segmenting and blending words (which increase in difficulty) and using these in the context of a picture book with a beloved character, such as *Froggy Goes to School* (London, 1996; see Learning From a Character box that follows) will add novelty to skill development.

1. Sound matching—Show boys several pictures in the book and ask which words begin with a specific sound.

2. Oddity detection—Turn to a page and ask which object's name does not end with the same sound.

3. Same/different judgment—Ask students, for example, Does *desk* start with the /d/ sound? When you put these sounds together do they make the word *race*: /r/ /a/ /s/?

4. Segment isolation—Ask students, What is the first sound of *bus*? What is the first part of *sidewalk*? What is the sound at the end of *bus*?

5. Production—Say to students, Tell me a word that begins with /b/. Tell me a word that ends with the same sound as *tip*. Tell me each sound in the word *book*.

6. Counting—Tell students to count the number of parts they hear in the word *Froggy*.

7. Compound production   Ask students, What word do you get when you change the /n/ in *man* to /p/? Say *peel;* now say *eel.* What sound did you omit?

LEARNING ABOUT TOLERANCE FROM A PICTURE BOOK CHARACTER

Froggy Goes to School (London, 1996)

The first part of *Froggy Goes to School* provides a glimpse into the life of a forgetful yet lovable frog. The story opens with Froggy forgetting to get dressed and boarding the school bus in his underwear! His day revolves around trying to hide this fact—he hops behind bushes, hides behind an umbrella, and pretends to be a flowerpot. But the call, "Frrrooggy," that he thought was his teacher calling his name was really his father waking him up. Forgetting to get dressed was only in Froggy's dream.

The second part of the story takes place on the first day of school. Froggy flop, flop, flops to the bus stop, fully clothed, and makes it to his class. At school, Froggy sees his name on his desk and is able to pronounce it by stretching out each phoneme, "Frrrooggy." During class Froggy has a difficult time paying attention, and he needs his teacher and peers to be tolerant of his behavior. But at circle time, when Froggy gets to tell the class what he did last summer, he shines. He talks about how he learned to swim, and he sings a catchy song—so catchy that everyone, including the principal, joins in.

Froggy is a colorful and interesting character young boys enjoy. His antics capture boys' attention and the drawn-out phonemes in Froggy's name can be used to teach phonemic awareness skills. Using picture books to place this important skill in context is important. Learning phonemes in isolation and devoid of text may be difficult and much less fun for young boys, but helping boys hear phonemes spoken by favorite characters helps them make meaningful connections between oral language and texts in a fun and interesting way.

Placing phonemic awareness activities in the context of a story will help boys better understand this important language component. Froggy's story can also teach young boys about tolerance. When he was in the classroom, Froggy was distractible. When it came time to share his ideas, Froggy, like many other students, was very impatient. His teacher Mrs. Witherspoon modeled tolerance for an enthusiastic boy.

- Do you ever consider how difficult it can be for some boys to be patient when they, like Froggy, have an exciting story to tell?

Phonemic awareness is an important precursor to learning to read and spell. Unfortunately, phonemic awareness is a skill many young boys lack. Boys who need instruction in phonemic awareness must be taught in active and interesting ways. The next sections provide several strategies to do this with young boys. These ideas are drawn from best practices and recommendations from the IRA but they are not exhaustive. These ideas are provided as examples of how you can make activities you are already using more conducive to the learning of young boys.

Sound Cards

We recommend always using books as starting points for phonemic awareness activities. Phonemic awareness activities should be based on words boys hear in stories and words that are of interest to them in their world. Although some boys pick up phonemic awareness by hearing stories, others need language to be made concrete. In these instances it is important to use hands-on materials like sound cards, which are useful because they make the sounds in words explicit. You can develop cards with a boy-friendly focus as follows:

1. Glean words for sound cards from books you read to boys on topics of interest to them. (Although you will want to carefully choose picture books with good words for phonemic awareness activities, remember that these books can also be used to teach social, emotional, and moral lessons.) For example, if the boys in your classroom are interested in baseball you may read a fiction story like *Baseball Saved Us* (Mochizuki, 1995) to your class and use words from this text to create sound cards. Remember that boys like action words and have preferences for words they can use in their world.

2. After you have developed a list of interesting words, prepare sound cards like the one shown in Figure 2 for the word *ball* (clip art on the Internet provides a rich source for pictures). Print the illustrations on

FIGURE 2
Example of Sound Card for the Word *Ball*

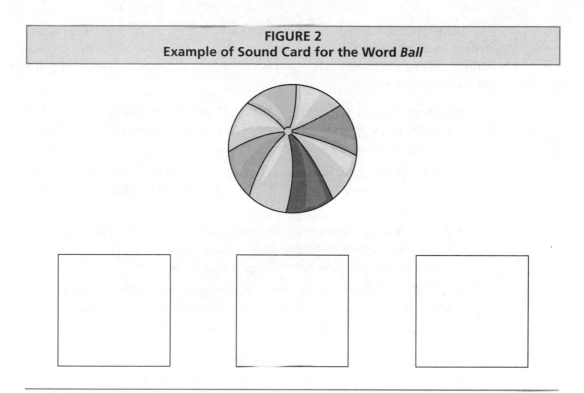

cardstock and laminate them so they will last. Find tokens (such as plastic bingo chips, pennies, cardboard squares) to place in the boxes.

3. Instruct boys in a small group so you can offer scaffolding and support. At first, guide boys through the task by modeling what is to be done. Slowly pronounce the word on the card sound by sound while you push the tokens into the boxes that correspond with each sound. For example, the word *ball* shown in Figure 2 would have three phonemes, /b/ /a/ /l/, so three tokens would be pushed. When you say /b/, push one token into the first box, then say /a/ and push another token into the second box, and finally, say /l/ and push a token into the third box.

4. Repeat the activity, but this time, ask one boy to be your assistant. Instead of you pushing the tokens into the boxes have your assistant do it for you.

5. Provide a second sound card for the word *bat* with an image and three boxes, and transfer responsibility for the activity to the boys. Ask one boy to identify the picture and pronounce the word slowly (this provides the auditory feedback). Encourage the boys to stretch the sounds as they move the tokens into the boxes, /b/ /a/ /t/.

Remember that the brain needs novelty to stay alert and interested. It will habituate or tune out when the same activities are used day after day or when things are not meaningful. You can vary the Sound Cards activity with some of the following ideas:

- Instead of using bingo chips as tokens use plastic letters (using letters crosses the bridge between phonemic awareness and print, so it is more like a phonics activity).

- For an auditory and kinesthetic focus say a word out loud (stretching the sounds) and have boys repeat the word and count the phonemes on their fingers.

- A more abstract activity to use after boys have had time practicing with the Sound Cards is to simply show them a card and ask them to hold up fingers to indicate how many sounds they hear.

- After boys become proficient at counting the number of sounds, ask questions about sounds such as What is the first (or last) sound you hear in *player*? What sound do you hear after the /p/ in *player*?

After students have worked with Sound Cards for a while, begin to help them make the speech-to-print connection by writing sentences to go along with the cards. For example, a card showing an image of a baseball player can be used to write a sentence like *Jackie Robinson was a great hitter* on a sentence strip, and this can become part of a class story.

Activities such as these help boys develop the foundational literacy skills they need in an interesting and meaningful way. Varying activities, making learning active, and using boys' interests, including their passion for male characters, help them develop phonemic awareness and learn positive character traits. Because boys vary in their development, language abilities, and many other ways, they sometimes have difficulty fitting in. Young boys often need to develop courage just to be themselves. The following Learning From a Character box describes a book with a young boy who shows courage in a difficult time. The Appendix contains many more books you can use to help boys learn about the trait of courage.

LEARNING ABOUT COURAGE FROM A PICTURE BOOK CHARACTER

Baseball Saved Us (Mochizuki, 1995)
Baseball Saved Us shows the courage of a group of Japanese Americans in an internment camp during World War II. This story explains how building

a baseball field keeps this group active, alive, and strong. When one young Japanese American boy gets out of the internment camp he faces discrimination. But he uses the skills he learned while in the camp to be strong and to prove he is as good as everyone else. When prejudice rages against Japanese Americans, the boy's skills in baseball give him courage and he realizes the strength he has inside.

- Consider the power of this story and the important message it provides. How do you promote social equity in your classroom?

- In today's society boys are often expected to show a tough exterior. Reflect upon how the classroom climate you develop helps boys develop empathy and respect for all.

- What do you do to help young boys be themselves and stand up for who they are?

- What do you do to help young boys find courage?

Using Movement in Instruction

Neuroscience indicates that instruction that stimulates multiple brain areas (auditory, visual, kinesthetic) helps learners with different styles. Using multiple forms of input aids memory because multiple representations of the concept are produced (Willis, 2007). Learning with one's senses can be fun and active and is just what young boys need to build their literacy skills and self-esteem. Young boys learn by doing and they have boundless energy. Their gross motor skills are advancing and they love to jump, skip, throw, and kick. Cooper et al. (2006) offer an idea for combining practice in phonemic awareness with movement in a game-like atmosphere:

1. Have boys stand in a circle.

2. Say a word with a consonant-vowel-consonant pattern such as *man*. (It's preferable to use words with which they're familiar.)

3. Toss a beanbag to a boy and have him segment the sounds.

4. Have the boy toss the beanbag to a friend who blends the sounds back into the word.

5. Have that boy say another word and toss the beanbag to another boy who segments the word into sounds.

6. Continue until everyone has had a turn segmenting and blending words.

More active learning ideas include the following:

- Tell boys to jump once for each sound in a word. For example, with the word *ball* (/b/ /a/ /l/), boys would jump three times.

- Set up a basketball game with a clean wastepaper basket and a soft, spongy ball so boys can shoot a basket for every challenge they get right. For example, when a boy rhymes the word *bike* with *hike,* hand him the ball and let him toss a winning shot.

- Some boys love competition, so use this in a positive way. Have boys set goals and compete to see if they can achieve them. For example, a boy may set the goal to find four words that rhyme with *ball* in the room or in a book.

- Have boys compete in small groups against one another when they do phonemic awareness activities. For example, when a team is given a challenge the team members must all brainstorm and come to consensus before an answer is accepted for the team. Although correct answers are important, it is just as important for boys to focus on being part of the team and competing for their personal best.

It is vital to always provide consistent and constructive feedback. Explain what is right, and model ideas that still need work. Praise effort and hard work, and do not focus on ability (Dweck, 1999).

Developing Fluency

Fluency is the ability to read with accuracy, expression, and speed (Johns & Lenski, 2005). Fluency is important to comprehension because when boys automatically decode text their precious working memory space can be devoted to making meaning. Freed working memory space allows a boy to process new information, and this builds a deeper understanding of what is being read. Fluency affords children time to make connections between what they are reading and their own lives. Making connections motivates children to read and be transformed by text (Wolf, 2007). If reading does not offer boys this enlightenment or spark their curiosity it is just another skill learned in school. Boys who lack fluency sound choppy when they read because they are stumbling on many words. To build fluency, young boys need to develop their sight vocabulary. They need to read a lot, and when appropriate, read out loud to others (Rasinski, 2003). But round-robin reading can be another esteem buster for young boys (Stipek, 2002). According to Opitz and Rasinski (2008) round-robin reading provides students with an inaccurate view of reading's purpose and causes ineffective habits and embarrassment. In short, it wastes precious classroom time and does little to help boys gain important literacy skills. Better ways to promote fluency include shared reading with a partner and Readers Theatre.

Read-alouds performed by competent and fluent readers help boys hear what fluent reading sounds like. When we read to boys we make a character's voice come alive and help boys understand that reading needs to be expressed smoothly and clearly. Sharing reading with a partner also helps build fluency but in a nonthreatening way. When a boy buddies up with a trusted classmate he knows will not make fun of him he is more likely to take risks and commit to practicing his part to fluency.

Readers Theatre

Boys do not enjoy doing a task that makes them look weak. Asking a young boy to read in a round-robin session could make him develop negative attitudes toward reading. Young boys who struggle with reading are very aware of the effect this has on their social status. They know they are in the low group, hear that they do not read very well, and begin to feel stressed about reading because it is a direct blow to their self-esteem. Neuroscience tells us that stress, anxiety, and boredom interfere with learning. When the amygdala, the brain structure that registers emotion and stress, is in an overactive metabolic state it delays or blocks electrical activity en route to higher cognitive centers. In other words, negative emotional reactions take over and learning just shuts down (LeDoux, 1996; Zambo & Brem, 2004). Remember Ronald Morgan and his reading experience in the Learning From a Character boxes in Chapter 3?

We also know that experiences that are relevant to one's life, interests, and prior knowledge are captivating and motivating. When it comes to boys and reading, the key is to help them feel relaxed when they read and see that reading is an important learning tool. Readers Theatre is the perfect means to do just this because it gives boys an authentic reason to read, makes them part of a community, helps them develop fluency, and has the potential to be fun.

Readers Theatre is the dramatic production of a script by a group of readers (Martinez, Roser, & Strecker, 1999). Scripts can be developed from a wide range of texts such as traditional literature, comic books, informational texts, and websites. When it comes to reading, boys like choices, and they like to feel a sense of competence and control over what they do (Brozo, 2002; Smith & Wilhelm, 2002), so let boys develop a Readers Theatre script using texts they enjoy.

In a Readers Theatre activity, each child assumes a role and reads the character's lines. Practicing one's lines over and over again to get them right and sound like the character builds fluency, an important part of comprehension. When boys read fluently, smoothly, and with prosody, they are better able to comprehend and they feel better about themselves as readers. To cause these changes in perception it is important to use stories that appeal to boys in Readers Theatre.

Although some descriptions of Readers Theatre note that children do not need to use much action, it is important to let boys move to enact scripts because they like to do so and have the energy. Let them dress as the character they are portraying and use the character's voice, gestures, facial expressions, and body language. The beauty of Readers Theatre comes from its simplicity and its reliance upon imagination and creativity. Performances do not need fancy costumes, elaborate props, or scenery, and scripts can be developed from almost any type of text (Campbell & Cleland, 2003). The following are some ideas for developing scripts from literature and from comics.

Readers Theatre From Literature. If there are character traits you want boys in your classroom to develop such as tolerance, honesty, or cooperation, choose a story where the characters display these traits. For example, in *The Boy Who Held Back the Sea* (Locker, 1993; see also the Learning From a Character box on page 86) Jan, the main character, faces a challenge and learns about honesty. This would be an appropriate book to use for Readers Theatre with young boys because its plot is exciting, boys can identify with the main character, and the story teaches a valuable trait. To create a Readers Theatre performance we suggest using the ideas of Johns and Lenski (2005) and Tompkins (2005) but adapting them for young boys.

First, choose a story, poem, or song that appeals to boys. Stories should have a positive male character. Look for characters facing difficult choices and doing honorable things. Be sure that the story is at students' independent reading level and can be broken into sections and read in parts. Consider starting with some of the books in the Learning From a Character boxes throughout this book and in the Appendix.

Have the boys read the story silently. Then discuss critically and deeply the story's characters and plot. Encourage students to talk about the characters and how they act and feel. Ask the boys to read it again. Remember that reading aloud can be a real esteem buster for young boys, so assess what they need to make the activity a success. Teach vocabulary and scaffold reading with strategies.

Now develop a script from the piece. Depending on your grade level, boys may use the entire story, or they may choose to develop and extend one scene. If you teach first grade you will likely need to do a lot of scaffolding. The following is a sample script from *The Boy Who Held Back the Sea*:

Narrator: Jan knew he would be in trouble if his mother discovered he had never gone to Mr. Schuyler's house, but still he ran to get help.

Scene: *Policeman talking with teacher.*

Jan:	[enters running and shouting] The dam is leaking! The dam is leaking!
Policeman:	[laughing] Go back to watching for sea monsters.
Teacher:	A leaking dam is silly. Lying boys who don't obey their parents come to bad ends!
Jan:	But it's true, it's true! The dam is leaking! It's leaking!
Policeman:	Such conviction. If what you say is true go back to the dam, boy, and I will send help.

After the script is developed, prepare for the performance. Allow boys to choose their parts and have them work in small teams to rehearse. Encourage boys to develop their character's voice (tone and volume), gestures, facial expressions, and body language. This will help boys learn to read emotions in others and interpret social cues. Rehearse the script several times in several ways. Strive for accurate pronunciation, voice projection, and inflection. Character interpretations should be developed as fully as possible.

The goal is to perform the script for an audience. Readers Theatre can be presented in a corner of a classroom or on an auditorium stage. Costumes and props are unnecessary, but a few items that help boys step into character can be used to enhance interest as long as they do not interfere with the performance. Students stand or sit in rows and read and act out their lines. They remain in position through the production or enter and exit as characters come and go. If boys are sitting they should stand to say their lines; if they are standing they should step forward to stand out.

Readers Theatre is not a polished production. It should be fun and interesting. The ultimate goal of Readers Theatre is to give boys an authentic purpose to read and the opportunity to actively produce something of meaning to them. It also helps boys learn how to cooperate and can boost their self-esteem when they experience the thrill of a live performance and hear an audience clap for them.

Readers Theatre From Comics. Young boys enjoy comic books because they are humorous, visual, and unique. These qualities make them very different from traditional texts. For struggling male readers, comic books look less threatening. Scripts based on comic books can be used in Readers Theatre to build fluency, develop sight words, increase awareness of phonics, and improve grammar skills. Because they typically have a story line, comic books help boys develop story structure and sequencing skills and these benefits will be realized when developing a Readers Theatre script from them. Furthermore, if boys speak a language other than English, or speak nonstandard English, the visual clues in comics enhance their learning of English syntax and vocabulary.

For young boys, short, interesting comics are best. Comic strips with favorite characters like Garfield or the children in *The Family Circus* work well and are easily accessible on the Internet. To develop a script from a comic, simply follow the steps described in the literature example on page 84. However, you or the students writing the script may want to extend the simple ideas in a comic and enrich the part and vocabulary.

Readers Theatre activities are especially important for boys because they engage them physically and encourage them to develop responsibility, especially when their performance becomes part of a larger project and extends beyond classroom walls. Performing Readers Theatre in another classroom, at a school assembly, or for elderly adults in the community encourages boys to learn their part to fluency, take ownership in their learning, and develop a learning community. To ensure the boys in your class are ready for their performance, verify that they each have the skills they need to read their part fluently, have the social skills they need to work cooperatively, and are part of a peer group that models and expects responsibility from each of its members. Use natural consequences to help boys understand how important it is for them to act responsibly. Picture books can also be used to help boys better understand responsibility and the disappointment those who care feel when one is dishonest and does not act responsibly. The following Learning From a Character box provides an example of this, and the Appendix contains many more books you can use to help boys learn about responsibility.

LEARNING ABOUT RESPONSIBILITY FROM A PICTURE BOOK CHARACTER

The Boy Who Held Back the Sea (Locker, 1993)
The Boy Who Held Back the Sea can be used in a Readers Theatre activity because it contains an exciting tale that appeals to the hearts and interests of boys. The book contains a story within a story about two young boys facing consequences because of their lies. Pieter is in his room when his grandmother tells him the story of Jan, a boy with an imagination who struggles to tell the truth and act responsibly. One day Jan lies to his mother and tells her he is going to read to a blind miller, but he goes into the woods instead. Jan has a grand time until he realizes that the dike that holds back the water from flooding the town has a small leak. Of course, no one believes Jan because he has a reputation for being a liar so he is forced to act responsibly and to hold his finger in the dike all night. Fortunately, on his way to work the schoolmaster sees Jan and realizes that he has saved the town. In the end Jan realizes that his past ways were hurting others so he makes amends.

Hearing this story from his grandmother also makes Pieter aware that he needs to be honest and responsible.

- Think about ways you can use this book in a Readers Theatre activity.

- How can you use it to help boys become part of a learning community?

- How could this story help the boys in your class learn about honesty and responsibility?

- How can you use this book to help boys understand that once a lie is told, one must face consequences and make amends?

Developing Attention

To understand oral language, hear phonemes in words, read a short story, and comprehend what has been read, a boy must be able to focus and sustain his attention. He must tune out external noises in the environment (e.g., other students talking) and internal noises (e.g., a voice in his head telling him to think about something else). A boy that has never been read to as a small child or engaged in activities requiring sustained attention may not understand that he needs to pay attention. Attention, like other cognitive functions, can improve over time with practice—but not through rote drill and repetition, which will cause the brain to habituate and tune out. For some boys, you will need to use the same strategies again and again. This does not have to be dull, because even though a routine is consistent the books and activities that accompany it should vary. Attention can improve with sound, structured, and systematic instruction. Earlier is better, but it is never too late!

Attention can be broken down into a series of behaviors as follows:

- Becoming alert and aware

- Shifting or changing one's focus and orienting to something new

- Maintaining or sustaining focus as long as necessary and tuning out other distracting information and thoughts

Visual attention improves significantly during preschool and early elementary years and at this age many young boys become drawn to television, video games, movies, and other quick-changing media. The brain is use-dependent, so when this happens boys' brains adapt to a shift-and-scan processing style (Stamm, 2007). They are constantly looking around the room (shifting their focus) and investigating (scanning) what is there, which is detrimental to their learning because their minds jump and wander. Boys who develop this processing style have difficulty self-regulating or inhibiting their impulses. They have trouble keeping their attention on the task at hand and ignoring other things going on in the classroom.

Even if a boy does not engage with media entertainment he still may have difficulty focusing. Attention develops with practice, and if it is never used consistently a boy may encounter problems when this cognitive resource is needed in school. A boy who has never been read to may not realize he needs to focus on the print on the page. He may have a difficult time sustaining his focus long enough to sit still and listen to a short story. The lack of focus may get boys in trouble, and if this happens repeatedly this can cause them to believe they will never read. This may cause stress for young boys and start them in a cycle of failure early in their school careers. Combine all of this with the fact that the frontal lobe—necessary for sustained attention—develops later in boys than in girls, and it is no wonder that the number of young boys getting diagnosed with attention problems is rising and that many of them lose motivation and drive.

Structured Read-Aloud Sessions for Boys With Severe Attention Difficulties

In a structured read-aloud the book being read is placed consistently in a certain space so the boy knows where to focus his attention. The idea of focusing a boy's attention on a particular spot comes from Stamm (2007), who uses it to train the attention of infants, toddlers, and preschoolers. A structured read-aloud is important and developmentally appropriate for boys in kindergarten through third grade.

There are several ways you can create a focus space. You can lay down a placemat (dark, plain, without letters, words, or pictures) or a piece of construction paper, or you can create a box with masking tape on a desk and place the book in it. You want to create this space to provide a visible, concrete cue that alerts the boy that it is time to settle down for reading and focus his attention here. The marked-off space helps a boy with attention difficulties focus on a narrowed spot instead of shifting and scanning the room. The keys to its success are clear directions, repetition, consistency, and an interesting book.

This activity needs to be conducted in a one-on-one situation, which is not an easy task for a teacher with a full classroom. However, because of the importance and urgency of helping young boys understand and train their attention we encourage you to get creative in soliciting helpers to work with young boys. Parent volunteers and older students can easily learn the following steps and procedures if you develop an environment conducive to success. You will need a boy-friendly, interesting book, and a clearly delineated space.

Before Reading. Choose a book the boy suggests he would like to read or one you believe he will be interested in reading. Remember that boys like to read exciting stories, mysteries, or texts with personal significance. Boys will resist reading (and not pay attention) if they encounter unfamiliar or dull stories. Boys want to understand boyhood, so books with positive male characters should be used in this activity because they can be springboards to discussions about challenges the boy may be facing, like being responsible for his behavior, focusing on a task, or postponing desires until work is complete.

Choose a book that is at the boy's listening and attention level. If the book is beyond the boy's maturity, contains a drawn-out story, or has complicated vocabulary, it is likely that the boy you are working with will have difficulty focusing and sustaining his attention on the story.

Prepare as you would for any read-aloud, with a few exceptions. Select vocabulary the boy will need to comprehend the story and teach him these words prior to the read-aloud. Consider how you will activate prior knowledge and also prepare one or two questions to ask at the beginning and end of the read-aloud. Do not use questions as you read because they may distract the boy from your objective of training his brain to focus on the task at hand.

Select a quiet and comfortable area away from noises, blowing fans, classmates doing other things, or eye-catching stimuli that may distract the boy. Boys learn best when they are side-by-side, not face-to-face (Gurian & Ballew, 2003; Sax, 2005, 2007), so select a place where the boy and you can sit side-by-side at a table or desk. Create an emotionally safe situation by using the notion of a learning community, even if in this instance the community is of only two members. Remember that a boy with an attention problem may associate reading with failure and humiliation. The best state for a boy to be in for reading and learning from print is a relaxed and alert one.

Keep the structured sessions consistent. Consistency reinforces feelings of security by letting the brain predict what will happen next so it can focus on challenging tasks like reading. Also, keep the sessions controlled and short. Boys want reasonable limits and need appropriate expectations. Remember that the attention span of young boys is shorter than that of girls, and that boys with disabilities often have even briefer attention spans.

During Reading. Define the reading space and place the book in it, modeling interest and enthusiasm about the book and the reading session about to take place. As in any read-aloud, activate the boy's prior knowledge. Show the boy the cover and ask him one or two questions to help him connect what he already knows to the text he is about to hear. Sit next to the boy and give a verbal cue like "It's time to read. Look at the book and follow along with me." This will alert him that you are going to begin and that he needs to settle down and focus his attention on the book.

Read the story orally with the following points in mind:

- Boys tend to not hear soft or high sounds very well, so if you have a soft, quiet voice increase your volume. Caution: Reading too loudly may cause the boy to become loud in return, distracting him from the story.
- Boys tend to respond slower to auditory sources of information, so speak clearly and slow the rhythm of your reading down a bit. This will help his brain tune in and process the meaning from the print. Caution: Do not read so slowly or monotonously that you become dull.

As you read, slide your finger under the words and encourage the boy to do the same. If he becomes distracted tap your finger on the page to alert him that he needs to bring his focus back to the book.

After Reading. When you are finished, ask a few questions to make sure the boy understands the story. Allow him to move; let him retell the story or his favorite part in an active way. Ideas include the following:

- Getting up out of his chair to imitate favorite characters or scenes
- Joining other students for Readers Theatre
- Drawing the meaning of vocabulary words, a synopsis of the story, or his favorite characters or scenes

Remember, this is a very controlled situation and you should use it with the following two objectives in mind:

1. To help a boy who is experiencing problems learn how and where to focus his attention when he is reading a book
2. To catch the boy's attention with a good picture book so he, like his peers, will be exposed to good literature

A structured read-aloud is a specific strategy that will not be necessary after a boy learns where to attend. Make the transition slowly but continue to provide support. Ideas include the following:

- Have the boy sit on a small rug during reading circle time. This visual and tactile aide can cue him to the fact that it is time to sit and listen to the story being read.
- As the boy practices reading on his own have him use a clear plastic ruler to know where to focus and keep track of his place.

Focusing one's attention and putting distracting thoughts out of one's mind requires self-regulation and responsibility. These are important needs of young boys, but ones many struggle to attain. The next Learning From a Character box contains a character boys can learn from because he struggles with his focus. The Kenyan boy in the story is not responsible; instead of doing what he was asked, he does as he pleases until he gets caught. This book is interesting to young boys and because it has engaging illustrations and few words per page, it can be used for the structured reading activity mentioned above.

LEARNING ABOUT RESPONSIBILITY FROM A PICTURE BOOK CHARACTER

For You Are a Kenyan Child (Cunnane, 2006)
For You Are a Kenyan Child helps boys learn the importance of acting responsibly. In this story, a young Kenyan boy is asked by his mother to take his grandfather's cows to pasture and watch them carefully. But instead of acting responsibly, the boy becomes distracted. He visits friends, chases monkeys, and enjoys milk sweetened with charcoal. The cows wander. When the boy discovers that the cows are not in the meadow, he panics. There is a marvelous illustration that captures this and shows the worry on his face. Fortunately, his grandfather comes to the rescue and does not scold him. Instead of demeaning the boy he hands the cow switch back to him as a symbol that he has learned a lesson and needs to accept responsibility once again.

- Think about ways you can use this book to help boys understand that they must stay focused on a task.

- Think about ways you can use this book to help the boys in your classroom develop responsibility. What literacy experiences can you give to them to help them transfer what they learned about responsibility from the Kenyan boy to their own lives?

- How do you react when boys let you down? Are you forgiving like the Kenyan boy's grandfather? Instead of getting angry do you hand responsibility back to them?

The previous strategy was for boys with severe attention problems. Although most boys might not need such drastic measures, many boys may need a bit of support. The next section is for those boys.

Boy-Friendly Strategies for Gaining and Maintaining Attention in a Read-Aloud

Before reading, select an area and prepare it. Think about comfort—dim lights, and a quiet corner away from loud noises, blowing fans, and eye-catching distractions. Provide quiet props such as stuffed animals, pillows, and soft blankets so boys can get comfortable.

As you plan your read-aloud, identify an issue of interest, a behavior that needs to be addressed, or a positive character trait the boys in your class need to know more about. Select a picture book with a character experiencing the same issues. Aim to find a book with a human character that is like the child in some significant way. Books with animal characters are fine as long as students can identify with their actions and thoughts (such as Froggy in the Learning From a Character box on page 77). Be sure to carefully examine illustrations for facial expressions and body language. Choose stories or illustrations that have the potential to encourage lively discussions, problem solving, and critical thinking skills. Boys like to be challenged and to problem solve.

Plan read-aloud sessions to be short. Create structure and routine (same time, same place). Have rules in place and consistently enforce them. Focus on what boys do right. Lavish praise and supply specific feedback when necessary.

During reading, provide cues to gain attention (such as "All eyes on me."). Position boys near you and allow those who need it to stand (beside or behind you). As you read, be sure boys can see the words and pictures. Allow them to draw if they need to, and provide opportunities for movement (e.g., show me what the character did, use your face to show me how he looked). As you read, activate prior knowledge. ("Look at this book's cover. What do you think it might be about? Have you ever felt this way? Has this ever happened to you?"). Read the story with expression and at a slow and steady pace, and make explicit connections between ideas you want the boys to learn and the character. Remember to praise boys profusely with specific feedback for listening and appropriate behavior. Boost self-esteem whenever possible.

After reading, engage boys in grand conversations and help them see connections between the character and themselves. Continue this throughout the day and week. Encourage students to rehearse and practice skills and behaviors they learn. Supply plenty of specific, constructive feedback as they practice. Help them have mastery experiences.

Boys sometimes miss things the first time around, so reread books and repeat information as needed. Encourage other individuals that work with your class, such as the school principal or counselor, to reread and extend ideas. Boys enjoy listening to favorite stories, and it is good for their vocabulary and fluency to hear multiple readings.

You need to gain and keep boys' attention. Boys, in turn, need to focus and sustain their attention on the task at hand. The following ideas, which are based on the work of Woolfolk (2006) but have been adapted for young boys, can be used to gain and maintain boys' attention when they read or work on other tasks. Keep in mind as you read this list that although it's important to grab attention, constant attention is counterproductive for both boys and girls—neurons need time to rest. You cannot expect to have students' attention all the time. Students can either be making meaning in their minds or focusing on you. Students need time to think, to go internal. Give boys some down time. Cramming too much content in too little time equals little retention.

- Intensity—The brain takes note of contrasts. It pays attention to extremes more than to the midrange or average. If boys are to be interested in reading, reading needs to stand out from the daily routine. Books can stand out visually when they look interesting and have props to go along. Books on topics of interest to boys (e.g., trucks, other boys, animals), large books, pop-up books, and other books that stand out for some physical reason may capture boys' attention and make them want to explore the book. Intensity can be fostered auditorily by making your voice loud or soft when you read.

- Size and shape—Use a variety of books—big books, miniature books, and oddly shaped books—to capture boys' interest.

- Novelty—The brain habituates or adapts to the same old materials it sees day after day. If the same books are used day after day they will be perceived to be boring to the brain and the boy will simply tune out. On the other hand, the brain learns when it is alert and aroused with new, exciting, or interesting experiences and ideas. Think of ways you can incorporate these ideas to enhance boys' literacy. Bring in various people to read to the class (especially male role models) and keep the classroom library full of new and interesting books. More books typically lead to more reading. Public and school libraries are good and free sources of new books to bring in. Let favorites hibernate for a time, then bring them back for a second round of investigation and interest. Also keep and rotate a variety of writing tools, including computers.

- Challenge—Boys pay better attention when they are challenged, when things do not fit with what they know. Puzzling and challenging ideas can lead boys to discover the fun and humor in books. For example, in *Cloudy With a Chance of Meatballs* (Barrett, 1982), meatballs rain from the sky, an incongruous event guaranteed to capture any boy's attention. Try causing surprise by creating disequilibrium. Present confusing and mind-jogging questions and activities to go along with the reading of books, such as What will happen if...? Which one does not belong...? Disequilibrium, even though cognitively uncomfortable, motivates a boy to search for a solution, to use the strategies you are teaching to try to figure things out for himself. This causes deeper processing of the materials and both cognitive and literacy growth.

- Difficulty—Of course, disequilibrium must be at an appropriate level. Young boys will not be interested in books with complex language or ideas they cannot grasp. If a boy lacks prior knowledge it is unlikely that he will attend to what is being read. Build prior knowledge with realia, pictures, computer simulations, and other means. Also remember that when you want a boy to stay on task and read alone, he needs to understand the vocabulary and have a book at his independent level.

- Anticipation—Before reading, set your class up for an unexpected turn of events with a cue such as "Just wait until you read this book...!"

- Personal significance—Boys pay more attention to stories they can relate to and stories that are personally significant to them. In Chapter 5 you will learn several strategies that can be used for this. Boys want to understand who they are and who they can become, so books with these themes are likely to catch their interest. Another way to bring in personal significance is to use books that contain the child's own name. Boys love to hear stories with characters that have their names. If the boy has an unusual name and no books can be found, change the name of the main character to the boy's. This will add humor to the story and will help keep the boy's interest as you read.

- Similarity between tasks—When two voices sound alike a boy may have difficulty tuning in to one and eliminating the distraction of the other. If the room in which a boy is being asked to listen to a story is noisy with two or more similar-sounding voices (especially if they are female and the person reading the story is female) he may have difficulty keeping his attention on the correct voice. Keep distracting conversations clear of read-aloud areas.

- Cues and signals—Sometimes boys need direct auditory or visual cues and signals to help them understand when and where to attend. Explicitly state that it's time to attend by using words such as "watch" and "all eyes and minds on the book." Use visual signals like flashing lights or soft music to assist boys in making the transition to a new activity and understanding it is time to attend.

- Differences—The ability to attend, like many things, varies along a continuum. Some elementary-age children can sustain genuine attention at a high constant level for 10 minutes, but others for much less. Young boys with learning disabilities will have a harder time attending for long periods of time.

- Emotions—Emotions drive attention and attention propels learning (LeDoux, 1996; Stamm, 2007; Zambo & Brem, 2004). Emotional stories that have personal significance to a boy will help him maintain his attention for a longer period of time. Furthermore, if a boy is nervous or worried about something when you want him to attend to reading, he will find it difficult. Conditions for optimal learning are to be relaxed yet alert. Reading for young boys works best when they are fed, rested, and comfortable. If a boy is distraught over reading because of previously negative experiences, be patient and allow time for him to understand that when it comes to reading you will not humiliate him.

Strong emotions such as anxiety, sadness, or fear can cause learning to shut down just as positive emotions help us to feel better about ourselves. In Chapter 3 you learned about the importance of healthy emotional development and how some boys, for various reasons, do not develop emotionally. Many times young boys put on a front to show they are tough, when in reality they care very much. Boris in the Learning From a Character box that follows demonstrates this well. Boris is tough and mean on the outside but is really very caring and loving inside. When boys hear about Tough Boris they will feel empathy for him and learn that even tough guys can show generosity toward those they care about. You also can use *Tough Boris* to help boys understand it is courageous to show how they feel.

LEARNING ABOUT GENEROSITY FROM A PICTURE BOOK CHARACTER

Tough Boris (Fox, 1994)
Tough Boris is about a pirate named Boris von der Borch who is tough, fearless, and greedy—that is, until his parrot dies. Boris's emotional connection to a small bird reveals that even though he was tough on the outside he was really very generous with his love inside. You can use *Tough Boris* to help boys learn that it is important to care about others. It is a book that shows that love can be generous because when you love someone, you do it with all your heart.

- What do you do to encourage young boys to show that they care about other people?
- How do you help the boys in your class develop emotionally?
- How can you use role models like Tough Boris to help the boys in your classroom understand it is OK for them to cry?

Many boys distance themselves from reading and this is occurring earlier than ever before. As a teacher of young boys you have an important job. We believe the strategies in this chapter align with best practices, will make your job easier, and can help young boys get off to a bright start.

QUESTIONS FOR DISCUSSION

- Think about what you have learned about boys as learners and then consider how you teach reading skills. Do your teaching methods match boys' needs?

- How might small changes, like the ones suggested in this chapter, make the learning of reading better for boys?

- Reflect on the boys you teach. Which positive values do they exhibit? Which ones would you like to see them exhibit to a greater extent? How might this be achieved through the picture books suggested in Chapter 4?

CHAPTER 5

Matching Literacy Activities to Boys' Interests: Real-World Examples

With a variety of narratives showing effective real-world instructional examples, in this chapter we make suggestions that can help you to craft more responsive literacy instruction for young boys by

- Realizing that the more information we as teachers have about boys' preferences, the greater our chances will be to teach effectively to their interests

- Learning about boys' interests by inviting them to talk about preferences for particular toys and games, about what they like and don't like, about their dreams and desires, about the kinds of print experiences they have at home, and how they spend their time when the school day ends

- Taking advantage of helpful adults in the community and older students to mentor young boys and to share enjoyable reading experiences

- Using information about boys to employ a range of strategies for introducing them to books and print that match their interests, that create the time and space for boys to have sustained print encounters with self-selected material, and that use boy-friendly texts to embed needed skill development

What Boys Find Interesting, Boys Will Do: Interest, Motivation, and Reading

A friend who is a children's book author said to us once, "If you want students to be interested, you have to be interesting." By this he did not mean that we as teachers had to transform ourselves into entertainers, but that to grab students' attention and keep them focused we have to select engaging reading material and ensure our classroom experiences engender student enthusiasm (Gambrell, 1996). Getting boys interested is the key to gaining and keeping their attention.

Research tells us that children who have interests are engaged, and engaged thinkers and readers are better students (Guthrie & Humenick, 2004). This is because children who are motivated to read spend more time reading than their less motivated peers (Guthrie, Wigfield, Metsala, & Cox, 1999; Mullis, Martin, Gonzalez, & Kennedy, 2003; Wigfield & Guthrie, 1997). Children who read often are better overall readers (Cipielewski & Stanovich, 1992; Taylor, Frye, & Maruyama, 1990). Furthermore, engaged readers as children have a greater chance of becoming lifelong readers (Morrow, 1992), which makes it all the more critical that we capture boys' imaginations at an early age with print that sustains their attention and keeps them reading into adolescence and beyond (Brozo, 2002). This may be especially important for young boys in poverty who are at a disadvantage in terms of school readiness (Coley, 2001, 2002) but who can make up for low family income and reach expected levels of achievement if they become highly motivated readers and learners (Brozo, Shiel, & Topping, 2007/2008).

Most children when they first enter school are excited about learning and are highly motivated (Edmunds & Bauserman, 2006). But then as they advance through the grades motivation begins to decline (Guthrie & Wigfield, 2000). This phenomenon is so pervasive in the United States and around the globe that it has come to be called the fourth-grade slump (Brozo, 2005; Cummins, 2001; RAND Reading Study Group, 2002). This slump is most pronounced for boys and appears to have a direct and negative correlation to their reading achievement (Mullis et al., 2003). Declining academic motivation in the intermediate years has been attributed to two main causes.

First, children's increasing awareness of their capabilities compared with others influences their motivation. Differences in ability are made more obvious in competitive and stratified learning environments (Wigfield et al., 1997). Within these types of environments, it's easy to understand why young boys who see themselves as less able readers and writers will quickly lose enthusiasm for participating in activities that require these skills (Martin, 2003).

A second explanation centers on the types of texts children are exposed to as they progress through the grades. With the narrowing of curriculum standards and an increased focus on content knowledge and acquisition, attention to and time for personal, interest-driven literacy activities decreases. Children are less motivated to read and write texts that are not of their choosing (Guthrie & Humenick, 2004).

To help boys avoid a slump in motivation and achievement, we need to use books and strategies that will engage and sustain effort. The goal is for all young boys to have exciting print experiences that impel them to continue to seek similar enjoyable experiences with print. To do so, we need to discover personal interests, expose boys to a great variety of print material that relate to those interests, and make the time and space for texts to be read and enjoyed. Finding an entry point to literacy, as discussed in Chapter 1, may be the highest goal when working with a young boy. Once engaged by text, regardless of the particular material that initially captures his imagination, there can only be optimism about his chances for becoming a lifelong reader.

Entry-point texts can come from virtually any source. Just ask Patrick Jones, who while growing up in Flint, Michigan, USA, in the 1960s was a self-described avid nonreader until he discovered wrestling magazines. Photographs and stories about how professional wrestlers such as The Sheik and Johnny Valentine cracked heads with folding chairs and threw bodies out of the ring kept Jones riveted. Over time his reading interests and tastes grew, but he credits wrestling magazines with sending him down the path of lifelong reading (Jones, Gorman, & Suellentrop, 2004). Eventually, Jones earned a library science degree at the University of Michigan, became a librarian, and is now head of outreach programs for the Minneapolis Public Library system. But Jones isn't your average librarian. He's also an author of books for young readers and librarians and recipient of the Scholastic Library Publishing Award for lifetime achievement. He earned this award primarily for his efforts to encourage young people to make greater use of libraries and spend more time reading.

The lesson learned from Jones's story of entry-point texts is that although each of our literacy journeys is unique, there is one common characteristic that binds all readers. Like Patrick Jones, all of us who are active readers and writers in adulthood began modestly on our own paths. Yet if from the first stirrings of excitement brought about by print encounters as children we continue down the path of lifelong reading, eventually we arrive at a point where the life-altering and consciousness-expanding power of literacy is realized. Why some boys stay the course of reading and others do not, we are prepared to argue, has to do with whether very early on they are offered or discover an entry point to literacy.

In the next section of this chapter we present strategies for discovering boys' interests and ways of exploiting those interests to motivate boys to read and keep them reading. These strategies derive from the literature on reading and learning engagement (Guthrie & Humenick, 2004; Guthrie, Schafer, Von Secker, & Alban, 2000; Guthrie & Wigfield, 2000), as well as our own experiences and the experiences of numerous teachers working with young boy readers.

Learning About Boys' Interests

It's not uncommon these days to hear us talking about the new 3 Rs—Relationships, Relevance, and Rigor. The logic is that before anything like rigorous learning can take place in schools, we must establish meaningful relationships with students and make academic experiences relevant to students' needs and desires. As we form relationships with boys we get to know them in ways that offer important clues to how reading and learning can be made more relevant to them. In turn, the more boys participate in reading activities because they're engaged, the more we learn about the best ways to further develop their skills.

In the following pages we present several strategies and practices that have been found to offer teachers direct evidence and insights on who boys are, what excites them, what sustains their attention and energy, and what they will read when given the prerogative and time.

My Bag

Six-year-old Antonio's reading tutor was stymied. Antonio was the child of immigrant parents, yet all indications were that his English language skills were developing appropriately. Nor was there any record of speech pathology. And yet Antonio was so diffident and uttered so few words it was impossible to determine what he liked or disliked. It was only after his tutor had Antonio share a "my bag" activity that she discovered his areas of interest and converted them into activities and experiences in the reading center.

My Bag is a strategy that allows students to share who they are and what they like to do outside of school. With this knowledge, we can make literacy and curricular links. Students put items in a bag or any container they can carry to represent their out-of-school interests and activities. For example, Antonio's bag held photographs of his parents and brother. He also had a baseball and book of *Garfield* cartoons. What stood out among the items he removed from his bag, however, was a toy telephone. In the limited conversation his tutor had with Antonio about his items, she discovered that he really enjoyed talking with friends and family on the phone. This surprised her because he seemed so averse to conversation in their sessions. Nonetheless, she took the clue to heart and the next session came in with a couple of old telephones, one for Antonio and one for her. After reading a story aloud to him, she pretended to call Antonio on the phone and proceeded to have a conversation about the story with him. Never before had she witnessed such language production from him, such animation, and such evidence of Antonio's ability to recall story details and sequence.

If it hadn't been for this strategy, Antonio's tutor might never have discovered his interest in talking on the telephone and then turned this knowledge into a way of restructuring the tutorial context to maximize language production for him. The more Antonio talked about the stories they read together, the more his tutor learned about his strengths and areas of need as a beginning reader, which she translated into responsive instructional activities.

To help students prepare for a My Bag experience it is helpful first to model it for them. Students enjoy getting to know their teachers, and this strategy offers an ideal opportunity to forge relationships with them by talking on a personal level about interests and experiences. We recommend that as items are removed from your bag, children should be encouraged to ask questions about what they mean to the sharer. In this way, questioning and listening skills can be taught through the strategy. Above all, you should model the process of explaining what the items represent and why they are important.

Modeling the My Bag activity can be followed by a brainstorm activity to give children the opportunity to reflect on what they would want to include in their own bags. These should be written down as reminders to take home. This process also gives children advance time to think about themselves as individuals with unique interests, hobbies, and experiences and consider how these might be represented as My Bag items.

Because the goal of the strategy is to uncover boys' outside-of-school interests and experiences as potential links to reading and classroom activities, it's important to have students share early in the school year. We also recommend that the activity is shared at least once or twice again during the year to learn about new interests, hobbies, and experiences. Exactly how students share will depend upon their level of independence and how much time is available for the strategy. Using several small groups, all the students in a classroom can share their bags during the same time while you rotate around the room to monitor, encourage, and ask questions. With this approach, students should leave their items on the desks or tables so that you can see what each has included. It's also helpful with this approach to have students write down what they included in their bags. This list can be put into the student's file as a reminder. For example, as author Jon Scieszka points out (personal communication, May 6, 2008) in describing his new Trucktown collection, big vehicles like trucks are fascinating, especially to boys, and should be exploited by teachers to excite the imaginations of their young boy readers. Truck books seem to have become a genre of their own, as growing numbers of them show up each year in print. If it's discovered that a boy has an interest in trucks and other big machines, then the book featured in the following Learning From a Character box is the book for him.

LEARNING ABOUT GENEROSITY FROM A PICTURE BOOK CHARACTER

Hush Little Digger (Olson-Brown, 2006)
In Olson-Brown's enjoyable variation of the traditional "Hush Little Baby" lullaby, the narrator, the young boy's father, takes on the persona of Papa and recounts the lullaby using trucks and other heavy machinery he knows will appeal to his son. Papa keeps upgrading to a bigger and more powerful vehicle, from front-end loader to dump truck to bulldozer, and so on, when

the little digger and the succeeding ones aren't enough for the job. Within this delightful rendition of the lullaby, Papa's generous spirit is always on display, as he seeks to assure and help each anthropomorphized vehicle when the going gets too tough for it. Papa's son exhibits his own brand of generosity when he's lifted up by a cherry picker machine and thoughtfully offers a bright red apple to a hungry giraffe.

- What are some ways you can teach boys the importance of being generous through a story such as *Hush Little Digger*?

- How can boys' outside-of-school interests in trucks and large vehicles be linked to activities around this story?

My Favorite Things Inventory

Another approach to learning about boys' interests and experiences is by using a simple inventory that asks them to make drawings to go with sentences (Flippo, 2003). For example, some typical favorite things sentences include the following:

- When school is over these are my favorite things to do.
- When I am on school vacation these are the things I like to do.
- If I could do anything in the whole wide world, this is what I would do.
- When I am in school, this is my favorite thing to do.
- If I could read about anything I wanted to, this is what it would be.
- This is my favorite hobby.
- This is my favorite toy.

Leave ample space between sentences to allow boys to make their drawings. Boys who are capable readers can complete the inventory individually. For less capable and beginning readers, we or more capable classmates may need to read the sentences to them. Once boys have completed their drawings, there are options for acquiring further information about their favorite things. You can ask them to write or dictate a descriptive sentence that can be written next to the drawing. You might ask individual boys to describe their drawings and use what they tell about them to create a language-experience story. This process allows you to observe a boy's level of language production as well as his enthusiasm for various favorite things to do.

Seven-year-old James was already a reluctant reader, though his skill level according to test scores was actually slightly above his second-grade placement. His teacher was having difficulty finding an entry-point text for James until she gave him a My Favorite Things Inventory and noticed his response to the statement, *If I could do anything in the whole wide world, this is what I would do.* Though simple and lacking detail, James's stick figure illustration clearly depicted a person flying across the sky like Superman. When his teacher asked James to tell her a story about his drawing, he said he wished he could fly like a bird or an airplane. Armed with this knowledge, she introduced James to Dav Pilkey's irreverent but hilarious Captain Underpants series. Captain Underpants is about two fourth graders, George Beard and Harold Hutchins, and the aptly named superhero they accidentally create by hypnotizing their principal, Mr. Benny Krupp. When Captain Underpants drinks a carton of Super Power Juice it gives him super strength and he has the ability to fly.

It's this quixotic main character's ability to fly that James's teacher thought would entice him to read these zany books. And it worked. James was completely taken in by the polka-dotted-cape–clad superhero who flits around dueling Dr. Diaper, foiling talking toilets, and clashing with cafeteria ladies. This kind of humor and action kept James laughing and begging for more. It truly served as his entry-point text.

Listening to Boy Talk

Researchers (Lee, 1999; Wasley, Hampel, & Clark, 1997) remind us that by gathering students' input about their own learning we can better appreciate their lifeworlds and make teaching more responsive to their experiences and perspectives. Moreover, when students feel their input matters they are motivated to participate constructively in their education (Corbett & Wilson, 1995; Heshusius, 1995).

The benefits of going to the source—that is, conversing with children about what motivates them to read—have been well documented in the professional literature (Edmunds & Bauserman, 2006; Gambrell, Palmer, Codling, & Mazzoni, 1996). Holding an individual conference with a young boy is an ideal way to gain an in-depth understanding of whether he reads, how and why he reads, and what might make reading more enjoyable for him.

Unique questions can be crafted by us for each boy interviewed, or a general questionnaire such as the Conversational Interview portion of the Motivation to Read Profile (Gambrell et al., 1996) can be used intact or in modified form (see Figure 3). Regardless of format, getting boys to talk about what books and other print material interest them, and why, will provide us with valuable information for instructional decisions that are responsive to boys' literacy and learning needs.

Marcus, an 8-year-old, was interviewed by his third-grade teacher. She had become concerned about his lack of interest during free reading time. While most of the children quickly found books and magazines and settled into the

FIGURE 3
The Motivation to Read Profile

Name _____ Date _____

Reading Survey

Sample 1: I am in _____ .
- ❑ Second grade
- ❑ Third grade
- ❑ Fourth grade

Sample 2: I am a _____ .
- ❑ Boy
- ❑ Girl

1. My friends think I am _____ .
- ❑ A very good reader
- ❑ A good reader
- ❑ An OK reader
- ❑ A poor reader

2. Reading a book is something I like to do.
- ❑ Never
- ❑ Not very often
- ❑ Sometimes
- ❑ Often

3. I read _____ .
- ❑ Not as well as my friends
- ❑ About as well as my friends
- ❑ A little better than my friends
- ❑ A lot better than my friends

4. My best friends think reading is _____ .
- ❑ Really fun
- ❑ Fun
- ❑ OK to do
- ❑ Not fun at all

5. When I come to a word I don't know I can _____ .
- ❑ Always figure it out
- ❑ Sometimes figure it out
- ❑ Almost never figure it out
- ❑ Never figure it out

6. I tell my friends about good books I read.
- ❑ I never do this
- ❑ I almost never do this
- ❑ I do this some of the time
- ❑ I do this a lot

7. When I am reading by myself I understand _____ .
- ❑ Almost everything I read
- ❑ Some of what I read
- ❑ Almost none of what I read
- ❑ None of what I read

(continued)

FIGURE 3 (continued)
The Motivation to Read Profile

8. People who read a lot are _____ .
   - ❑ Very interesting
   - ❑ Interesting
   - ❑ Not very interesting
   - ❑ Boring

9. I am _____ .
   - ❑ A poor reader
   - ❑ An OK reader
   - ❑ A good reader
   - ❑ A very good reader

10. I think libraries are _____ .
    - ❑ A great place to spend time
    - ❑ An interesting place to spend time
    - ❑ An OK place to spend time
    - ❑ A boring place to spend time

11. I worry about what other kids think about my reading _____ .
    - ❑ Every day
    - ❑ Almost every day
    - ❑ Once in a while
    - ❑ Never

12. Knowing how to read well is _____ .
    - ❑ Not very important
    - ❑ Sort of important
    - ❑ Important
    - ❑ Very important

13. When my teacher asks me a question about what I have read, I _____ .
    - ❑ Can never think of an answer
    - ❑ Have trouble thinking of an answer
    - ❑ Sometimes think of an answer
    - ❑ Always think of an answer

14. I think reading is _____ .
    - ❑ A boring way to spend time
    - ❑ An OK way to spend time
    - ❑ An interesting way to spend time
    - ❑ A great way to spend time

15. Reading is _____ .
    - ❑ Very easy for me
    - ❑ Kind of easy for me
    - ❑ Kind of hard for me
    - ❑ Very hard for me

16. When I grow up I will spend _____ .
    - ❑ None of my time reading
    - ❑ Very little of my time reading
    - ❑ Some of my time reading
    - ❑ A lot of my time reading

(continued)

Matching Literacy Activities to Boys' Interests: Real-World Examples

FIGURE 3 *(continued)*
The Motivation to Read Profile

17. When I am in a group talking about stories, I _____ .
- ❑ Almost never talk about my ideas
- ❑ Sometimes talk about my ideas
- ❑ Almost always talk about my ideas
- ❑ Always talk about my ideas

18. I would like for my teacher to read books out loud to the class _____ .
- ❑ Every day
- ❑ Almost every day
- ❑ Once in a while
- ❑ Never

19. When I read out loud I am a _____ .
- ❑ Poor reader
- ❑ OK reader
- ❑ Good reader
- ❑ Very good reader

20. When someone gives me a book for a present, I feel _____ .
- ❑ Very happy
- ❑ Sort of happy
- ❑ Sort of unhappy
- ❑ Unhappy

Conversational Interview

A. Emphasis: Narrative Text

Suggested prompt (designed to engage students in a natural conversation): I have been reading a good book...I was talking with...about it last night. I enjoy talking about good stories and books that I've been reading. Today I would like to hear about what you have been reading.

1. Tell me about the most interesting story or book you have read this week (or even last week). Take a few minutes to think about it. (Wait time.) Now tell me about the book or story.

   Probes: What else can you tell me? Is there anything else? _____

   _____

   _____

   _____

   _____

2. How did you know or find out about this story? _____

   _____

   _____

   - ❑ Assigned   ❑ In school
   - ❑ Chosen   ❑ Out of school

3. Why was this story interesting to you? _____

   _____

   _____

(continued)

FIGURE 3 *(continued)*
The Motivation to Read Profile

B. Emphasis: Informational Text

Suggested prompt (designed to engage students in a natural conversation): Often we read to find out about something or learn about something. We read for information, for example, I remember a student of mine...who read a lot of books about...to find out as much as he or she could about.... Now I'd like to hear about some of the informational reading you have been doing.

1. Think about something important you learned recently, not from your teacher and not from television, but from a book or some other reading material. What did you read about? (Wait time.) Tell me about what you learned.

   Probes: What else can you tell me? Is there anything else? _____

   _____

   _____

   _____

   _____

   _____

2. How did you know or find out about this book/article? _____

   _____

   _____

   □ Assigned   □ In school

   □ Chosen   □ Out of school

3. Why was this story interesting to you?_____

   _____

   _____

   _____

C. Emphasis: General Reading

1. Did you read anything at home yesterday? _____ What?

   _____

   _____

2. Do you have any books at school (in your desk/storage area/locker/book bag) today that you are reading? _____. Tell me about them.

   _____

   _____

3. Tell me about your favorite author.

   _____

   _____

   _____

(continued)

FIGURE 3 (continued)
The Motivation to Read Profile

4. What do you think you have to learn to be a better reader?

_____

_____

_____

5. Do you know about any books right now that you'd like to read? Tell me about them.

_____

_____

_____

6. How did you find out about these books?

_____

_____

_____

7. What are some things that get you really excited about reading books?

_____

_____

_____

Tell me about...

_____

_____

_____

8. Who gets you interested and excited about reading books?

_____

_____

_____

Tell me more about what they do.

_____

_____

_____

Note. From Gambrell, L.B., Palmer, B.M., Codling, R.M., & Mazzoni, S.A. (1996). Assessing motivation to read. _The Reading Teacher, 49_(7), 518–533. Reprinted with permission.

comfortable bean bag chairs and cushions spread out in the room, Marcus took a long time searching for a book and was easily distracted even after he sat down with something to read. His teacher knew he was reading below grade level, so she wanted to make sure he was taking full advantage of the time she set aside each day for self-selected material. To discover potential ways of increasing Marcus's enthusiasm for reading, she held a short conference with him. Using questions and prompts selectively chosen from the Motivation to Read Profile, she and Marcus had a rich and informative conversation that yielded the following information:

- Marcus's favorite book was *The Wishing Chair* (Dupre, 1993) about Eldon's Sunday visits to his grandmother's house, where he sits in the wishing chair while listening to stories about African American emancipators and civil rights leaders. Marcus selected that book most often during free reading time. He liked the story because it was about a boy similar to him who had dreams of meeting interesting people and doing interesting things.

- He preferred books that he could choose himself, but he sometimes wasn't sure what interested him.

- He liked books that were about boys doing things that he might be able to do.

- He also said he would like stories about "real things."

Although Marcus's responses did not include any other favorite authors or titles beyond *The Wishing Chair* (Dupre, 1993), they gave his teacher abundant clues to topics, books, and other print material that he might find enjoyable. With the help of the school librarian a number of titles and a couple of magazines were gathered for Marcus, including

- *Bill Pickett: Rodeo-Ridin' Cowboy* (Pinkney, 1999)
- *How I Became a Pirate* (Long, 2003)
- *Satchel Paige* (Cline-Ransome, 2003)

These materials helped keep Marcus occupied during free reading time. He was especially excited about the story of Bill Pickett and asked for more books like it. His teacher and the school librarian continued to search for stories on this topic and found the wonderfully illustrated book *African-Americans in the Old West* (McGowen, 1999). Marcus was finding an entry point to active reading through tales about an interesting and relatively unknown piece of the past. His curiosity aroused, his teacher and the school librarian continued to serve as conduits to engaging texts for Marcus. Although his teacher might have eventually learned of Marcus's interest in certain books and topics, engaging him in "boy talk" to gather information about his tastes in print made it possible to quickly and efficiently identify material he enjoyed reading.

Teaching to Boys' Interests in the Classroom

Boys and men who become disaffected readers have the same stories to tell (Worthy, 1998): Reading was exciting and pleasurable once but now is boring, tedious, and decidedly not fun; or reading has always been a chore and will never compete with the other things they like to do. Those who (re)discover the joy and excitement of reading have stories, too (Brozo, 2002), from which lessons can be extracted and turned into useful teaching guidelines and strategies. What follows are strategies based on what we've learned about the importance of gaining and holding boys' interest. These strategies derive from years of observing, interacting, and talking with boys and their teachers.

Give Personal Introductions to Books With Book Talks

Once you are aware of boys' interests, you can bring material related to those interests to their attention through book talks. A book talk is a short, exciting glimpse of a book or other text delivered with enthusiasm, expressive excerpting, and a conclusion that keeps listeners guessing (Angelillo, 2003; Trelease, 2006). An exciting book talk can be delivered in as few as 3–5 minutes, which makes it possible to give them frequently (see Table 3 for a list of book talk guidelines).

Once book talks are given, the books or other reading material should be readily available and accessible to young boys for independent, recreational reading. We suggest that a special section of the class library be set aside for good reads for boys. Some teachers dedicate particular shelves or a separate bookcase for this purpose. These books are clearly labeled, such as Guys' Rack or Best Bets for Boys, so as to make a young boy's search for something to read more efficient. Girls should never be discouraged from selecting books from this section; nor should boys be forced to select only books from it. The ultimate goal is to whet boys' appetites with an engaging book talk then make it clear to boys where they can locate the book and others they might also enjoy.

A first-grade teacher discovered that several of her boys liked playing with toy cars based on their responses to a My Favorite Things Inventory, so she made sure to find and give book talks on several related books. With help from the school librarian, she selected books that were at various levels of readability, because her boys had a range of reading abilities from emergent to well beyond their first-grade placement. Some were wordless books while others were print-rich and challenging even for the boys who were quite capable readers, but she shared them anyway because of their exciting and informative

TABLE 3
Guidelines for Effective Book Talks

- Read the book and prepare a book talk based on the following critical features:
  - An attention-grabbing introduction
  - Broad-stroke information about the book
  - Contextual information about a scene to be excerpted
  - An exciting excerpt read aloud
  - A conclusion that leaves listeners eager to learn more
- Do not say too much about the book (a book talk is not a book report).
- Do not provide a synopsis of the book!
- Avoid basing your talk around the climax of the story. This will force you to say too much about it.
- Do not give away the ending.
- Rehearse. Practice keeping the talk within a timeframe of 5–7 minutes.
- Repeat author and title as often as possible to help listeners find the book for self-selected reading.
- Show enthusiasm!
- Use an effective oral reading voice.
- Use appropriate simple gestures and simple props.
- Make frequent eye contact throughout the room.
- Take your talk to your listeners by moving around the room.
- Share the book's photos and illustrations.
- Do not use notes or scripts. Book talks should be rehearsed and planned so that they appear natural and spontaneous.
- Make the book available and accessible in the classroom for recreational reading.

illustrations and photographs. See Table 4 for a list of books about cars that young boys will love to read.

The more often boys are provided with personal introductions to books and other reading material the greater the likelihood their curiosities will be aroused by a particular title and that boys will select it for independent reading. Regularly sharing material of high interest to boys in short, attention-grabbing book talks allows us to demonstrate that we care about what matters to boys and shows boys that they can read about their interests. An added benefit of booktalking is that students are more likely to select books to read on their own based on personal recommendations from teachers (Kragler & Nolley, 1996).

Create Time in School for Self-Selected, Recreational Reading

Putting the right books and other print material in boys' hands or making text available from the computer will not always guarantee they will read. You can take an important additional step to enable active reading by creating the time and space before, during, and after the school day for students to enjoy texts

D'Aulaire, I. (2007). *The Two Cars*. New York: NYRB Children's Collection.
Herzog, B. (2006). *R Is for Race: A Stock Car Alphabet*. Chelsea, MI: Sleeping Bear.
Huff, R. (1998). *The Making of a Race Car*. New York: Chelsea House.
Lord, T. (1992). *Amazing Cars*. New York: Knopf.
Mitton, T. (2005). *Cool Cars*. Ashmore, QLD, Australia: Kingfisher.
NASCAR. (2004). *Wild Wheels!* Fairfield, IA: Reader's Digest.
Rex, M. (2000). *My Race Car*. New York: Henry Holt
Scarry, R. (2001). *Cars, Trucks, and Things That Go*. New York: Picture Lions.
Van Dusen, C. (2005). *If I Built a Car*. New York: Dutton.
Zane, A. (2005). *The Wheels on the Race Car*. New York: Orchard.

of interest. The easier the access to interesting print materials, the more frequently students read (McQuillan & Au, 2001).

Time and again in formal and informal surveys and questionnaires boys express interest in topics most commonly found in nonfiction (Sullivan, 2003; Worthy, Moorman, & Turner, 1999). Yet informational text is scarce in primary-level classrooms (Duke, 2000) and not nearly as abundant as it should be in school libraries. One librarian explains it this way:

> Because we're primarily women, and I hate to stereotype us, but...we're just not particularly interested in...or aware that's what boys want to read about, then we don't buy it and so it's not available. Then, the boys say, "Eh, this library doesn't have anything worth reading." (McGowan, 2008)

If boys fail to have regular and frequent print experiences because they can't find or aren't exposed to books and other reading material they deem worth reading, their skills may develop more slowly than expected, contributing to the gender-based achievement gap that widens over time (National Assessment of Educational Progress, 2005; Stanovich, 1986). On the other hand, if school libraries are well stocked with books that boys prefer, if classrooms are enriched with these selections, and if programs are in place that ensure boys have regular opportunities to read and hear such books, reading achievement can be expected to rise (Lonsdale, 2003).

To ensure that boys have frequent opportunities to interact with books and print they like, independent reading time must be planned just as other instructional time in a literacy program is planned. As Combs (2002) points out, children know whether teachers really value self-selected, independent reading by the time and attention it's given. Boys will not become better readers unless they read often and for sustained periods of time. There is a variety of ways that time can be made during the school day for boys and girls to read for pleasure. Among the most common are the following:

- School- or classroomwide Sustained Silent Reading (SSR) or Drop Everything and Read (DEAR) programs. It is critical that boys have their preferred reading material on hand for quick access, so precious minutes of SSR or DEAR time aren't wasted in searching for a suitable text.

- Provisions within the reading/language arts curriculum for independent reading and for time spent with self-selected text to be equivalent to that spent on paper-and-pencil tasks.

- Independent reading time that is built in to other instructional blocks, such as social studies and math, and allowance for boys to read self-selected related texts during this time. For example, when learning in social studies about jobs that adults have in the community, boys could read books or articles about recycling or zoos.

Book Clubs as Contexts for Literacy Engagement and Prosocial Behavior

One way to increase valuable time boys spend in recreational reading is by involving them in school-based book clubs. An increase in language production around books (Geraci, 2003), improvement in reading and writing skills of linguistically diverse learners (Kong & Fitch, 2002), elevation of self-esteem (Jaeger & Demetriadis, 2002), greater leadership and independence (Bond, 2001), and tolerance of diversity (Raphael, Florio-Ruane, & George, 2001) are just some of the important benefits of book club membership documented in the literature.

In addition to these benefits, book clubs afford boys regular opportunities to learn rules for and gain linguistic abilities through structured group conversation. Schwarzchild (2000) points out that family mealtime talk—which he has shown promotes important conversational skills, more extensive vocabularies, superior ability to conceptualize, and adeptness at articulating meaning in spoken and written language—is a rare occurrence in the lives of many young boys today. Book clubs might serve as surrogates for this once taken-for-granted family ritual.

There isn't a single best model for constituting and scheduling book clubs for boys, so teachers often need to be creative and flexible to make them work within existing school structures. The issue of gender fairness and equal time for girls may also arise and require additional deft planning. In spite of the challenges and potential barriers, teachers and librarians should not be deterred from forming special reading clubs for boys and exploring their benefits.

The first step is to determine club membership and size. In an elementary school in the northern Virginia area, for example, 20 boys who were struggling readers were identified in grades 2 and 3 and handed personal invitations to participate in a book club. The next step in planning is to make time for regular club meetings. The same school presented three options in the invitations—convening book club 45 minutes before the start of the school day, meeting during lunchtime, or staying after school for book club and sending the participating boys home on the activity bus. The club would meet on Tuesdays and Thursdays. In the end, 12 of the parents agreed to allow their sons to participate in book club and preferred the after-school, two-days-per week format.

Another important book club consideration has to do with making it possible for older boys and men to join as regular members or serve as guests to provide role models for the younger boy members. Invitations and advertisements for a boys' book club should include special requests for male teachers, administrators, and coaches from the school and district and older male relations from home to come as often as possible. In the case of the school in northern Virginia, holding book club meetings between 3:30 p.m. and 4:30 p.m. turned out to be a much more convenient time for older brothers, uncles, grandfathers, and even some fathers to participate than if it had been scheduled before or during the school day. Every week at least one older male family member was able to go to club activities. The school principal, who is a man, also made it to book club at least once per week.

As much as possible, selection of material that boys read in book clubs should be made on the basis of what club members like. The material really does matter and can make or break a successful book club experience for boys. Young boys who may be reluctant readers may need "free rein" (Bond, 2001) on all matters related to what will be read in a book club context.

To ensure she was making the most interesting books possible available to her third-grade boys, a teacher gave them a questionnaire to determine their outside-of-school interests. The following were the most popular activities:

- playing on the computer
- playing sports
- watching television
- making things
- telling jokes

Along with this questionnaire, the teacher also asked the boys what they would like to read, and their responses were as follows:

- books that are funny
- books that are action packed
- mysteries

- books about "boys like us"
- books that tell you how to do things

These patterns of interest are not unlike those for similar boys documented in the literature (Chance, 2000; Doiron, 2003). Armed with this knowledge, the teacher was able to identify various books that would match the interests and book genres the boys specified in the questionnaires.

Book club members should be allowed multiple modes of expression. Typically, students are given a limited range of response options based on what they read. Answering the teacher's questions orally or in writing is most common. To help boy readers become more engaged with text, creative response formats should be made available to them. These might include drama, electronic presentations, art, and making real-world connections. We've even witnessed boys using walkie-talkies to converse about a book because that was the preferred mode of communication. Choice of books to read and choice in deciding how to respond to gratifying books (Turner, 1995) is critical to a successful book club experience.

Having fun with books should be a high priority in a school-based boys' book club. When reading is either difficult or unappealing for young boys, one of the best antidotes is to immerse them in experiences with simply told stories that are very funny (Scieszka, 2003). To make sure the boys never grew too weary of the selections for the book club, even when they were related to their interests, the third-grade teacher made humorous books available throughout the year. After reading Scieszka's *The Stinky Cheese Man* (1992), the boys couldn't get enough of it and went on to read several others by the same author, including *Math Curse* (1995) and *The True Story of the Three Little Pigs* (1996). Humorous books help book club members sustain their efforts to read, discuss, and respond to all selections. Exposure to this genre also impels some boys to seek similarly zany books to read on their own.

Our own experience in boys' book clubs has reinforced our convictions about the kinds of books young boys will read and why, when given the prerogative and support. "I didn't like to read before, but now I like reading even if my friends don't" is what Armando, a disinterested and struggling reader at the outset of second grade, wrote to us in May after participating in a book club since the previous January. Reactions like these have made us realize just how successful a boys' book club could be. Book club offered Armando's teachers a way of honoring his and the other boys' unique literacy needs and interests. And when young boys like Armando find entry points to literacy because their interests are matched with pleasurable books, we are left with the very real hope they will remain engaged readers throughout their lives.

Omar's second-grade teacher began the new school year by asking the class members to brainstorm a list of things they like to read and do outside of school. The teacher's goal was to gather these lists of interests and hobbies so she could plan classroom activities around them. Omar, however, had little to say to Maria, his table partner. As she walked around the room, his teacher overheard him comment, "We don't have books and stuff like that at my house. And we don't have a computer either...I don't have computer games or anything like that." When Maria asked what he enjoyed doing for fun, Omar shrugged his shoulders and replied, "I don't know...nothing much...I watch a lot of TV."

Omar's responses are indicative of a serious issue confronting teachers today. Growing numbers of young boys are entering our schools and classrooms with extremely limited traditional print experiences. In addition to coming from homes where there is an absence of print matter, many young boys may also be experientially deprived. This can lead to a condition in which they may seem to be unaware of what interests them. It is especially challenging for teachers to take advantage of boys' everyday literacies and competencies when they may only encounter print in school. Without expressed interests, without home-based experience with print, what resources do boys like Omar bring to school that can be honored and linked to reading material and classroom topics?

On your own or with colleagues, brainstorm answers to the following questions:

- Because Omar claims he isn't really interested in anything, what might you do to help him discover new interests?

- Omar lacks enthusiasm for anything except watching television; what are some ways of helping him find other activities he would enjoy?

- How might Omar's interest in television be exploited in classroom reading and writing activities?

- How might other students in the class, both boys and girls, help Omar expand his interests?

Connecting to the Life Experiences of Mentors From the Community

Another way to help young boys expand their repertoire of interests is by arranging systematic opportunities for them to interact with men from the community who are engaged readers and who have a wide variety of life experiences. Many young boys are in desperate need of direct contact with male role models who embody positive values and who are interested and regular readers ("Boys and Books," 2006; Gould, 2006). As sociologist Males (2001) stresses, youth act in ways similar to the adults around them, and Zirkel (2002) verifies that the best mentors are those who are a gender and racial match. So, if we expect young boys to be readers, they need to see brothers, fathers, uncles, and cousins, as well as all the other older boys and men with whom they come into contact, valuing reading in their daily lives (Kids and Family Reading Report, 2008).

Using a state-funded grant, a literacy specialist in a southern Texas elementary school organized a mentoring program for the most seriously struggling readers. Nearly 100% of the students in the school were receiving free or reduced-cost lunches. Many were from single-parent families. And the overwhelming majority of the school's lowest readers were boys. Consequently, the specialist, other teachers, and administrators were well aware of the need for boys to have encounters with men who could be a positive influence on their literacy development and academic achievement.

The program used community volunteers to read to and with the low-ability boy students. The primary goal of the program was for very young boys who were struggling readers to have enjoyable and memorable print experiences with a caring older male. The specialist challenged the volunteers to be as resourceful as possible in creating motivating reading experiences. It was hoped that these experiences would help boys become habitual readers, which would increase their skill level and improve overall academic achievement.

Antonio had recently retired from his career as an operations specialist for radar on aircraft carriers. In addition to the exciting and varied life experiences he had, he also loved to read, and so was happy to respond to the request for volunteers for the school's mentoring program. The literacy specialist quickly recognized the contributions Antonio could bring to the mentoring experience and teamed him with a third grader named Gilbert, who came from a particularly difficult home situation. Gilbert and his three younger brothers and sisters lived with their mother in a motel room on a noisy commercial thoroughfare. His father had left the family to return to Mexico.

Three days per week for 60 minutes Gilbert was excused from his classroom so he could meet with Antonio. Initially, they met in a small, private room adjacent to the library. Before long, however, they began to search out comfortable spaces anywhere on the school grounds to read and talk together, often finding themselves outside enjoying the mild coastal breezes. Gilbert asked many questions about Antonio's career in the Navy. Antonio shared photographs of aircraft carriers, airplanes, and radar rooms and talked about the various places around the United States and the world he had lived. Gilbert was so fascinated that Antonio decided to seek books about ships and airplanes to read and talk about during their sessions.

Together they enjoyed *Blue Angels* (Braulick, 2005) about precision jets and the Navy pilots who fly them. Antonio added a hands-on experience to the reading of this book by helping Gilbert decode and follow directions for assembling a model jet airplane, which they painted blue to imitate the jets in the photographs. They also enjoyed Roza's (2004) informative and carefully illustrated *The Incredible Story of Aircraft Carriers*. As they made their way through this book, Antonio used a computer to show the various routes carriers traverse and their major ports of call and naval bases around the globe. To extend and enliven their activity with this book, Antonio helped Gilbert maintain a ship's log in which he wrote entries about the seas, recorded location using lines of latitude and longitude, and made up interesting incidents on ship to report.

As the two progressed through selected books and related activities Antonio noticed patterns of difficulty and strength in Gilbert's reading and writing abilities. He shared this information with the reading specialist, and based on her suggestion, Antonio had Gilbert keep a notebook of words that he stumbled over and expanded these into word families to help him recognize and decode other words with similar spellings. They played games to quiz each other about the words, such as competing to see who could find the most words from a particular family on a page of the book they were reading. However, Antonio always made sure he never fell into the role of reading teacher. He understood his main purpose was to arouse Gilbert's interest and use print experiences to nurture that interest. As a result of the many fun and informative book encounters the two of them had, Gilbert showed marked improvement in attitude toward reading and reading skill, according to his teacher and the reading specialist. As Gilbert's reading skill improved he became more confident in his abilities and participated with more enthusiasm in classroom learning experiences.

Gilbert's fascination with airplanes is one that is shared by many boys. Teachers who learn of this interest would be well advised to put into boys' hands the book featured in the following Learning From a Character box.

LEARNING ABOUT COURAGE
FROM A PICTURE BOOK CHARACTER

Charles A. Lindbergh: A Human Hero (Giblin, 2007)
Charles Lindbergh was a hero, but like any real human hero, he had faults, too. This multidimensional portrayal of Lindbergh presents an ideal real-life

character that boys will enjoy reading about and whose positive achievements they may dream of emulating. Lindbergh's daring solo flight across the Atlantic Ocean from New York to Paris in an airplane is what springs to mind for most of us. But in this biography we also come to know his courage as an outspoken and tireless advocate for conserving the environment and protecting endangered species. Lindbergh's flaws will help young boys think about this famous American aviator in ways that acknowledge his courage while recognizing his complex personality.

- How can you demonstrate for young boys that they do not have to see themselves as great figures like Lindbergh to exhibit acts of courage?

- What can be done using books such as this to help boys who struggle as readers learn that they can keep trying and work hard to become better readers?

Building Skill and Motivation Through Cross-Age Tutoring

Peer-mediated instruction is another way to support young boys who are struggling or disengaged readers while providing role models of competent reading ability and positive masculinity. Cross-age tutoring has been shown to be a promising alternative to pull-out and remedial programs (Topping & Ehly, 1998). It is particularly beneficial for students who find it difficult to learn in whole-group contexts (Davenport, Arnold, & Lassman, 2004). Furthermore, it has been demonstrated that when older children work with younger children in a cross-age tutoring context both groups tend to make significant gains (Caserta-Henry, 1996). This occurs because successful cross-age tutoring programs imbue older struggling readers with a sense of responsibility and purpose for improving their own abilities (Avery & Avery, 2001), which in turn leads to better support for their younger reading buddies.

A high school in Illinois established a cross-age tutoring, or buddy reading, program to improve the reading skill level of boy students who had fallen significantly behind. Instead of relying exclusively on pull-out tutoring for the neediest of these boys, the curriculum specialists at both the elementary and the high school worked closely to match a struggling high school reader with a second or third grader who was also struggling with reading.

Because high school students' schedules were already set, it was impossible not to have those targeted for participation in the program take time out of one of their existing classes. The B-block faculty who had the students identified for the program agreed to allow them to leave during the second half of the period for two days per week. A total of 12 students were identified for and participated in the program. After a couple of orientation sessions, the students and curriculum specialist settled into a routine that began by gathering in the main hall outside the office at 10:30 a.m. to go to the elementary school, where the high school students met their younger partners in the library.

DeShawn, a tenth grader, was teamed with Mario, a second grader, who was experiencing difficulties with grade-appropriate materials. Like the other high school boys in the program, DeShawn spent the 45 minutes with his reading buddy involved in the following activities:

- Reading aloud from a favorite children's book
- Filling out a log sheet upon a book's completion
- Making an entry in a shared response journal
- Writing and illustrating a book of their own

DeShawn and the other participants were monitored to ensure they were reading material within or very close to the younger students' independent ranges and that they were making optimal use of their time together. With guidance, DeShawn learned to prepare for the read-aloud by orally rehearsing the story at least two times, identifying vocabulary that might pose difficulty for his reading buddy, and preparing strategies to assist in decoding and contextual understanding.

DeShawn learned that Mario lived in an apartment complex just a couple of streets away from his building. He also learned that Mario loved baseball, and because his father lived in Chicago, Mario wanted to play for the Cubs when he grew up. Armed with this knowledge, DeShawn found a biography entitled *Sammy Sosa* (Savage, 2005) about one of the greatest Cubs players of all time. This short biography helped get their cross-age buddy reading sessions off to an exciting start.

Virtually all of what DeShawn and Mario read and wrote about had to do with baseball. With the curriculum specialist's help in finding appropriately difficult, high-interest books, they enjoyed an engaging team history entitled *Chicago Cubs* (Stewart, 2006) with brief biographies of great Cubs players from the past, such as Ernie Banks, Ron Santo, and Mark Grace. They kept a scrapbook of the team, including newspaper stories and pictures of their favorite players. To go along with these they wrote captions, statistics, and bits of trivia from players' records.

While cutting out a magazine photo of the Cubs' premier player, Derrek Lee, Mario commented about his powerful physique, wondering out loud how he got so big. DeShawn thought they could find information on that topic using the Internet. Because the cross-age tutoring sessions were held in the elementary school's media center, computers were available throughout the large

Matching Literacy Activities to Boys' Interests: Real-World Examples

open room. With assistance they got their search started using descriptors such as *baseball players training*, and they found pages of sites concerned with bodybuilding and conditioning. What caught DeShawn's eye, however, were references to performance-enhancing drugs. The curriculum specialist helped them locate sites with straightforward, objective information about these supplements, which they printed for reading later.

The curriculum specialist talked with DeShawn about how he might share this information with Mario, cautioning him not to present it in a way that might inadvertently glorify drug use. DeShawn assured her he was going to "set him straight about that junk." Under the specialist's watchful eye, DeShawn planned ways he would read, write, and talk about performance-enhancing drugs in the next few sessions. Her own research yielded a book on the topic entitled *Steroids and Other Performance-Enhancing Drugs* (Aretha, 2005), which she found in the high school's library. The information in Aretha's book is presented in a colorful, easy-to-understand format, with many illustrative photographs. The curriculum specialist helped DeShawn develop strategies for sharing selected content from the book that would help Mario begin to appreciate drug-free ways of building muscle and stamina for athletic competition.

It was DeShawn, however, who came up with the idea of a digital activity related to the topic. Aware of Mario's keen interest in computers, he developed a plan for taking a closer look at the characters from popular computer games. His plan was inspired by reading that one of the most common pastimes among many American baseball players when on the road or during the off-season was playing action or wrestling video games. Typically, the heroes and villains in these games have exaggerated muscles that baseball players and bodybuilders must envy, and perhaps, strive to attain. DeShawn saw how these images might influence certain athletes to do whatever it takes, including using drugs, to achieve impressive physiques.

With assistance from the elementary school media specialist, DeShawn and Mario used the Internet to find pictures of popular action computer game figures. These pictures were then downloaded and altered using a popular image-altering computer program. DeShawn and Mario learned how to rework the main characters' physiques, reshaping them in ways that were more proportional to normal muscle development. They displayed their work in a slide-show presentation with "before" slides, accompanied by captions warning of the dangers of steroids and other illegal substances for building muscle, and "after" slides with statements about good health, diet, and fitness.

At the end of the tutorial program, a party was held to showcase the reading buddies' work. The principal, curriculum specialists, and other teachers attended and offered their praise and congratulations. Proud of the brief slide-show they had created, DeShawn and Mario were given special opportunities to share the slides at this event. The elementary school's principal was so impressed that she made sure the slides were shown to the students during drug awareness events that year.

During the three months of the program, DeShawn and Mario read several children's books, newspaper articles, and websites. These readings provided Mario with additional reading practice that seemed to improve his fluency and confidence. Participating in the cross-age tutoring program also helped DeShawn view himself as a reader in a new way. He came to enjoy his new-found status as a role model and "expert" reader for his younger buddy. DeShawn's heightened sense of responsibility ensured the time he spent reading with Mario was enjoyable. His "big brother" attitude motivated him to learn more about what they were reading, so he could be knowledgeable on the topics that were of interest to Mario. He learned how to uncover his reading buddy's interests and experiences and then locate appropriate print material to match. As a result of DeShawn's tutorial assistance, Mario had improved as a reader both in skill and motivation and was learning that reading could be used as a tool for information and pleasure.

Bridging Boys' Competencies With Familiar Texts to Academic Literacy

In the primary-grade classroom, you can take advantage of boys' outside-of-school interests and competencies to develop needed reading and writing skills. For example, librarians know that books with nonstop adventure, or shocking, sensational, fantastic, and even gory, slimy stuff are popular with younger boys (Fuoco, 2007; Prince, 2008), yet because this kind of material is often thought to be lacking in taste or doesn't come from a prescribed list of acceptable books, it's not easily found in school libraries or classrooms (Worthy et al., 1999). Because this material has immediate appeal to many young boys, there's no reason why it shouldn't be used to increase their exposure to print as well as to embed important skill building experiences. Furthermore, by eliminating barriers between students' competencies with outside-of-school texts and classroom practices it is possible to increase engagement in learning and expand literacy abilities (Alvermann, Swafford, & Montero, 2004).

Children enjoy many literacy and text-based activities in their everyday lives that could form the source material for engaging classroom lessons. For instance, at home boys play computer and video games that involve reading directions, "cheat sheets," and codes to improve play. Boys also read comic books and graphic novels, peruse print and online magazines related to their hobbies (e.g., skateboarding, collecting, sports), and listen to music and read song lyrics (Hull & Schultz, 2002).

Teaching vocabulary is one of the five pillars of instruction recommended by the National Reading Panel (National Institute of Child Health and Human

Development, 2000) and is a common feature in early literacy programs in elementary schools and classrooms across the United States. Vocabulary instruction for young and emergent readers is typically organized around word study activities that involve games, music, and read-alouds (Combs, 2002). For restless young boys who may be unmotivated by typical lessons and content, text and other material of high interest can serve as a vehicle for increasing recognition and expanding knowledge of words. This alternative approach is consistent with the overarching theme of this chapter and enjoys firm support (cf. Allington, 2005). In the example that follows, a teacher dismantles the barriers between outside- and inside-of-school literate practices to engage boys in successful vocabulary learning.

After a My Bag activity with her second graders, the teacher took note of the excitement generated by Zach's *Star Wars* video game. This version for children casts all the main characters of the movie as Lego figures. Like most other games it is interactive, allowing players to become any of the heroes or villains and to combine episodes into new storylines. The teacher allowed Zach to give the class a quick demonstration, and all the children, but especially the other boys, were agog. She had used the My Bag activity in previous years, but decided that this year she would make a concerted effort to link individual and shared interests to daily learning activities. Based on the enthusiasm she witnessed among her boys for the *Star Wars* game, this teacher crafted word-study and vocabulary lessons taken directly from the game.

First, the teacher transformed her classroom with *Star Wars* paraphernalia, putting up posters of Luke Skywalker, Darth Vader, Han Solo, and Princess Leia, and displaying character costumes on a table. Instead of a word wall, her class added words to the "Vocabulary Spaceport."

For specific vocabulary work, the teacher first listed the syllabic and phonemic units scheduled for study in upcoming lessons. She next identified actual words spoken by the narrator and characters in the *Star Wars* game and linked them with these units, creating a chart similar to that in Figure 4.

Students were given a similar chart with room to add other words with similar phonemic elements. After reviewing the words as a whole group, the

FIGURE 4
Example Phonemic Chart With *Star Wars* Theme

Phonemic Element	*Star Wars* Words
/sp/	*sp*ace station
/pl/	*pl*anet
/ck/	ro*ck*et

teacher directed students to several stations set up in the classroom to continue working with these new elements in small groups. One station had *Star Wars* comics, another had a *Star Wars* graphic novel, a third was a computer with a simple *Star Wars* WebQuest activity (webquest.org). But by far the most popular station for the boys was the Lego *Star Wars* video game Zach had loaned to the class. Students at this station were required to play five minutes of the game, writing down all the words they heard during that time that contained one of the phonemic elements under study.

To increase understanding of newly learned words, students worked with a partner to write their own *Star Wars* story using the words in context. One pair of boys wrote,

> Luke Skywalker sat in a <u>space station</u>. He was going to set off the <u>booster rockets</u> so he could travel to a <u>planet</u>. The <u>planet</u> was going to be <u>attacked</u> by the Jedi. Luke had to save it.

Linking boys' out-of-school literacies with academic literacy is a practice that honors who they are in all their diversity and demonstrates the value we place on their lifeworlds beyond the classroom walls (Hull & Schultz, 2002). There is a growing realization of the importance of creating spaces in schools for striving and listless boy readers' everyday literacies so they can showcase and build on their strengths with the print and digital media they use on their own (Livingstone, 2002).

QUESTIONS FOR DISCUSSION

- Does the finding that boys are less motivated to read than girls match your own and your colleagues' experiences?

- What reading material or strategies have you found successful in motivating boys to read? How could these successful materials and practices become part of a schoolwide program for boys?

- What barriers have you experienced or do you envision when planning programs and curricula focused on boys' literacy? How might these be overcome?

- What factors in your school and community may be contributing to boys' depressed reading motivation? How might you and your colleagues learn more about these factors and ways of improving or compensating for them?

CHAPTER 6

Making School–Home–Community Connections to Enhance the Literacy Development of Young Boys

This final chapter moves beyond school boundaries to families and neighborhoods. We do this to give a wider perspective on the literacy needs of boys so anyone who comes in contact with them can enhance their development. In this concluding chapter you will learn that boys become readers and good and honorable boys when

- Partnerships between teachers and caregivers are forged
- Relatives, coaches, librarians, and members of congregations of worship interact with young boys and help build their literacy skills
- Fathers and brothers become role models

Why We Need Partnerships

In Chapter 1 we presented a historical perspective of boys' underachievement in literacy. From Gates's (1961) initial study to today's boy crisis the debate about boys' achievement rages on. We believe that failing to meet the literacy needs of young boys isn't so much a crisis as it is an imperative educational challenge, a challenge that research demonstrates has a better outcome if it is dealt with early, when a boy first enters school. Literacy beginnings matter to future reading success, yet too many boys—especially those of color—are getting turned off to literacy early. Boys, and especially boys of color, struggle most to learn how to read, dominate the rolls of remedial reading programs, and suffer disproportionately as alliterate adults. The price is huge: Boys make up the majority of offenders in our juvenile justice system (Kipnis, 1999), and boys without literacy will miss opportunities to be changed by the new ideas, sympathies, and understandings literacy provides. Alliterate boys miss a key source of insight on becoming better and more thoughtful men.

In their book, *Ghosts From the Nursery: Tracing the Roots of Violence*, Karr-Morse and Wiley (1997) remind us that problems like reading failure or antisocial behavior do not suddenly appear in adolescence. They begin early, during infancy, when children are not nurtured, spoken to, read to, and loved. For many young offenders bullying, tantrums, and a lack of self-regulation are the only coping skills they have ever known and they are bringing these behaviors with them to school. As mentioned in Chapter 3, across the United States, 3- and 4-year-old boys, mostly boys of color, are being expelled from preschool for what is considered to be obscene and disrespectful acts (Gilliam & Shahar, 2006). Young boys are getting kicked out of the very place where they can receive the language, literacy, and nurturance they need to become smart, caring, and successful men. Good instruction in preschool, kindergarten, and early elementary grades makes a difference to oral language and literacy development and to social and moral skills (Ramey & Ramey, 1998, 1999).

Yet it would be foolish to believe schools can do it all. Just as it takes a village to raise a child, it takes a village—or an entire community—to develop honorable and literate boys. Research conducted by practitioners, psychologists, and policymakers indicates how difficult it is to disentangle the sphere of influence (school, family, culture, and community) from children who inhabit and influence each of these. The theoretical frameworks of Bronfenbrenner (1979, 1995) and Sherif (1982) help teachers, caregivers, and community members understand the multiple spheres of influences on children's lives. The brain, like any other organ, lives in a particular time and space and it adapts to these (Stamm, 2007). Family and community contexts are strongly associated with physical and psychological health and school achievement, so it is crucial to create bridges between schools, families, and the wider community.

The Influence of Families on Boys' Literacy

Families are the places where young boys begin their literacy journeys and they are the place where much learning occurs throughout their lifetime. When families are involved in their sons' literacy many benefits are found, especially in the early years as children adapt to the school environment and form identities as learners (Chavkin, 1993; Christenson & Conoley, 1992). Adult involvement at this time matters to learning and literacy because this is when young boys sit in caregivers' laps to hear their first stories, see reading being modeled by those they care for most, and are rewarded or punished for imitating what they see (Carter, 2002; Pipher, 1996). West (2000) reports that when parents read to their children for just five minutes per night, three nights per week, their children's reading skills, vocabulary, and motivation to become a reader increase. Books are a major source of new words for young children because they contain different and richer language than is typically found in everyday speech (Gambrell et al., 2007). Prior and Gerard (2007) explain how children in early classrooms make greater gains in reading and language abilities when families use teacher-suggested strategies. Likewise, Henderson and Berla (1994) suggest school achievement will be more likely when the following conditions are met:

- Home environments promote learning.

- Parents hold high expectations for their children.

- Parents are interested in and willing to participate in their children's education both at school and in the community.

An overarching theme in each of these studies is that time and parental involvement correlate with school and literacy success. Yet when it comes to families and gender some interesting facts arise. In a large study of academic assistance, or who receives help when it is needed, Carter and Wojtkiewicz (2000) found that parents offer more assistance to girls, have higher expectations for them, and engage them in more discussions about schoolwork. When it comes to school, parents attend more events with their daughters than with their sons. In contrast, parents are more likely to check their son's homework and be in contact with the school, not for events or celebrations, but for behavioral issues. As teachers, we can break this pattern by communication with parents not only when their sons are in trouble but also to celebrate their accomplishments and successes. In our interactions with parents we can model our beliefs and expectations that when it comes to reading, boys can and will succeed.

Engaging Parents and Caregivers

We know the interests of boys are important for motivating them to read and do well in school. While it is likely parents and caregivers know their sons' general interests, parents may not have insight on appropriate books or ways to work with their sons to make learning productive and fun.

In its position statement on Family–School Partnerships, IRA (2002) notes that collaborative partnerships focusing on literacy development are important because children, caregivers, and teachers all benefit. Collaboration between teachers and parents helps parents understand classroom demands and the important role they play in their children's academic success. This, in turn, helps parents become more invested and hold higher expectations for their sons. When teachers work with parents their morale receives a boost. Teachers who feel a close connection to parents hold higher expectations for their students and develop lessons focused on higher level thinking (Henderson & Berla, 1994). As teachers, our beliefs fuel our actions, the objectives we set, and the lessons we plan. Our perceptions of students are important because they filter down and influence how students perceive themselves. When we repeatedly give positive feedback about students' abilities, the students who receive it come to see themselves through our eyes (Marachi, Friedel, & Midgley, 2001). Students will then talk to their caregivers about their accomplishments. Unfortunately, too often school–family partnerships are never forged and parents only hear negative stories from their sons. We may not communicate effectively because we are not trained to create partnerships or work collaboratively with families and community members (Rothstein, 2008).

One way to encourage school–family partnerships is to communicate. Lines of communication should always be open and focused on what children are learning. One way to do this is to send monthly information bulletins to families based on topics about which your class is investigating, reading, and writing. These topics should be based on the interest inventories discussed in Chapter 5 and the standards you need to cover. Information bulletins should be eye catching but brief. They are not designed to give many facts, but instead should help caregivers understand what the boy is learning so they can reinforce learning at home. Be sure to provide information on inexpensive or free outside resources parents can use if they want more background materials. Cite credible websites from well-known organizations and supply titles of books at the proper reading level. Do not forget tips for parents because many times parents want to help their sons succeed, they just do not know how. Always end an information bulletin with a fun, real-world activity that involves reading or writing. A sample information bulletin on gray wolves is provided in Figure 5. Notice that it focuses on a topic of interest, offers sources to extend learning, contains a fun activity, and gives parents insight on a few learning tips. Creating bulletins with sound information, variety, and interesting facts builds motivation and literacy skills and bridges the gap between school and home.

Parents and caregivers of young boys are often busy, and even the most interested parent may not have time to keep up on the latest discoveries. As a teacher of young children it is important to share information you find with parents and caregivers. For example, share with parents the following keys we have adapted from the National Education Association to help their children become good readers:

- Begin sharing books early—From the moment they are born, children should own child-safe books, be read to as much as possible, and see others reading and writing all around them. Encourage children to talk about books they have heard and to elaborate on story lines, add their own characters, and create new endings.

- Surround your child with a reading-rich environment—Your home is your child's first school and it is a critical learning environment. Make it full of print and sounds. Put signs around the house with your child's name on them. Make writing tools, alphabet refrigerator magnets, and

FIGURE 5
Sample Information Bulletin for Parents

This week we have been learning about gray wolves.

In class we discovered that the gray wolf's story is one of the most interesting tales in American wildlife. Once, the wolf was plentiful in most of North America, but because of over hunting and misunderstanding it was nearly exterminated. Today, with protection, the wolf is making a comeback in some of its former habitats.

Wolf Facts:
- Wolves are social animals; they live in packs of 2 to 15.
- The strongest male of a pack is normally the leader, and he is called the alpha male.
- An alpha male can go anywhere he wants and take anything he wants.
- The beta male is second in line.

Words to Investigate: interesting, exterminated, comeback, alpha male, beta male

Connections: Learning this information connects to Arizona Science Standards for first grade.

Concept 1: Characteristics of organisms.

Websites to Learn More:
The above facts came from the National Wildlife Federation's website at www.nwf.org/kids. Other good sources with information about wolves can be found at:

National Geographic
kids.nationalgeographic.com/Animals/CreatureFeature/Graywolf
Yahoo Kids
kids.yahoo.com/animals/mammals/4030--Gray+Wolf

Parent Tip: Always be present and involved when your child is using the Internet.

Nonfiction Books to Read for More Wolf Facts:
Gray Wolves by Lynn M. Stone (2003)
Gray Wolves by Patricia A.F. Martin (2003)

Fiction Books to Read:
The Eyes of Gray Wolf by Jonathan London (1993). Written in poetic prose, this book tells the sad tale of a wolf who has lost his mate to man.
The True Story of the Three Little Pigs by Jon Scieszka (1996). Alexander T. Wolf gives his side of the story of the three little pigs whose houses he huffed and puffed to smithereens. Alexander claims to have gotten a bad rap. He was just in the wrong place at the wrong time, with a sneezy cold.

Cooking With a Wildlife Theme:
Children studying about wildlife need to keep up their strength. Below is a healthy tasty snack for you to make as you read or search the Internet about wolves.

Parent Tip: Encouraging children for their effort as opposed to getting things perfect helps children learn that hard work pays off. As your child works on the follow recipe offer specific feedback (e.g., you are spreading that peanut butter nice and evenly) and accept and enjoy less-than-perfect creations. Offer support only when requested or needed.

(continued)

**FIGURE 5 *(continued)*
Sample Information Bulletin for Parents**

Ants on a Log

To make them you will need:
- a jar of peanut butter (chunky or smooth)
- clean washed sticks of celery
- raisins (about 4–6 per log)
- plate and plastic knife

What to do:
1. Make a log by spreading the peanut butter in the curve of the celery stick.
2. Put 4–6 raisins (which are your ants) on top of the peanut butter.
3. Eat your Ants on a Log with your family or friends.

This recipe came from www.childrensrecipes.com.

Parent Tip: Research indicates that reading to children every day increases their achievement. Children who hear books read to them often and from an early age have bigger vocabularies, comprehend text easier, and enjoy reading across their lifetime.

audio books part of your child's environment. To find good books go to www.nea.org/readacross/parents.html or www.reading.org/resources/tools/choices.html.

- Talk with your child—Talking with others is extremely important in encouraging your child's language, basic knowledge, and literacy development. Shut off the television and talk. Also limit television time because it does not offer the rich language and vocabulary your child needs. Television talk is abstract and does little to help your child gain insight on his immediate world.

- Teach your child about reading as you read—When you read aloud, help your child learn rules about print. Point to words, point out spaces between words, and sweep your finger left to right across the page. Point to the question mark at the end of a sentence and say, "That mark lets me know a question has been asked."

- Encourage your child to think—As children move from toddlerhood to school age, they are increasingly able to grasp the meaning of language and think about increasingly complex ideas. When you read, stop to discuss the meaning of words so your child will learn them. Pause to ask questions to help your child predict what will happen next. Help your child to understand main characters and encourage them to think about why these characters act as they do. Linking questions to print helps boys learn that print carries important and interesting messages.

- Form a partnership with you child's teacher and school—Educating your child is a shared responsibility between you, your child's teacher, and the school. Take advantage of parent–teacher conferences and make time each day to become involved.

Parents and caregivers are the earliest teachers of boys, so it makes sense to tap into this tremendous resource. Caring families make a difference, and creating partnerships between teachers, parents, caregivers, and students forms a true learning community and allows everyone to play their part in developing a boy who loves reading and acts responsibly with honor and care. The following Learning From a Character box presents a book with a little boy who extends his love and respect for family to the elderly residents of a nursing home.

LEARNING ABOUT RESPECTFULNESS FROM A PICTURE BOOK CHARACTER

Wilfred Gordon McDonald Partridge (Fox, 1985)

Wilfred Gordon befriends the residents of a nursing home and makes them a part of his extended family. His favorite is Miss Nancy Alison Delacourt, a 96-year-old woman who has lost her memory. Wilfred feels sad about Miss Nancy's lost memories and wants to help her find them again. He goes to the residents of the home and asks each of them to describe what a memory is, and each resident gives him ideas. Wilfred gathers objects that have the qualities of memories, such as laughter and preciousness, and he gives these to Miss Nancy. She begins to remember warm thoughts, happy times, the day she met Wilfred Gordon, and all the secrets they have shared.

Young Wilfred Gordon is respectful of the feelings, beliefs, and opinions of the nursing home residents and in many ways makes them part of his family. He teaches us about the sensitivity and insight young boys possess. Young boys are often attuned to the people in their world. They watch and listen to them and they ask countless questions about what is going on.

- How can you use Wilfred Gordon's story and the illustrations in this book to model boys' respect for classmates, grandparents, and others in their world?

- How do you encourage boys to extend their care for family into the wider world?

Connecting Fathers to Classrooms

Research indicates that cognitive, social, and emotional development is stronger in children when both mothers and fathers are involved in their lives and in their learning, and involvement of both parents in the early years has a positive effect on children's later academic performance (Henderson & Berla, 1994;

U.S. Department of Education, 1994). Furthermore, boys will not be readers if their parents and caregivers tell them to read but are not themselves models of active reading.

From our experience working with families we have come to recognize an untapped resource. A growing body of evidence reveals the unique and important role fathers play in a boy's intellectual and social development, psychological well-being, and school readiness (Krampe & Fairweather, 1993). Too often our schools and classrooms have a mother-centric approach; fathers are not included in school activities or encouraged enough by teachers to work with their sons in constructive ways. We exclude and fear men on school campuses, do not keep men informed on their children's progress, and do little to help men understand how they can become involved. This is a tragedy because school readiness and father involvement are directly correlated. A school-age boy with an involved male in his life tends to have better verbal and communication skills and perform better on measures of cognitive skills (Biller, 1993; Bing, 1963).

Fathers are role models and have a unique part to play. They communicate, encourage, and discipline differently than mothers and this variety helps create a balance that broadens and enriches the lives of boys (Prior & Gerard, 2007). Boys who have male role models tend to be patient, curious, and confident (Prior & Gerard, 2007). Behaviorally, children with involved fathers are more likely to remain in their seats, wait their turn before speaking, and sustain focus on their schoolwork (Biller, 1993). A boy's self-image may suffer if there is no father figure or no intimacy with a male role model (Gonzalez et al., 1995). Boys whose fathers are not involved in their schooling get poor grades and are likely to be retained. When men do not model a love for learning boys are much less likely to enjoy school (Cooksey & Fondell, 1996). Modeling also affects literacy because boys do not become readers if the adult men around them are not readers.

But this influence on children is not only a one-way street, because men need connections and ties to their children as well. Nurturing children allows men to display their emotional and moral sides. Unfortunately, too often men have grown up without positive role models themselves. They are uncertain how to nurture their sons, and as a result, feel inadequate (Frieman & Berkeley, 2002). As educators and community members we must come to respect the important role male caregivers play, and we must encourage and provide opportunities for them to work with their sons. It is vital that we recognize and communicate with the men in our boy students' lives.

Research indicates that fathers are more likely to become involved in school activities when the link between these activities and their sons' progress is explicit and when they understand what they need to do (Hadadian & Merbler, 1995; Turbiville & Marquis, 2001). We can encourage this by directly and explicitly sharing information from research on the importance of a father's role. One way to do this is to send short fact sheets home to male caregivers. The fact sheet shown in Figure 6 was adapted from the work of Prior and Gerard (2007).

One idea that might get fathers more involved is to encourage them to play games with their sons. Boys look up to the men in their lives and when they compete with them they learn to strive to do their best. Mild competition helps young boys learn social and moral skills. They learn that friends play fairly, and that honesty is always best. And young boys get pleasure from playing challenging games. In Chapter 4 we explained the work of Mark Prensky (2001a, 2001b), who talks about the practicality of using video games to "turn on the lights" for students today. Prensky suggests that anyone working with 21st-century learners should uncover how they want to be taught and offer developmentally appropriate challenges. Encouraging fathers to play well-constructed, challenging games with their sons can advance literacy development.

FIGURE 6
Sample Fact Sheet for Male Caregivers

As a caregiver the things you do have a powerful influence on your son. Your influence is important to the following aspects of your son's development:
- Cognitive development and thinking skills
- Language and literacy development
- School readiness and school behavior
- Self-image and self-esteem
- Self-competence and willingness to try new things

You can learn more about how important you are by reading the following articles:
"Spending Time With His Kids: Effects of Family Structure on Fathers' and Children's Lives" (Cooksey & Fondell, 1996)
"How Fathers Care for the Next Generation: A Four-Decade Study" (Lamb, 1994)

Fathers are different than mothers! And these differences are very important.
- Fathers have special ways of communicating—they speak in brief and direct ways.
- Fathers challenge and enrich their sons' verbal skills.
- Fathers encourage their sons to push themselves to their limits, to become their best.
- Fathers stress fairness, justice, and duty when they discipline their sons.
- Fathers prepare their sons for real-world challenges.

You can learn more by reading books such as these:
Fathers and Early Childhood Programs (Fagan & Palm, 2003)
Better Dads, Stronger Sons: How Fathers Can Guide Boys to Become Men of Character (Johnson, 2006)
Fatherneed: Why Father Care Is as Essential as Mother Care for Your Child (Pruett, 2000)

ABOUT
A BOY

Kenny runs in the house clutching a quart-size plastic bag in his hand. Inside it is a book and two white envelopes. "Uncle Charlie, Uncle Charlie, here are some games we learned to play in school today. Wanna play? Please, please, please let's play. Let's play!"

Charlie smiles at his adopted nephew and says, "Hold it squirt, how about you first focus on your homework?" "But this *is* my homework Uncle Charlie, see?" Charlie reads the note explaining that this bag contains three activities students were to complete for homework that evening. Charlie thinks to himself, What will they think of next? as he begins to read the directions: This is a word game based on word walls. Word walls, thinks Charlie, do I have to paint my walls with words? What am I getting myself into? Charlie removes the first envelope from the bag and begins to read the directions on the card:

Game #1: Mind Reader

This first game is called Mind Reader because it will require the child you are working with to guess a word from the clues you give. Doing this will develop problem-solving abilities and increase vocabulary skills.

   To begin, remove the book from this bag. Read it with your child and pick out six words you believe your child needs to learn to be able to read the book alone. Choose words your child does not know yet but that are not too difficult. Write these words on the index cards supplied and place them in two rows. Then ask your child the following questions and see if he or she gets the word correct. Be sure to ask these same questions each time you play.

"The word I am thinking of is one of the words on the table." (always provide this clue)

"It has _____ letters." (state the number of letters)

"It begins with _____." (say the beginning sound)

"It has a _____." (give a clue about the word)

"It means _____." (give the definition of the word)

Easy enough, thinks Charlie, and he and his nephew go to the couch to read *Willy the Wizard* (Browne, 1996). "Wow, that's quite a book, squirt," says Charlie, and he tells Kenny about how he played soccer when he was young. After this discussion Charlie picks out six words for Kenny to learn: *uniform*, *cleats*, *sidewalk*, *kickoff*, *goalkeeper*, and *stranger*. Pretty big words, thinks Charlie, and he is amazed that his nephew does so well. They play for 25 minutes without stopping or even thinking about the time. "Let's do the next game. Let's try the next one," says Kenny. OK, thinks Charlie, I really enjoyed reading the book and playing the first game was actually kind of fun. Charlie takes the second envelope and reads the card for Game #2:

Game #2: Word in a Cup

This second game is called Word in a Cup because it will require your child to read a word drawn from a cup. Doing this will develop problem-solving abilities and increase decoding and vocabulary skills. Please get a coffee cup and let the fun begin. Start with the words on the index cards you used for the previous game (Mind Reader) but add approximately 10 more. Words can come from *Willy the Wizard* (Browne, 1996), or they can be words you know your child wants to learn. Words around you, called environmental print, are good choices. Also add 4 "SORRY" cards. These will be used to skip a turn.

Alternate turns pulling a card out of the cup. If the player can say the word correctly he gets to keep the card. The winner has the most cards.

This won't be much of a challenge, thinks Charlie, if I go up against the kid. So he has Kenny run next door to get a friend. When he returns, Robert is with him and Charlie is ready to mediate game play. Robert goes first but pulls a SORRY card. "Hey, no fair, I'm the guest." "Keep on trying," says Charlie, and he monitors the boys for about 25 minutes. Whew! I never knew homework could be so much fun, thinks Charlie. The boys are tired themselves, and ready to go out and play.

On your own or with colleagues, brainstorm answers to the following questions:

- How did Kenny's teacher successfully bridge the gap between school and home?

- In Chapter 4 you learned how important playing games can be to young boys. Explain how the games Kenny was playing encouraged literacy development and motivation.

- What do you notice about Uncle Charlie's attitude toward literacy? Did it change after playing the games?

- How did Charlie help Kenny develop both literacy skills and a positive view of literacy?

- Why do you think Kenny's teacher had Charlie and Kenny read that particular book?

Interacting With Brothers

In many families young children spend more time with their siblings than they do with their parents. Siblings play an important role in contributing to boys' cognitive, social, and emotional development (Peterson, 2002; Roberts & Blanton, 2001). In the early years, when siblings spend a lot of time together, their interactions are often emotionally charged and marked with both positive and negative experiences. Siblings cooperate, instruct, and nurture one another, and older brothers often become role models for young boys. Younger siblings imitate older brothers and often accept their advice without question or concern. Having an older brother who gives good advice can be of great benefit, but having an older brother who gives bad advice can do the opposite (Clark, 1984). For example, many boys join gangs at their brother's request. It is also inevitable that brothers sometimes fight. The emotions brought out by sibling rivalry provide opportunities for boys to learn how to handle conflict (negotiation skills), develop an identity (who they are and what they stand for), and become good fathers themselves (Bedford, Volling, & Avioli, 2000).

Given the special relationships formed by brothers we encourage you to consider ways to help brothers connect through literacy. Just as fathers need to understand the importance of their role, brothers need the same. We suggest that you hold a brothers' workshop at your school to help brothers realize their important role. To understand how this can be accomplished let's look inside a school, and then let's consider how to use a book about brothers in your instruction.

ABOUT
A BOY

The last two months have been rough ones at Sunset Elementary School. Because of a large number of teens living in the neighborhood and few recreational activities, there has been vandalism, several break-ins, and the school has been tagged with graffiti five times. A neighborhood task force decides to take action and the principal, Mrs. Harris, has become actively involved. Working with parents, community members, and teachers, Mrs. Harris has recruited 15 older brothers of students at her school (some of whom are thought to be causing the problems) to be part of Brothers' Night, which has been designed to keep the older boys off the streets with an activity to enhance their own and their siblings' literacy skills and build self-esteem. To accomplish this, several community members, including a coach, a librarian, and a few uncles, will train the older brothers to work with their siblings on literacy tasks at the public library. Volunteers will present workshops to older boys on ways they can work successfully and productively with their siblings.

After a brief welcoming ceremony and overview of rules and responsibilities, Mr. Zelweski, coach of a local high school football team, begins the first session using an activity based on a Top 10 List. Mr. Zelweski asks the boys to brainstorm their top 10 ideas for how older brothers should work with their siblings when they read a book. Mr. Zelweski begins with 1 and has the boys work up to 10. The list they generate, with Mr. Zelweski's guidance and support, is as follows:

10. Have FUN!

9. After you read, take time to discuss the book. Ask one another who, what, when, why, and how questions.

8. Ask the child his or her favorite part and character.

7. If the child is a reader, have him or her read to you. If you notice too many mistakes being made, check for readability. Ask the librarian or teacher in charge to make sure the book is at the proper level.

6. If the child does make an error while reading that distracts from the meaning of the story, prompt the child with a question that will help him or her recognize the error.

5. As the child reads, remember that some mistakes are OK. If the child says *house* for *home* it does not change the story's meaning. If meaning is not altered, let it go.

4. Encourage the child to ask questions about the story if the plot is confusing.

3. Identify and discuss unfamiliar words.

2. Encourage conversation. Ask the child if his or her initial predictions were correct.

1. Take time to discuss the book before you read. Look at the cover, point out the author and illustrator, and ask the child what he or she thinks the book will be about.

Other workshops focus on ways to select books, strategies to develop conversations and friendships, and games to reinforce reading and writing skills. The program has been going on for three months and six more boys have joined. Problems at the school and in the community have decreased. This school, library, and community partnership is working out better than anyone could have anticipated.

The scenario above reveals how important it is to have constructive things for older boys to do in their neighborhood and how positive it can be to their esteem when they become role models for their siblings. Providing insight for older boys and space for brothers to come together to read is worth the initial investment. Benefits will last a lifetime.

Brothers have special relationships and the meaning of brothers often extends from blood relatives to good friends. Brothers are in our homes and they are in our neighborhoods. Brothers look out for one another, help one another learn, and are tolerant of one another's differences, as the boys in the following Learning From a Character box reveal.

LEARNING ABOUT TOLERANCE FROM A PICTURE BOOK CHARACTER

Brothers (Yin, 2006)

Brothers is the story of Ming, who travels from China to San Francisco to live with his older brother, Shek. Unfortunately, Ming not only finds a strange country but also an intolerant and hostile place. Longing for a friend, Ming wanders near a school and meets Patrick, who accepts and respects him for who he is. Patrick teaches Ming how to speak in English and his family teaches Ming how to sing and have fun. Being with Patrick is one of the few happy things in Ming's life. In other parts of his life people are intolerant: No one wants to come to Chinatown to buy goods because the merchants do not speak English. So Patrick and Ming come up with a plan that turns things around. The story ends with Ming showing Patrick how to write the word *hing-dai*, which means *brothers*, in Chinese because the boys have become more than friends—they have become brothers.

- What message about different cultures does this book provide?

- What message about brothers does this book provide?

- How can you use this story to help the boys at your school, in your home, or in your neighborhood develop tolerance and respect?

- What do you do to model respect for everyone?

Accommodating Nontraditional Family Structures

Social and economic changes in society have brought about changes in family structures and support (Swick, 2003). Understanding family structures and backgrounds is important because literacy is nested within and influenced by each of them. The idea of a traditional nuclear family, consisting of a father, mother, and a few children living under one roof, with the father being the primary breadwinner, has changed. Today's family is likely to be very different. While some boys come from traditional families, many others come from homes where both parents work outside the home. There are blended, divorced, and single-parent families. In the United States today 1 in 5 first marriages ends in divorce, so many boys live in single-parent homes (Bramlett & Mosher, 2002). Divorce is difficult on any child but becomes especially difficult on young boys when a parent remarries and starts a new family. Although many fathers seek active roles despite divorce, many others leave physically and emotionally (Furstenberg & Cherlin, 1991).

Single parents carry out all the responsibilities of two parents, often with little support and few resources. Approximately 90% of single parents are women, and many single mothers have limited incomes (Fields, 2001). If a single parent feels emotionally drained and alone, with little support, he or she may be unable to invest the time and energy needed to promote positive social, academic, and emotional growth. Anyone can help a single-parent family by taking an interest in the boys who reside in it. For instance, supporting a grandson, cousin, nephew, or neighbor who lives in a single-parent family with the strategies and books we have provided may offer some needed mentorship. The following Learning From a Character box contains an example of a book that can be used to support young boys. The story is one of courage and shows boys how, even in difficult situations, they can be brave and strong.

LEARNING ABOUT COURAGE
FROM A PICTURE BOOK CHARACTER

Night Boat to Freedom (Raven, 2006)

Night Boat to Freedom is the story of 12-year-old Christmas John, who is asked by his Granny Judith to row slaves across the Ohio River to freedom. Christmas John is being raised by this courageous woman who helps her grandson fight injustice and find courage inside himself. Granny Judith tells how she was tricked with red flannel cloth and kidnapped into slavery. To Granny Judith red is a sad color, and she tells her grandson how he can learn the color of freedom by taking slaves across the river. Christmas John does this over and over again and each time he does Granny Judith asks him what color a dress or some other piece of clothing those being transported to freedom wore. Blue, indigo, and green each get woven into Granny Judith's quilt as Christmas John crossed the river.

Granny Judith then tries to convince her grandson that he should make a final trip and stay in Ohio without her because she is too old. Christmas John rejects this idea. He tells her, "Freedom's got no color for me without you." Despite the hunters and their dogs, the small family of two makes it to freedom and when they do, Granny Judith raises the quilt she has been sewing that contains the colors of freedom she has heard about each night.

- How can this book be used to help young boys living in traditional and nontraditional families learn about courage?
- How might a grandmother or grandfather use this book to help her or his grandson learn about prejudice?

The Influence of Neighborhoods on Boys' Literacy

During the 1990s researchers in developmental psychology, public health, family studies, and sociology joined forces to study the links between families, schools, neighborhoods, and communities. Their initial focus was to disentangle each of these and provide information on the influence of each. The theoretical frameworks of Bronfenbrenner (1979, 1995) and Sherif (1982) did much to help us understand the effects of multiple spheres of influence on children's lives. We believe it is important to focus on neighborhoods' influence on boys' lives and literacy development because just as schools and families influence social and psychological development, the economic opportunities, physical conditions, institutional capacities, and values a neighborhood provides lead boys on very different paths (Nettles, Caughy, & O'Campo, 2008). Boys make friends with youngsters in their neighborhoods, attend schools and worship in churches nearby, and read books in libraries near where they live.

Boys living in poor neighborhoods tend to display lower verbal abilities, reading scores, and overall academic achievement, which often makes them at risk for failure (Caughy, O'Campo, & Muntaner, 2003; Leventhal & Brooks-Gunn, 2004). If boys live far from a library or if their public library lacks resources, they experience fewer literacy opportunities. As a result of less access, especially during the summer months out of school, they experience a greater setback when they return to the classroom (Constantino, 2005; Fryer & Levitt, 2002). This is compounded by the fact that families living in poverty must often send their children to dilapidated schools with poor academic records. These schools get labeled as failing, pay teachers lower salaries, have fewer experienced teachers, and have limited access to technology (Gorski, 2003; Karoly, 2001). Boys attending schools in impoverished neighborhoods are placed in larger classes and the curriculum they receive is less rigorous, focusing on lower level skills.

Just as we must not let the boy crisis cloud our thinking, we must not let myths of poverty pervade. Unfortunately, there are far too many stereotypes about people living in poverty that are used to divert responsibility. Teachers, parents, and neighbors develop low expectations for certain boys and do not recognize what boys in poverty have in common—inequitable access to resources and rights. The most destructive mindset anyone can hold is a deficit one, that of defining boys by their weaknesses rather than their strengths. Those with a deficit view often use two strategies to propagate their beliefs: they draw on stereotypes that support the cycle of poverty, and they ignore systematic conditions such as unequal access to quality schools and teachers (Gorski, 2008). If boys' own deficiencies and choices are assumed to cause failure, antipoverty programs and policies are much less likely to get funded and implemented successfully. If families living in poverty are believed to devalue reading and education it becomes easy to dodge responsibility (Gans, 1995). The questions all of us, as educators, parents, relatives, and neighbors must ask ourselves are, What can we do to eliminate this deficit mindset? What can we do to stop trying to fix the poor and start demanding the best for each and every child? What can we do in our own neighborhoods to get books into boys' hands, help them learn how to read, and help them find productive paths to manhood? We wish there were simple answers but there are not. However, if each of us would spend some time with a young boy in need things would be much better. Using the ideas and books we have set forth here could be a productive place to start. We believe the key is spending time with boys in productive ways. We must reach out to boys and nurture them each and every day.

ABOUT A BOY

Sacred Heart and Blood is a small parish church in Gary, Indiana, USA, run by Father Semanski. Many of the church's parishioners are facing difficult times because the steel mills and oil refineries have shut down or cut back. Many parishioners lost good paying jobs and are working two minimum wage jobs just to make ends meet. As a result, many of the boys in the neighborhood are unsupervised for long periods of time. Father Semanski realizes this, and creates a neighborhood task force to hit the problem head on. He connects with community outreach programs and health organizations to bring resources into his church. He also establishes a homework hotline, and to get the boys off the streets, begins a church Book Club. Several parish members are teachers, and they have been more than glad to lend their expertise to this enterprise. With humble funding and the help of one teacher's book club points, the parishioners purchase a small collection of books.

Book Clubs occur on Friday evenings and Saturday and Sunday afternoons after services. This week's book is *My Ol' Man* (Polacco, 1995), and the boys are excited about this choice because many have read it in school. The story is about a divorced family that has fallen on hard times. After the boys read, Father Semanski engages them in a discussion about the courage the family in the book displays and the important role cooperation plays. Hal, a boy living in a divorced household with his father, talks about how he and his father do the shopping, laundry, and lawn mowing together as a team. Father Semanski shows us how a neighborhood leader can make a difference in the lives of boys.

- How might a Book Club discussion such as this one help boys break stereotypes?
- How might a discussion with a neighborhood leader help boys learn positive character traits such as cooperation, perseverance, and respectfulness?
- What are some other ways a neighborhood leader could help boys find personal value in their own unique family situations?

Our Ending and Your Beginning

Bill has worked for many years to advocate for the literacy needs of adolescent boys, and Debby has worked with young boys with disabilities. These varied ends of the developmental spectrum have helped us see the importance of understanding the development and needs of young boys and the importance of starting early. If we wait until the middle grades to introduce boys to activities that address their unique learning needs and to introduce positive male characters to help them envision a role for themselves we run the risk of losing boys early, perhaps even before their journey into literacy begins. Research shows that by first grade, girls are likely to be ahead of boys in reading and they continue to make more progress in reading throughout the elementary years (National Center for Education Statistics, 2001). Answers as to why so many young boys are becoming disenchanted with literacy are complex and likely to be symptoms of a constellation of problems. However, we believe the information we have provided, boy-friendly strategies, and books addressing the things boys want to know about are productive steps in the right direction. Helping boys find entry points into literacy must be a priority and must happen early, when boys first become acquainted with literacy. If you, too, believe this we ask you to join us to spread the word and do the hard work. Just as we came together from distant parts of the country and varied environments we ask you to do the same: to bring literacy skills and wonder to the boys in your classroom, in your home, down the block, and across contexts and time.

Learning From a Character boxes have played an important part in helping us convey our message, so it seems fitting we should end with a discussion about the final box. *The Three Questions* (Muth, 2002) asks some very important questions. When is the best time to do things? Who is the most important one? What is the right thing to do? The boys in our schools and neighborhoods ask questions like these every day and literacy can help them find answers. Unfortunately too many boys are encouraged or allowed to be aliterate or they are turned off to literacy because of the way it is presented to them. Throughout this book we have argued that expecting less from boys and failing to meet their unique literacy needs, and meet them early, is wrong. Changing this mindset must become an imperative educational challenge.

If we are going to help boys make a bright beginning, boys need to learn literacy skills in active, contextualized ways. Boys need to be immersed in print-rich environments that keep them engaged and allow them to learn in communities that offer respect, responsibility, and brotherhood. It is our job as teachers, caregivers, siblings, neighbors, and friends to answer the questions boys ask and to care for the boys in our lives. The most important ones are the boys in our schools, homes, and neighborhoods. The best time to lead boys to literacy is right now. The right thing to do is to use books and authentic activities that help boys learn how to decode and at the same time learn positive character traits. The young boys in our lives deserve nothing less, and we pass this challenge on to you. As our journey writing this book ends, we hope your journey with young boys and literacy begins.

LEARNING ABOUT COURAGE
FROM A PICTURE BOOK CHARACTER

The Three Questions (Muth, 2002)

In *The Three Questions* Nikolai feels uncertain about how he should act. To find the answer, he asks three questions of his friends Sonya, Gogol, and Pushkin. When is the best time to do things? Who is the most important one? What is the right thing to do? Although each friend provides answers, Nikolai feels that these answers are not quite enough. So he decides to ask Leo, the wise turtle, because he has lived a very long time. When Nikolai meets Leo, he sees him digging a garden. Nikolai helps until a great storm blows in and he hears a cry for help from an injured panda who has fallen from a tree. Nikolai takes the panda home and learns she has a child left in the storm. Nikolai rushes to the infant and brings her back to the safety of her mother's arms. Feeling a great sense of satisfaction, yet still wondering about his questions, Nikolai once again turns to Leo for solace and this wise old turtle helps Nikolai understand how circumstances link. If Nikolai had not helped him dig his garden he would never have heard the panda's cry for help, learned about her baby, and rescued the little one. From this simple connection Nikolai learns the best time to do things is now. The most important person is the one you are with, and the right thing is to do good for the person who is standing at your side.

- How can you use this book to help young boys find courage and inner strength?
- How can you use this book to help boys question their world?
- How can you use this book to help boys get a bright start?

QUESTIONS FOR DISCUSSION

■ Parents are the first teachers of literacy. How can parents connect with others to help broaden the literacy experiences of their sons?

■ What roles do families play in the social and emotional development of their sons, and how might literacy help?

■ Fathers play important roles in their sons' early literacy experiences. Where and how can fathers incorporate literacy into their daily routines with their sons?

■ How do family structures influence boys' literacy development and needs?

■ What roles do neighborhoods play in the social and emotional development of young boys, and how might literacy help?

■ Why should we think broadly and comprehensively about the needs of young boys?

■ In this chapter we have profiled several community members who may have opportunities to work with young boys. Whom have we omitted, and what other opportunities are there in the community to bring literacy into the lives of boys?

Books That Demonstrate Positive Values for Boys

Positive Male Value	Bibliographic Information	Description
Cooperation	Agee, J. (2001). *Milo's Hat Trick*. New York: Hyperion.	Milo the Magician needs a spectacular new trick and turns to a bear to rescue his failing show. Through cooperation, the two quickly become a smash sensation.
	Burns, L.G. (2007). *Tracking Trash*. New York: Houghton Mifflin.	Aided by an army of beachcombers, oceanographer Dr. Curtis Ebbesmeyer tracks trash in the name of science. From sneakers to hockey gloves, Curtis monitors the watery fate of human-made cargo that has spilled into the ocean. And with careful analysis, Curtis—working cooperatively with a community of scientists, friends, and beachcombers—is using his data to understand and protect our ocean.
	Harris, E. (2006). *Elephant on My Roof*. San Diego, CA: Red Cygnet.	Lani turns to the people in his village to help get an elephant off his roof after he realizes that he cannot do it alone. At first everyone refuses, but the youngster convinces them to lend a hand. He and the rescued elephant reciprocate by assisting the fisherman, some children, and an old woman.
	Katz, K. (2003). *Daddy and Me*. New York: Little Simon.	The story of cooperation between a father and his son as they do a home-improvement project together.
	Laminack, L.L. (2008). *Jake's 100th Day of School*. Atlanta, GA: Peachtree.	Mr. Thompson's class is preparing for the 100th day of school. Jake is working on a scrapbook with 100 pictures of his family but is so excited when the big day comes that he forgets his book bag with his album in it. The principal works with Jake to help him assemble a second collection.
	Medearis, A.S. (2004). *Seven Spools of Thread: A Kwanzaa Story*. Morton Grove, IL: Albert Whitman & Co.	In an original Kwanzaa tale, seven bickering brothers must work together and use the seven principles of Nguzo Saba to make gold from thread and claim their inheritance.
	Mills, C. (2001). *Gus and Grandpa at Basketball*. New York: Farrar, Straus & Giroux.	Gus, with the cooperation of his Grandpa, is able to close his ears to the yelling crowds so that he can finally score in a basketball game.
	Pilkey, D. (1999). *The Paperboy*. New York: Scholastic.	This is the cooperative story of a young boy and his dog who responsibly complete their rounds delivering newspapers.
	Raschka, C. (1993). *Yo! Yes*. New York: Orchard.	With very few words and using short sentences, subtle punctuation hints, and body postures, two boys communicate, cooperate, and become friends.
	Rathmann, P. (1995). *Officer Buckle and Gloria*. New York: Scholastic.	Officer Buckle is hilariously upstaged by his canine partner, Gloria, when they team up to give safety tips to children.
	Reiss, M. (2008). *The Boy Who Wouldn't Share*. New York: HarperCollins.	Edward has oodles of toys but doesn't share any of them with his little sister, Claire. Then one day Edward finds himself stuck under his enormous pile of toys and can't move! With a little help, he learns that if he cooperates with others, they'll share right back with him.

(continued)

Positive Male Value	Bibliographic Information	Description
Cooperation (*continued*)	Steig, W. (1998). *Pete's a Pizza*. New York: Joanna Cotler.	When Pete is in a bad mood because it is raining and he can't play ball with his friends, his father decides that he might cheer his son with a pizza. Father and son cooperate and make a pizza together.
	Williams, M. (2005). *Brothers in Hope: The Story of the Lost Boys of Sudan*. New York: Lee & Low.	This is the story of a boy who cooperates with many other young people to survive the civil war that ravaged Sudan in the 1980s.
	Wynne-Jones, T. (2007). *The Boat in the Tree*. Honesdale, PA: Front Street.	An unnamed 8-year-old boy is passionate about boats of all kinds. He builds one out of junk parts and sails to imaginary Bongadongo and away from Simón, a slightly younger boy. When the weather turns bad, his boat ends up in a tree. The boys work together, cooperating, to get the boat down.
Courage	Bannerman, H. (1996). *The Story of Little Babaji*. New York: HarperCollins.	Delicate comic art shows how a small boy in India outsmarts four tigers, each more vain than hungry, in this handsomely designed book.
	Blumberg, R. (2003). *Shipwrecked! The True Adventures of a Japanese Boy*. New York: HarperTrophy.	Rescued by a whaling ship, 14-year-old Manjiro becomes the first Japanese person ever to visit the United States and becomes a bridge between two cultures.
	Bradby, M. (1996). *More Than Anything Else*. London: Orchard.	A fictionalized story about the life of young Booker T. Washington. After emancipation, 9-year-old Booker travels to the salt mines to work. Throughout the book, Booker glows with his desire to read, and the inspiring tone of the language predicts a bright future.
	Bruchac, J. (2000). *Crazy Horse's Vision*. New York: Lee & Low.	Embodying the spirit and culture of the legendary Lakota warrior, this fictionalized biography focuses on his journey to adulthood and the courageous life paths that created the man he was.
	Carbone, E. (2002). *Storm Warriors*. New York: Yearling.	Nathan longs to become a surfman with the only African American life-saving crew on 1890s' Pea Island. When confronted with his own personal limitations and courage, he discovers a better way to contribute.
	Carbone, E. (2008). *Night Running: How James Escaped With the Help of His Faithful Dog*. New York: Knopf.	James has a plan to escape his life of slavery on Master Graham's farm. He tells his dog to stay behind; he's too noisy to bring along on a dangerous nighttime journey. But when James is captured soon after he runs, he's grateful his faithful hunting dog has followed him. The scrappy hound rescues James from his captors.
	Cowan, C. (1997). *My Life With the Wave*. New York: Lothrop, Lee & Shepard.	A boy brings home a wave from the seashore in this highly imaginative picture book that uses magically realistic art to credibly present the incredible.
	Crews, N. (2006). *Below*. Austin, TX: Henry Holt.	One day Guy falls through a hole in the stairs, and Jack worries about what might be happening to him below. Fearful that Guy might have to deal with dragons, wild horses—or worse, be all alone—the child shows great courage and uses his crane and other action figures to affect a rescue.
	Davis, K. (2008). *Kindergarten Rocks!* New York: Voyager.	Dexter Dugan is about to start kindergarten, and his stuffed dog, Rufus, "is an eensy teensy beensy bit scared" about it. Thankfully, Dex's third-grader sister, Jessie, sees that her brother is really the scared one and sets out to help him find the courage to get through his fears.
	Davol, M.W. (1997). *The Paper Dragon*. New York: Simon & Schuster.	Cut tissue paper art elegantly unfolds across triple-page spreads in the dramatic story of a Chinese artist who saves his village from a fearsome dragon.

(continued)

Positive Male Value	Bibliographic Information	Description
Courage (*continued*)	DeFelice, C. (2007). *The Apprenticeship of Lucas Whitaker*. New York: Farrar, Straus & Giroux.	A touching novel about a 12-year-old Connecticut farm boy who courageously becomes a doctor's apprentice after his family dies of consumption in 1849.
	DiCamillo, K. (2006). *Mercy Watson Goes for a Ride*. Somerville, MA: Candlewick.	Every weekend, Mr. Watson takes his pig Mercy for a ride in his pink convertible. One Saturday, their elderly neighbor, Baby Lincoln, stows away in the backseat. Man and pig speed happily along until Baby reveals her presence. Surprised, Mr. Watson takes his eyes off the road, and Mercy seizes her chance, jumps into his lap, and grabs the wheel. With Mr. Watson unable to reach the brake, it takes some heroics from Baby to save the day.
	Fradin, D.B. (2003). *The Signers: The 56 Stories Behind the Declaration of Independence*. New York: Walker and Company.	Each of the signers of the Declaration of Independence had a life before, during, and after his historical act, yet most of them are unknown. This book gives brief, fascinating glimpses into the people who have been overlooked as well as those with whom readers might be familiar, portraying their courage and perseverance.
	Gerstein, M. (2007). *The Man Who Walked Between the Towers*. New York: Square Fish.	This true story recounts the daring feat of a spirited young Frenchman who courageously walked a tightrope between the World Trade Center twin towers in 1974.
	Giblin, J.C. (2007). *Charles A. Lindbergh: A Human Hero*. New York: Clarion.	A multidimensional portrait explores the courage and achievements of this famous American aviator as well as the controversies and tragedies that surrounded his life.
	Henderson, K. (2007). *Lugalbanda: The Boy Who Got Caught Up in a War*. Somerville, MA: Candlewick.	The story of an ancient Iraqi, Lugalbanda, and his heroic deeds to assist the kingdom of Uruk during a war. Lugalbanda's courage, kindness, and prescience contributed to his heroism.
	Himelblau, L. (2005). *The Trouble Begins*. New York: Delacorte.	Fifth-grader Du recounts his difficult adjustment to life in the United States when he emigrates from a Vietnamese refugee camp after a 10-year separation from his family.
	Holub, J. (1999). *The Robber and Me*. Austin, TX: Henry Holt.	On his way to live with his uncle, Boniface is helped by a mysterious stranger named Robber Knapp. He must find the courage to stand up to his uncle and the town authorities to clear the name of the stranger.
	Klise, K. (2006). *Why Do You Cry? Not a Sob Story*. New York: Henry Holt.	A 5-year-old boy rabbit decides no one who cries will be asked to his birthday party. However, he finds this a difficult requirement because even his big, best friend the horse cries when a bee stings him. In the end Little Rabbit's mother helps him understand that even she, as a grown-up, sometimes cries.
	London, J. (2001). *Where the Big Fish Are*. New York: Walker and Company.	The narrator and his friend Bill know that the big fish are out in the sea, not near the dock where they sit. One day they decide to build a raft and go after the fish. The night before the launching, Bill wakes to find the raft destroyed. Bill, who really doesn't want to go, finds his courage and encourages his friend to repair the raft.
	Look, L. (2008). *Alvin Ho: Allergic to Girls, School, and Other Scary Things*. Schwartz & Wade.	Alvin Ho is a second grader who is afraid of *everything*— elevators, tunnels, girls, and, most of all, school. But at home he's a superhero named Firecracker Man, a brother, and a gentleman-in-training. He learns to translate his courage at home into facing his fears in the world.
	Mochizuki, K. (1995). *Baseball Saved Us*. New York: Lee & Low.	Building a baseball field helps a group of Japanese Americans in an internment camp during World War II keep active, courageous, and strong. This strength and courage endures even after they are released and face prejudice.

(*continued*)

Positive Male Value	Bibliographic Information	Description
Courage (*continued*)	Morpurgo, M. (2007). *Kensuke's Kingdom*. London: Nick Hern.	Eleven-year-old Michael is washed over the side of his family's yacht and awakens on what he believes is a deserted island in the Pacific Ocean. In this riveting survival story, Michael discovers he is not alone.
	Muth, J.J. (2002). *The Three Questions*. New York: Scholastic.	Nikolai asks three very important questions: When is the best time to do things? Who is the most important one? What is the right thing to do? He seeks a wise Turtle for the answer and finds him digging a garden—until a great storm blows in. During the storm Nikolai is forced to summon his courage and save a mother panda and her child. In the end Nikolai learns how circumstances and people link together and how bonds of love are formed.
	Pinkney, A.D. (1999). *Bill Pickett: Rodeo-Ridin' Cowboy*. New York: Voyager.	This is the story of Bill Pickett, an African American cowboy, who exhibits courage as a cowboy and later as a famous rodeo star.
	Rappaport, D. (2007). *Freedom River*. New York: Hyperion.	John Parker, a courageous ex-slave and successful businessman from Ohio, is also a conductor on the Underground Railroad. On one of his trips, Parker must convince Jim and his family to leave the plantation for freedom.
	Raven, M.T. (2006). *Night Boat to Freedom*. New York: Farrar, Straus & Giroux.	Twelve-year-old Christmas John is asked by his Granny Judith to row slaves across the Ohio River to freedom. Christmas John summons all his courage to carry out this very dangerous wish.
	Rumford, J. (2001). *Traveling Man: The Journey of Ibn Battuta*. New York: Houghton Mifflin.	This is the story of Ibn Battuta, who shows great courage when he decides to travel across Africa and Asia. He begins his 29-year journey in 1325 at the age of 21. He first decided to go to Mecca as a pilgrim, and then he goes through Africa, across the steppes of Asia, into India and China, and back to Morocco.
	Santiago, C. (2002). *Home to Medicine Mountain*. San Francisco: Children's Book Press.	In this poignant and powerful picture book, homesickness plagues two Maidu brothers forced to find courage while attending a government boarding school for Indians in 1930s' California.
	Schachner, J. (2003). *Skippyjon Jones*. New York: Scholastic.	Skippyjon Jones is a boy kitty with a very active imagination. When he gets sent to his room he imagines he is Skippito Friskito, the sword fighter who courageously battles a humongous "bumblebeeto" and saves a roving band of Mexican Chihuahuas.
	Shea, G. (2005). *First Flight: The Story of Tom Tate and the Wright Brothers*. New York: HarperTrophy.	Tom Tate was a boy who assisted the Wright brothers with experiments for their historic flying machine. Tom is identified as a real person who courageously volunteers to try out the glider when there wasn't enough wind to lift the grown men.
	Simms, L. (1997). *The Bone Man: A Native American Modoc Tale*. New York: Hyperion.	In this story of a boy's rite of passage Nulwee is told by his grandmother that one day he must kill the Bone Man. The skeletal creature lies asleep, but if awakened will drink the river dry and devour all of the people. When Nulwee mistakenly awakes the Bone Man, the boy gathers his courage and destroys the evil creature.
	Taulbert, C.L. (2003). *Little Cliff's First Day of School*. New York: Puffin.	In this second story about Little Cliff, an African American boy growing up in the rural South in the 1950s, it is time for his first day of school. He is so frightened when it's time to leave that he tries hiding under the house—a favorite refuge from the heat of summer.
	Thaler, M. (2008). *The Principal From The Black Lagoon*. New York: Scholastic Cartwheel.	Hubie has been sent to the principal's office, and he's lost his courage! Does Mrs. Green really feed kids to the alligator she keeps in her office? Does she really keep kids locked in cages under her desk? Will Hubie be able to hear kids screaming for help from down the hall?

(continued)

Positive Male Value	Bibliographic Information	Description
Courage (*continued*)	Thaler, M. (2008). *The Teacher From the Black Lagoon*. New York: Scholastic Cartwheel.	Hubie faces his comically horrific fears during his first day of school and his first trip to the school library. Featuring a fire-breathing teacher and a library where all the books are bolted to the shelves, these stories are sure to amuse and quell fears of new experiences at the same time.
	Wallace, B. (1999). *The Eye of the Great Bear*. New York: Pocket.	A 12-year-old boy growing up in pioneer Texas overcomes his fear and gains courage when he encounters a bear.
	Winter, J. (2005). *Roberto Clemente: Pride of the Pittsburgh Pirates*. New York: Atheneum.	Black-and-white drawings interspersed with full color paintings depict the life and career of this Puerto Rican baseball player and the struggles he bravely faced on and off the field.
Generosity	Arnold, T. (2005). *Hi! Fly Guy*. New York: Scholastic.	A beautiful friendship begins when Buzz proves that a fly can be one smart pet. This slim, reader-friendly tale has a robust humor and wacky cartoon art featuring an eye-popping cover.
	Banks, K. (2000). *Night Worker*. New York: Farrar, Straus & Giroux.	Alex follows his Papa, a construction worker on the night shift, and helps him all night long until morning when he comes home to bed.
	Chinn, K. (1997). *Sam and the Lucky Money*. New York: Lee & Low.	Passing a homeless man huddled on the street in Chinatown, Sam decides to give him the "lucky money" he received for the New Year.
	Compestine, Y.C. (2001). *The Runaway Rice Cake*. New York: Simon & Schuster.	As part of the Chinese New Year celebration, Mama Chang cooks a rice cake that comes to life and runs away. Once caught, generous Da, the youngest son, offers the cake to an old woman who is hungry, leaving the Chang family with nothing for their feast—but their kind-heartedness brings them greater benefits.
	Couric, K. (2000). *The Brand New Kid*. New York: Doubleday.	Lazlo S. Gasky is unhappy and friendless at his new school—until a classmate decides to help him.
	Farr, D., & Van Dyke, D. (2005). *Mr. Finnegan's Giving Chest*. Salt Lake City, UT: Shadow Mountain.	Mr. Finnegan is no ordinary toymaker. His providential meeting with Maggie, a resentful girl who doesn't believe in the magic of Christmas, is the beginning of a series of miracles that will change her heart forever.
	Fleischman, S. (2000). *Bandit's Moon*. New York: Yearling.	In this robust adventure set during the California Gold Rush, outlaw Joaquin Murieta rescues the orphaned Annyrose, who generously repays his kindness.
	Fox, M. (1994). *Tough Boris*. New York: Voyager.	A rough and tough pirate named Boris von der Borch becomes saddened by the death of his beloved parrot and shows he is really very generous with his love and care.
	Gibfried, D. (2006). *Brother Juniper*. New York: Clarion.	This is the story of Brother Juniper, a follower of Father Francis of Assisi, who is beloved because he is simple and generous. When Juniper gives away almost everything from the church, he is faced with his responsibilities to his order.
	Grodin, E. (2006). *Oscar Wilde's* The Happy Prince. Farmington Hills, MI: Sleeping Bear.	A swallow comes to rest on the base of the Prince's statue and notices his tears. The Prince reveals that when he was alive he never ventured beyond the palace but now that he is a statue he is able to see all the suffering of the people below. The Prince asks the swallow to help him remedy this and the swallow complies by removing all of the Prince's outward treasures. The Prince generously gives away all his gifts until he has no more.
	Heap, S. (1999). *Cowboy Baby*. Somerville, MA: Candlewick.	Sheriff Pa says it's time for bed, but his little "deputy-to-be" must first round up his "gang." At bedtime, the little boy shows generosity when he makes sure his stuffed animals all get hugs and kisses.

(continued)

Bright Beginnings for Boys: Engaging Young Boys in Active Literacy by Debby Zambo and William G. Brozo.
© 2009 International Reading Association. May be copied for classroom use.

Positive Male Value	Bibliographic Information	Description
Generosity (*continued*)	Hoog, M.E. (2006). *Your Song: The First Growing Field Adventure*. Manhattan, KS: Sunflower.	A boy named Maxx learns he has much in common with Nightingale, a young eagle living in the Growing Field. Maxx experiences the magic of flying and learns to look deep inside himself for his gifts and talents, building his self-esteem.
	Kerrin, J.S. (2005). *Martin Bridge, Ready for Takeoff!* Toronto: Kids Can.	Martin Bridge learns about friendship and kindness as he encounters two very different school bus drivers, struggles with the death of a neighbor's pet, and reconciles with a friend as they decorate model rockets.
	Krensky, S. (2002). *How Santa Got His Job*. New York: Aladdin.	A contemporary, funny, and truly original look at how Santa Claus acquired all the skills that have made him the great success he is today. Santa's diverse background and generous heart prepared him perfectly for his Christmas Eve duties.
	Lasky, K. (2002). *Marven of the Great North Woods*. San Diego, CA: Harcourt.	During the flu epidemic of 1918, a Jewish boy from Duluth, Minnesota, is sent to live at a frozen logging camp staffed by French Canadians in this true story about family, love, and friendship.
	Olson-Brown, E. (2006). *Hush Little Digger*. Berkeley, CA: Tricycle.	A whimsical father-and-son story inspired by the traditional lullaby "Hush Little Baby." Papa adds bigger and more powerful machines to help the others get the work done, and the boy generously feeds an apple to a giraffe from his seat in the bucket of a shoveling machine.
	Stanley, D. (2002). *Saladin: Noble Prince of Islam*. New York: HarperCollins.	The biography of Saladin, a Persian who enhanced the lives of this people during the time of the Crusades, shows the great Muslim leader's courage and generosity.
	Taulbert, C.L. (2002). *Little Cliff and the Cold Place*. New York: Dial.	The day Cliff's teacher, Miss Maxey, tells his class about a cold place called the Arctic, where children live in houses made of snow, the boy is enthralled and determined that Poppa Joe should drive him there. When his bemused grandfather explains why this is impossible, the boy is heartbroken. Poppa Joe has a solution, though.
	Wojciechowski, S. (2007). *The Christmas Miracle of Jonathan Toomey*. Somerville, MA: Candlewick.	An isolated woodcarver finds healing and hope as he generously carves a wooden crèche for a widow and her 7-year-old son.
Honesty	Beechen, A. (2002). *Board Games*. New York: Simon Spotlight/Nickelodeon.	Otto has a new snowboard, and he's sure he'll win the upcoming competition with it. Twister borrows it without asking Otto, and the snowboard breaks. Twister comes up with a cover-up plan because he's afraid to tell his best friend what happened.
	Breathed, B. (2000). *Edwurd Fudwupper Fibbed Big*. Boston: Little, Brown.	Fannie, who hates lying, tries to befriend Edwurd, who is busy fabricating stories. Edwurd breaks a ceramic pig, lies about the deed, and draws hostile attention from a three-eyed alien whose purple potbelly could easily contain the entire Earth. When Fannie tells a "fat fib" of her own and saves the planet, she finally earns Edwurd's affection.
	Bunting, E. (1997). *A Day's Work*. New York: Clarion.	Francisco is trying to find a job for his grandfather, a carpenter, who has just arrived from Mexico and does not speak English. Francisco translates for his grandfather and tells a lie to Ben, who needs a gardener, that his grandfather is a skilled gardener. After a disaster that leaves Ben's fields bare, Francisco redeems himself and learns an important lesson in honesty.
	Cosby, B. (1999). *My Big Lie*. New York: Scholastic Cartwheel.	Little Bill retells the traditional "Boy Who Cried Wolf" tale, and relates how he has been banished to his room for making up a "big fib" to cover up his tardiness. Once he confesses and sees himself in the folk tale, he realizes that he deserves his parents' anger and punishment.

(continued)

Positive Male Value	Bibliographic Information	Description
Honesty (*continued*)	Demi. (2007). *The Empty Pot.* Austin, TX: Henry Holt.	When the Chinese emperor proclaims that his successor will be the child who grows the most beautiful flowers from the seeds the emperor distributes, Ping is overjoyed. Ping's seeds do not grow even though other hopefuls produce pots of lovely flowers. The emperor chooses honest Ping and reveals that all the seeds had been cooked and would not grow.
	Gemmen, H. (2004). *But It's True! Lying.* Colorado Springs, CO: Faith Kidz.	With the help of his father and his schoolteacher, Ben explores and learns the difference between telling "creative" stories and telling the truth.
	Gerstein, S. (2008). *Sokka, the Sword Master.* New York: Simon Spotlight/Nickelodeon.	When Sokka feels bad that he is not a master of anything, he decides to master the sword. Dishonestly, he disguises himself as a member of the Fire Nation and convinces Piandao, the master Fire Nation swordsman, to teach him the art. When he confesses to being from the Water Tribe, he is challenged to a duel.
	Greene, S. (2005). *Owen Foote, Super Spy.* New York: Clarion.	Owen Foote, a second grader, plays on a big-time town soccer league. Owen talks his friend Joseph, who has never played soccer before, into signing up for the team. When the team bully ridicules Joseph's abilities, Owen denies he's Joseph's friend. The message is one of honesty and the importance of being a true friend.
	Sis, P. (2000). *Starry Messenger.* New York: Farrar, Straus & Giroux.	The courage and honesty of a famous scientist is revealed through intricate ink drawings, maps, timelines, and samples of Galileo's own writings in this inventive biography.
	Taback, S. (2001). *Joseph Had a Little Overcoat.* New York: Viking.	This is the story of a resourceful, honest, and resilient tailor who transforms his worn-out overcoat into smaller and smaller garments.
Perseverance	Agee, J. (2005). *Terrific.* New York: Hyperion.	Eugene Mudge, from Dismal, North Dakota, has a problem with negativity. When he wins a free trip to Bermuda, and nothing goes right for him, he perseveres. No matter how horrible the experience—a wrecked cruise ship, a deserted island, a talking parrot, and almost dying of thirst—his response is always, "Terrific."
	Alexander, L. (1997). *The Iron Ring.* New York: Dutton Juvenile.	In this novel of high adventure, young Prince Tamar goes on a journey to recover his honor after losing everything in a game of chance.
	Anderson, M.T. (2001). *Handel, Who Knew What He Liked.* Somerville, MA: Candlewick.	A light-hearted yet informative picture-book biography of the noted composer. Whimsical illustrations extend the humor and historical details.
	Babbitt, N. (1998). *Ouch! A Tale From Grimm.* New York: HarperCollins.	In this retelling of a Grimm Brothers' story, a king sets a baby boy afloat in a river after he hears a prediction that the baby will eventually marry his daughter. Destiny kicks in as the baby, now grown, outwits the devil and wins himself a princess.
	Bardoe, C. (2006). *Gregor Mendel: The Friar Who Grew Peas.* New York: Abrams.	Mendel overcame poverty and obscurity to discover that animals, plants, and people all inherit and pass down traits through the same process. He is now regarded as the world's first geneticist. Children will be inspired by Mendel's never-ending search for knowledge, and his famous experiments are easy to understand.
	Bateman, T. (2006). *Keeper of Soles.* New York: Holiday House.	When Death comes calling for his soul, Colin the cobbler thinks on his feet and promises the Grim Reaper a new pair of sandals—then boots, then walking shoes—in a lighthearted variant of a traditional tale about outwitting death.
	Bernier-Grand, C.T. (2006). *César: ¡Sí, se Puede! Yes, We Can!* New York: Marshall Cavendish.	Using free verse, Bernier-Grand chronicles the compelling story of César Chávez. Luminous illustrations help make the activist hero accessible to young readers.

(*continued*)

Positive Male Value	Bibliographic Information	Description
Perseverance (*continued*)	Cline-Ransome, L. (2003). *Satchel Paige*. New York: Aladdin.	The life of one of baseball's greatest pitchers and the first African American inducted into the Baseball Hall of Fame is detailed here. The story tells of how he persevered and earned a place of honor in U.S. history.
	DeBeers, H. (2004). *Leonardo's Dream*. New York: North-South.	Penguin Leonardo never gives up on his dream to fly. And finally, as a result of determination and helpful friends, he takes to the sky in an old airplane. This experience helps Leonardo recognize the joy of "flying" underwater as a normal penguin.
	dePaola, T. (2001). *26 Fairmount Avenue*. New York: Putnam Juvenile.	In this book, dePaola looks back to 1938 when his family, overcoming fire and flood, built a new house. That year Tomie "quits" kindergarten, shares "chocolates" with Nana upstairs, critiques a movie, practices mural art, and finally moves to 26 Fairmount Avenue.
	Dungy, T. (2008). *You Can Do It!* New York: Little Simon Inspirations.	Tony Dungy's little brother, Linden, is a third grader who is having a bad day at school. Linden is the youngest and is the only member of the family who does not know what his talents are, but he knows he wants to make people happy.
	Frame, J. A. (2008). *Yesterday I Had the Blues*. Berkeley, CA: Tricycle.	An African American boy laments about the blues he had the previous day but tells about how he perseveres against these feelings. This book interprets the everyday life of the young boy's neighborhood and his family.
	Giblin, J.C. (2006). *The Amazing Life of Benjamin Franklin*. New York: Scholastic.	An illustrated biography traces the life, accomplishments, disappointments, and triumphs of one of the United States's greatest scientists and statesmen.
	Giff, P.R. (1980). *Today Was a Terrible Day*. New York: Puffin.	Ronald Morgan is struggling in school, especially in reading. Things change for Ronald as he perseveres to read a special note and realizes that if he has an authentic reason to read, and is not under stress, he is capable.
	Graham, B. (2000). *Max*. Somerville, MA: Candlewick.	Although Max has been born into a family of flying superheroes, he just cannot seem to get the hang of flying.
	Hurst, C.O. (2001). *Rocks in His Head*. New York: Greenwillow.	A young man pursues his love of collecting rocks until the director of a museum discovers his passion and appoints him curator despite his lack of formal education. Persevering through the Great Depression, he turns his hobby into a career.
	Isadora, R. (2005). *Luke Goes to Bat*. New York: Putnam Juvenile.	Luke idolizes Jackie Robinson, who plays for the Brooklyn Dodgers in this summer of 1951. When Luke finally gets a chance to substitute in stickball, he strikes out twice. His grandma takes Luke to a game where he watches his hero, two strikes down, deliver the tie-breaking run. Luke realizes the keys to success are determination and perseverance.
	Kinerk, R. (2005). *Timothy Cox Will Not Change His Socks*. New York: Simon & Schuster.	"What would happen, I wonder," muses little Timothy Cox, "if I went a whole month without changing my socks?" (n.p.). Rhyming couplets describe Tim's experiment, which quickly veers into tall-tale territory as the increasingly smelly socks prompt evictions by his classmates, by his adoring parents, and even by forest animals.
	Kraus, R. (1971). *Leo the Late Bloomer*. New York: HarperCollins.	A late-blooming lion name Leo is behind his peers in reading, writing, and speaking, causing his father distress. But Leo's mother never makes comparisons or watches Leo with a critical eye. With perseverance Leo does bloom and is able to catch up with his peers.

(continued)

Positive Male Value	Bibliographic Information	Description
Perseverance (*continued*)	Lasky, K. (2003). *The Man Who Made Time Travel*. New York: Melanie Kroupa.	In 1707, after losing numerous ships at sea, England's Parliament passed the Longitude Act guaranteeing 20,000 pounds sterling for a method to navigate the seas with certitude. John Harrison, a village carpenter and a self-taught polymath, took more than 35 years and five prototypes to develop a device that worked—but he refused the King's prize.
	Levine, E. (2007). *Henry's Freedom Box*. New York: Scholastic.	This is the true story of Henry Brown, a slave who mailed himself to freedom. When Henry watches his family being sold away from him, he enlists the help of an abolitionist doctor and mails himself in a wooden crate "to a place where there are no slaves!" (p. 17). This is a powerful illustration of a resourceful man and his extraordinary story.
	McGhee, A. (2008). *Little Boy*. New York: Atheneum.	Watching his son navigate a typical day, a father reflects on his own boyhood pleasure and the endless possibilities presented by a big cardboard box. Confident, independent, and inexhaustible, the boy perseveres to turns the cardboard box into a pirate ship, a stepladder, a spaceman's costume, and a crash pad.
	Mills, C. (2004). *7 x 9 = Trouble*! New York: Farrar, Straus & Giroux.	Third grader Wilson Williams struggles but perseveres to learn his multiplication tables, stay ahead of his math-whiz kindergarten brother, and convince his parents that he needs a pet.
	Mills, C. (2007). *Being Teddy Roosevelt*. New York: Farrar, Straus & Giroux	Fourth grader Riley O'Rourke wants to play saxophone in instrumental music, but his mother can't afford to rent one. He can't possibly make enough money to buy one, and even if he could, Mom might not let him, "because he was having enough trouble getting his regular homework done." This is a lesson about achieving a goal.
	Mollel, T.M. (1999). *My Rows and Piles of Coins*. New York: Clarion.	Aaruni, a Tanzanian boy, wants a bicycle to help carry his mother's daily load to market. Only by saving coin after coin does he come to realize his dream.
	Montes, M. (2000). *Juan Bobo Goes to Work: A Puerto Rican Folk Tale*. New York: Rayo.	This retelling of a traditional Puerto Rican folk tale humorously depicts Juan Bobo's determined-but-disastrous antics at work.
	Pinkney, A.D. (2006). *Duke Ellington: The Piano Prince and His Orchestra*. New York: Jump At The Sun/Hyperion.	The story of Duke Ellington's life and his "hot buttered bop" music. Ellington perseveres in the 1920s to become a respected jazz musician.
	Rosen, M.J. (1995). *A School for Pompey Walker*. San Diego, CA: Harcourt.	This is the true narrative of an escaped slave who returned to the South to raise money for a school by selling himself back into slavery again and again.
	Shannon, D. (2001). *David Goes to School*. New York: Scholastic.	A young boy named David encounters much difficulty regulating his behavior and fitting in at school. But he always seems to know he must try.
	Stanley, D. (2000). *Leonardo Da Vinci*. New York: HarperTrophy.	This is the story of Leonardo's extraordinary, productive life, focusing on his perseverance in contributing to the world of art and science. It describes his notebooks in conversational narrative and includes his accomplishments as a painter, scientist, and researcher.
	Wax, W. (2007). *Diego and Papi to the Rescue*. New York: Simon Spotlight/Nickelodeon.	When two baby pygmy marmosets get separated from their father, Diego and his *papi* take an adventure together in order to find them and bring them home.
	Winter, J. (2006). *Dizzy*. New York: Arthur A. Levine.	Jazz great Dizzy Gillespie's life—from his difficult childhood through the creation of bebop—is told in syncopated rhythms in this picture-book biography. This is a book that has a message, that one's weaknesses can be turned to strengths.

(continued)

Positive Male Value	Bibliographic Information	Description
Perseverance (continued)	Wolff, P.R. (2000). The Toll-Bridge Troll. New York: Voyager.	Every time the troll tries to keep Trigg from crossing the bridge to get to school, Trigg outwits him with a riddle—until the troll's mother decides that he too should go to school and become smart.
Respectfulness	Adler, D.A. (1997). Lou Gehrig: The Luckiest Man. Orlando, FL: Harcourt.	In this picture-book biography, a beloved baseball star stricken with a debilitating illness earns respect and admiration for his on-field stamina and off-field courage.
	Barton, B. (2001). My Car. New York: Greenwillow.	Sam shows readers his car, describing its features, its many uses, and how he drives it.
	Denslow, S.P. (2002). Georgie Lee. New York: Greenwillow.	In this pleasing early chapter book, 9-year-old J.D. shares a surprisingly unquiet summer on the farm with his grandmother, her intelligent cow Georgie Lee, and Boots the cat.
	Diakité, B.W. (2005). The Hunterman and the Crocodile: A West African Folktale. New York: Scholastic.	In this traditional West African tale, a cautious hunter helps some clever crocodiles and learns a lesson about respecting the relationship between man and nature.
	Fenner, C. (2005). Snowed in With Grandmother Silk. New York: Puffin.	Ruddy and his grandmother learn to be best friends and to respect each other when a surprise storm strands them without electricity or telephone.
	Fox, M. (1985). Wilfred Gordon McDonald Partridge. La Jolla, CA: Kane/Miller.	Wilfred Gordon befriends a 96-year-old woman named Nancy Alison Delacourt who has lost her memory. Wilfred feels sad about Miss Nancy's loss and gathers objects that have the qualities memories contain. Wilfred's respect and love for Miss Nancy help her remember warm thoughts.
	Fraustino, L.R. (2003). The Hickory Chair. Berkeley, CA: Tricycle.	When Gran dies, Louis, a young blind boy, finds all the notes she left for her loved ones except for one—his own.
	Giff, P.R. (1990). Ronald Morgan Goes to Bat. New York: Puffin.	When it comes to baseball, Ronald is an eternal optimist. He practices every day despite the fact he shuts his eyes every time he is at bat. Ronald's positive attitude changes when he realizes he is the worst hitter on the team. He's ready to give up baseball until his father intervenes and helps him gain self-respect and the respect of his teammates.
	Hoose, P., & Hoose, H. (1998). Hey, Little Ant. Berkeley, CA: Tricycle.	A boy converses with the tiny ant he wants to squish. This parable about mercy and empathy asks the reader to look at life from an insect's point of view.
	Jeffers, S. (1991). Brother Eagle, Sister Sky. New York: Dial.	In this Native American tale, Chief Seattle points out the destruction inflicted on the Earth and asks what will happen when the buffalo are all slaughtered, the horses are all tamed, and the hills, eagles, and ponies are all gone?
	Karr, K. (1999). Man of the Family. New York: Farrar, Straus & Giroux.	Istvan works alongside his father on their farm and learns about the resilience and pride of Hungarian heritage. Istvan learns to respect his father and his heritage.
	Kroll, V.L. (2006). Ryan Respects. Morton Grove, IL: Albert Whitman.	Elementary student Ryan learns how to be respectful of his friend Doug. At school, Ryan calls out "Doug the Slug" after Doug places last in a running race. At home, Ryan's older brother, Judd, calls him "Cryin' Ryan" because Ryan needs his toy rabbit to fall asleep. In both cases, a third party offers a not-so-subtle reminder to be more respectful.
	Lester, H. (1999). Hooway for Wodney Wat. New York: Houghton Mifflin.	A rat named Rodney has a difficult time articulating the letter r, and his classmates taunt him. Rodney becomes the shyest rodent in his class, and things only get worse when a bully named Camilla Capybara moves in. In the end, things work out for Rodney because he stands up to Camilla and gains the respect of his classmates.

(continued)

Positive Male Value	Bibliographic Information	Description
Respectfulness (*continued*)	Levy, J. (2005). *Alley Oops*. Brooklyn, NY: Flashlight.	J.J. has been bullying an overweight boy named Patrick, calling him Pig-Pen and Porky. Mr. Jax, J.J.'s father, tells his son how he was also a bully and had fun at another boy's expense. He recently met that same boy, and Mr. Jax tells how he feels sorry for what he did in the past.
	Long, M. (2003). *How I Became a Pirate*. San Diego, CA: Harcourt.	Jeremy joins a pirate crew and finds that no baths or vegetables are required, but sadly he learns that there is no one to tuck him in or read a good night story. Jeremy develops a deep respect for his family when he comes to realize that a life away from his parents lacks some of the niceties that he is used to.
	Mathis, S.B. (2006). *Hundred Penny Box*. New York: Puffin.	Michael loves his Great-Great-Aunt Dew, even if she can't always remember his name. He especially loves to spend time with her and her beloved hundred penny box, listening to stories about each of the hundred years of her life. Michael's mother wants to throw out the battered old box that holds the pennies, but Michael learns the importance it has in helping Dew's memory.
	Rumford, J. (2004). *Sequoyah: The Cherokee Man Who Gave His People Writing*. New York: Houghton Mifflin.	The story of Sequoyah, the man who created a writing system for the Cherokee language, shows how he gains the respect of his people and enables the Cherokee nation to learn and write in their own language.
	Rylant, C. (1996). *Mr. Putter and Tabby Pick the Pears*. San Diego, CA: Harcourt.	Mr. Putter and his cat Tabby are too old and creaky to climb ladders but still find a way to enjoy pear jelly!
	Steptoe, J. (1997). *In Daddy's Arms I Am Tall: African Americans Celebrating Fathers*. New York: Lee & Low.	Strong collage illustrations and 10 emotional poems express the depth, respect, and range of the father–child relationship
Responsibility	Barasch, I. (2000). *Radio Rescue*. New York: Farrar, Straus & Giroux.	In an exciting story about the heroism of ordinary people, a 10-year-old boy earns his amateur radio license and aids in the rescue of hurricane victims.
	Bynum, E., & Jackson, R. (2004). *Jamari's Drum*. Toronto: Groundwood.	Young Jamari lives at the base of a volcano called Chafua. He often sits in the village square, listening to Baba Mdogo play the great *djembe*, the drum that keeps the peace with the volcano. Years later, Baba selects Jamari as his successor, telling him to play the drum every day, but Jamari marries and has children and eventually stops playing the drum.
	Christopher, M. (2002). *All Keyed Up*. Boston: Little, Brown.	When Stookie Norris asks Jerry Dinh to take care of his gerbils while he's away on vacation, Jerry is happy to help. But then something terrible happens that forces Jerry to face his new responsibility.
	Cunnane, K. (2006). *For You Are a Kenyan Child*. New York: Atheneum.	A young Kenyan boy is asked by his mother to take his grandfather's cows to pasture and watch them carefully. But instead of acting responsibly the boy gets distracted, and after many playful antics he realizes he has shunned his responsibility—and the cows are not in the meadow.
	Garay, L. (2002). *The Kite*. Toronto: Tundra Books.	Since his father's death, Francisco's small earnings are essential to his family. Each morning he has three wishes: that he will sell all of his papers in the marketplace, that his mother's baby will be born soon, and that the kite that he longs for will still be hanging in Señor Gonzalez's toy stall. Even though he can't afford it, he wants the kite. Eventually, his responsible behavior does not go unnoticed and Señor Gonzalez gives him the kite.

(continued)

Positive Male Value	Bibliographic Information	Description
Responsibility (*continued*)	Gershator, P. (2007). *Sky Sweeper*. New York: Farrar, Straus & Giroux.	In this gentle tale, "Young Takeboki needed a job, and the monks in the temple needed a Flower Keeper" (p. 1). The boy is humble, responsible, and shows pride in his task that lasts through his long lifetime and into his afterlife.
	Graves, K. (2001). *Pet Boy*. San Francisco: Chronicle.	An obsessive young pet collector suffers a change of heart after an extraterrestrial hunter seizes him and sells him to a giant, three-eyed, purple alien boy. Having seen the bars from the inside, Stanley frees his own pets, but makes them an offer they can't refuse: regular meals in exchange for their company.
	Hunt, E.S. (2008). *Secret Agent Jack Stalwart: The Pursuit of the Ivory Poachers*. New York: Weinstein.	Jack receives an anonymous note that his brother Max is in trouble and receives a coded message from Max possibly detailing his whereabouts. But soon duty calls, and Jack responsibly goes on an adventure to Kenya to stop poachers and search for his brother.
	Kerley, B. (2004). *Walt Whitman: Words for America*. New York: Scholastic.	This book relates a poetic and visual story of Walt Whitman's experiences during the U.S. Civil War, including his responsibilities as a nurse.
	Kimmel, E.A. (2000). *Gershon's Monster: A Story for the Jewish New Year*. New York: Scholastic.	Gershon never makes reparations for the wrongs he commits. Instead, he throws his misdeeds into the sea each year until they grow into a monstrous demon that threatens the life of his children. He is finally forced to face his responsibilities to others, himself, and his family.
	Locker, T. (1993). *The Boy Who Held Back the Sea*. New York: Puffin.	Jan lies to his mother about reading to a blind miller and goes into the woods instead. Jan has a grand time until he realizes the dike that holds back the water from flooding the town has a small leak. Of course, no one believes Jan because he has a reputation for being a liar, so he is forced to act responsibly and to hold his finger in the dike all night.
	Singh, V. (2006). *Younguncle Comes to Town*. New York: Viking.	Younguncle visits his nieces and nephews after two years traveling. His brother invites Younguncle to live with the family to talk him into settling down. While visiting, Younguncle responsibly rescues his sister from marrying a man she does not love, tricks pickpockets as a deputy-stationmaster-in-training, and calms a ghost that lives in a tree.
	St. George, J. (2007). *Make Your Mark, Franklin Roosevelt*. New York: Philomel.	Franklin grew up in extreme luxury, but rather than turning into an idle country gentleman, he found outlets for his energy in social and civic responsibility, following in the footsteps of his cousin Teddy.
	Van Allsburg, C. (2002). *Just a Dream*. New York: Houghton Mifflin.	When Walter returns from a nightmare in which he dreams of a future world filled with garbage and pollution, he becomes responsible recycling and caring for the environment in his own home and neighborhood.
	Warren, A. (1998). *Orphan Train Rider: One Boy's True Story*. New York: Houghton Mifflin.	The true story of Lee Nailling and the early work of the Children's Aid Society in relocating orphans is told in poignant alternating chapters.
	Willems, M. (2003). *Don't Let the Pigeon Drive the Bus*. New York: Hyperion.	A bus driver leaves his bus in the reader's care with the plea that he or she not let the pigeon drive the bus. But the pigeon is very persistent and persuasive. Will the reader act responsibly or be swayed by the lovable pigeon?
Tolerance	Christensen, B. (2001). *Woody Guthrie: Poet of the People*. New York: Knopf.	A telling portrait of folk musician Woody Guthrie, whose life and work was highly influenced by his tolerant and intimate experiences with the struggling poor of the Great Depression.

(*continued*)

Positive Male Value	Bibliographic Information	Description
Tolerance (continued)	English, K. (2007). Francie. New York: Square Fish.	While waiting to move north, spunky Francie navigates the segregated society of rural Jim Crow–era Alabama, helping an African American boy who has been accused of assault to escape.
	Fierstein, H. (2002). The Sissy Duckling. New York: Simon & Schuster.	Elmer stretches traditional gender boundaries and his behaviors make the other ducks, and his own father, very uncomfortable. Elmer is labeled a sissy and banished from his home, but he proves he is brave and just as much a man when he saves his father from hunters. In the end Elmer's father and the other ducks learn to be tolerant of this unique boy.
	Frank, J. (2008). The Toughest Cowboy: Or How the Wild West Was Tamed. New York: Aladdin.	Grizz Brickbottom, toughest cowboy in the West, yearns for a companion and convinces his cattle-rustling cohorts that they need a dog to help with the work. When they finally get a dog, it is a miniature poodle named Foofy. They learn to be tolerant of the poodle, even though it is afraid of cows and won't chase away mountain lions.
	Fudge, B. (2008). Enrique Speaks With His Hands. Munster, IN: Hilton.	Enrique is deaf and must use sign language to speak. His family knows he is special but no one is sure why until a stranger introduces them to other children who are just like Enrique. Enrique's story teaches others to tolerate children who are different.
	Golenback, P. (1992). Teammates. New York: Voyager.	Baseball great Jackie Robinson is befriended by southern teammate Pee Wee Reese, whose act of tolerance inspires others players and fans to accept this first African American in the major league.
	Graham, B. (2005). Oscar's Half Birthday. Somerville, MA: Candlewick.	Oscar's dad, mom, and 4-year-old sister can't wait for his first birthday, so they celebrate with a picnic when he is 6 months old. Amusingly detailed watercolors depict the very real relationships of a mixed-race family and their acceptance in an urban environment.
	Harris, R.H. (2008). Mail Harry to the Moon. Boston: Little, Brown.	A brother has to tolerate a new addition to his family, a little brother. He just wants to mail his brother away so that his life can go back to the way it was before. But along the way, he learns that being a big brother is not a big nuisance, but an adventure and source of friendship.
	Isadora, R. (2007). Yo, Jo! San Diego, CA: Harcourt.	Set in an urban neighborhood, this is the story of two brothers waiting for their grandfather to come home for dinner. The book depicts the reality of inner-city life including graffiti, loud music, litter, and garbage cans, as well as friendly greetings and a warm, family-oriented environment. It is a story of Jomar's world, and the text communicates his simple joy and tolerance for his way of life.
	Lester, J. (2000). Sam and the Tigers: A Retelling of Little Black Sambo. New York: Puffin.	Sassy Sam is a comically streetwise hero, who outwits five conceited tigers. The tale is told in a humorous southern black storytelling voice.
	London, J. (1996). Froggy Goes to School. New York: Viking.	During class, Froggy has a difficult time paying attention, but at circle time his teacher and peers are tolerant and hear about Froggy's summer adventures. Froggy sings a catchy song and everyone, including the principal, joins in.
	McCann, J.T. (2002). There's a Skunk in My Bunk: Helping Children Learn Tolerance. Far Hills, NJ: New Horizon.	When a young boy finds a shivering skunk snuggled in his bunk bed on a cold autumn night, he is horrified and orders the animal out of his house. But as these two strangers come to know each other, the boy learns that he must think for himself and not prejudge others.

(continued)

Positive Male Value	Bibliographic Information	Description
Tolerance (*continued*)	Morimoto, J. (1999). *The Two Bullies*. New York: Knopf.	Ni-ou, the strongest fellow in Japan, sets out to challenge his Chinese counterpart, Dokkoi. Ni-ou travels across the sea and settles in to wait for Dokkoi, but after being told that what sounds like an earthquake is actually the returning Dokkoi's footsteps, he experiences a sudden change of heart and hightails it back to Japan. Both bullies become so intimidated by one another that they lose their will to fight.
	Myers, L. (2000). *Surviving Brick Johnson*. New York: Clarion.	Fifth grader Alex discovers that the classmate he fears is not a bully. They become friends, and both learn not to be judgmental but tolerant of others.
	Neubecker, R. (2006). *Courage of the Blue Boy*. Berkeley, CA: Tricycle.	Young Blue and his blue calf, Polly, dream about all the other colors of the world not found in their blue land. They set off to explore and encounter a purple village, orange hills, a red town, and other monochromatic places. When he moves to the multihued city, he finds no blue. Over time, Blue contributes to the city and changes himself with an array of new shades, but retains his blue heart.
	Rappaport, D. (2007). *Martin's Big Words: The Life of Dr. Martin Luther King, Jr.* New York: Hyperion.	Martin Luther King Jr.'s "I Have a Dream" speech is portrayed for its significance to being tolerant of others and as an event in which "his big words are alive for us today" (back cover).
	Rylant, C. (2006). *Henry and Mudge and the Great Grandpas*. New York: Aladdin.	In four simple, joyful chapters, Henry and his sweet-natured dog experience a memorable visit with Great-Grandpa Bill and his buddies at the "grandpa house." This is a story of a young boy showing respect for older people.
	Say, A. (1993). *Grandfather's Journey*. New York: Houghton Mifflin.	Home becomes elusive in this story about immigration and acculturation, pieced together through old pictures and salvaged family tales. Both the narrator and his grandfather, who longs to return to Japan, have to be tolerant of the changes they encounter.
	Say, A. (2005). *Kamishibai Man*. New York: Houghton Mifflin.	An elderly retired Japanese storyteller relives the days before television, when children would flock to hear his stories and sample his sweets. Ironically, he is featured on the television news—the very technology that replaced him. This is a story of how the old must be tolerant of the new and how the new must respect the old.
	Tietelbaum, M. (2008). *Aang's School Days*. New York: Simon Spotlight/Nickelodeon.	Aang and his friends are living in the Fire Nation, disguising themselves as natives in an attempt to blend in. When Aang is dragged off to a Fire Nation school and his own beliefs clash with traditional customs, he must learn to tolerate different ways of doing things.
	Wiesner, D. (1999). *Sector 7*. New York: Clarion.	This book tells the story of a small boy on a class trip to the Empire State Building who is transported by a friendly cloud to Sector 7, a great cloud factory high in the sky. Once there, they conspire with clouds that are bored with their shapes and long for a new way to express their individuality.
	Williamson, G. (2005). *Why Do I Have to Wear Glasses?* Pleasant Ridge, MI: Peerless.	Young Freddy wants to be a football star, but he has difficulty seeing things clearly. Freddy gets glasses, and although they solve his vision problems, the glasses make him uncomfortable. In the end, his hero Touchdown Joe helps Freddy learn how to cope with his vision difficulties and be comfortable with himself.
	Yin. (2006). *Brothers*. New York: Philomel.	A young Chinese immigrant named Ming arrives in San Francisco to live with his older brother Shek. Unfortunately, Ming not only finds a strange country but also finds an intolerant and hostile place—until he meets Patrick, who accepts and respects him immediately and helps others learn tolerance.

Adams, M. (1990). *Beginning to read: Thinking and learning about print.* Cambridge, MA: MIT Press.

Alexander, G.M. (2003). An evolutionary perspective of sex-typed toy preferences: Pink, blue, and the brain. *Archives of Sexual Behavior, 32*(1), 7–15. doi:10.1023/A:1021833110722

Allington, R.L. (2005, June/July). The other five "pillars" of effective reading instruction. *Reading Today, 22*(6), 3.

Alloway, N., Freebody, P., Gilbert, P., & Muspratt, S. (2002). *Boys, literacy and schooling: Expanding the repertoires of practice.* Sydney, NSW, Australia: Department of Education, Science and Teaching.

Alvermann, D.E., Swafford, J., & Montero, M.K. (2004). *Content area literacy instruction for the elementary grades.* Boston: Allyn & Bacon.

American Academy of Pediatrics. (2001). Children, adolescents, and television. *Pediatrics, 107*(2), 423–426.

American Speech-Language-Hearing Association. (1993). *Definitions of communication disorders and variations* [Relevant Paper]. Retrieved from www.asha.org/docs/pdf/RP1993-00208.pdf. doi:10.1044/policy.RP1993-00208

Anderson, J.R. (2005). *Cognitive psychology and its implications* (6th ed.). New York: Worth.

Angelillo, J. (2003). *Writing about reading: From book talk to literary essays, grades 3–8.* Portsmouth, NH: Greenwood.

Applebee, A., Langer, J., & Mullis, I. (1990). *The writing report card, 1984–1988.* Princeton, NJ: National Assessment of Educational Progress/Educational Testing Service.

Atkinson, R.C., & Shiffrin, R.M. (1968). Human memory: A proposed system and its control processes. In K.W. Spence & J.T. Spence (Eds.), *The psychology of learning and motivation: Advances in research and theory* (Vol. 2, pp. 89–195). New York: Academic.

Avery, C.W., & Avery, K.B. (2001). Kids teaching kids. *Journal of Adolescent & Adult Literacy, 44*(5), 434–435.

Bandura, A. (1965). Influence of model's reinforcement contingencies on the acquisition of imitative responses. *Journal of Personality and Social Psychology, 1*(6), 589–595. doi:10.1037/h0022070

Bandura, A., Ross, D., & Ross, S.A. (1963). Imitation of film-mediated aggressive models. *Journal of Abnormal and Social Psychology, 66*(1), 3–11. doi:10.1037/h0048687

Bedford, V.H., Volling, B.L., & Avioli, P.S. (2000). Positive consequences of sibling conflict in childhood and adulthood. *International Journal of Aging & Human Development, 51*(1), 53–69. doi:10.2190/G6PR-CN8Q-5PVC-5GTV

Benenson, J.F., Apostoleris, N.H., & Parnass, J. (1997). Age and sex differences in dyadic and group interaction. *Developmental Psychology, 33*(3), 538–543. doi:10.1037/0012-1649.33.3.538

Bergen, D., & Mauer, D. (2000). Symbolic play, phonological awareness, and literacy skills at three age levels. In K.A. Roskos & J.F. Christie (Eds.), *Play and literacy in early childhood: Research from multiple perspectives* (pp. 45–62). Mahwah, NJ: Erlbaum.

Berk, L.E. (2005). *Infants, children, and adolescents* (5th ed.). Boston: Allyn & Bacon.

Biller, H.B. (1993). *Fathers and families: Paternal factors in child development.* Westport, CT: Auburn House.

Bing, E. (1963). Effect of child-rearing practices on the development of differential cognitive abilities. *Child Development, 34*(3), 631–648.

Bond, T.F. (2001). Giving them free rein: Connections in student-led book groups. *The Reading Teacher, 54*(6), 574–584.

Booth, D. (2006). *Reading doesn't matter anymore...: Shattering the myths of literacy.* Portland, ME: Stenhouse.

Boylan, M., & Donohue, J.A. (2003). *Ethics across the curriculum, a practice-based approach.* Lanham, MD: Lexington.

Boys and books. (2006, August/September). *Reading Today, 24*(1), 1.

Bramlett, M.D., & Mosher, W.D. (2002). Cohabitation, marriage, divorce, and remarriage in the United States. National Center for Health Statistics. *Vital and Health Statistics, 23*(22).

Brizendine, L. (2006). *The female brain.* New York: Broadway.

Bronfenbrenner, U. (1979). *The ecology of human development.* Cambridge, MA: Harvard University Press.

Bronfenbrenner, U. (1995). The bioecological perspective from a life course perspective: Reflections of a participant observer. In P. Moen, G.H. Edler, Jr., & K. Luscher (Eds.), *Examining lives in context* (pp. 599–618). Washington, DC: American Psychological Association.

Bronson, M.B. (2000). *Self-regulation in early childhood: Nature and nurture.* New York: Guilford.

Brooks-Gunn, J. (2003). Do you believe in magic? What we can expect from early childhood intervention programs. *Social Policy Report of the Society for Research in Child Development, 17*(1), 3–14.

Brooks-Gunn, J., Duncan, G.J., & Aber, J.L. (Eds.). (1997). *Neighborhood poverty: Context and consequences for children* (Vol. 1). New York: Russell Sage Foundation.

Brozo, W.G. (2002). *To be a boy, to be a reader: Engaging teen and preteen boys in active literacy.* Newark, DE: International Reading Association.

Brozo, W.G. (2004). It's okay to read, even if other kids don't: Learning about and from boys in a middle school book club. *The California Reader, 38*(2), 5–13.

Brozo, W.G. (2005). Avoiding the "fourth-grade slump." *Thinking Classroom/Peremena, 6*(4), 48–49.

Brozo, W.G. (2007). Helping boys find entry points to lifelong reading: Book clubs and other strategies for struggling adolescent males. In J. Lewis & G. Moorman (Eds.), *Adolescent literacy instruction: Policies and promising practices* (pp. 304–318). Newark, DE: International Reading Association.

Brozo, W.G., & Schmelzer, R.V. (1997). Wildmen, lovers, and warriors: Reaching boys through archetypal literature. *Journal of Adolescent & Adult Literacy, 41*(1), 4–11.

Brozo, W.G., Shiel, G., & Topping, K. (2007/2008). Engagement in reading: Lessons learned from three PISA countries. *Journal of Adolescent & Adult Literacy, 51*(4), 304–315. doi:10.1598/JAAL.51.4.2

Brozo, W.G., & Simpson, M.L. (2007). *Content literacy for today's adolescents: Honoring diversity and building competence.* Upper Saddle River, NJ: Merrill/Prentice Hall.

Cain, K.M., & Dweck, C.S. (1995). The relation between motivational patterns and achievement cognitions through the elementary school years. *Merrill-Palmer Quarterly, 41*(1), 25–52.

Campbell, M., & Cleland, J.V. (2003). *Readers theatre in the classroom: A manual for teachers of children and adults.* Lincoln, NE: iUniverse Inc.

Campos, J.J., Frankel, C.B., & Camras, L. (2004). On the nature of emotional regulation. *Child Development, 75*(2), 377–394.

Canadian Council on Learning. (2007). *State of learning in Canada: No time for complacency.* Ottawa, ON: Author.

Carter, R.S., & Wojtkiewicz, R.A. (2000). Parental involvement with adolescent education: Do daughters or sons get more help? *Adolescence, 35*(137), 29–45.

Carter, S. (2002). *The impact of parent/family involvement on student outcomes: An annotated bibliography of research from the past decade.* Eugene, OR: Consortium for Appropriate Dispute Resolution in Special Education.

Caserta-Henry, C. (1996). Reading buddies: A first-grade intervention program. *The Reading Teacher, 49*(6), 500–503.

Caughy, M.O., O'Campo, P.J., & Muntaner, C. (2003). When being alone might be better: Neighborhood poverty, social capital, and child mental health. *Social Science & Medicine, 57*(2), 227–237. doi:10.1016/S0277-9536(02)00342-8

Chance, R. (2000). SmartGirl.com reading survey: What are the messages for librarians? *Journal of Youth Services in Libraries, 13*(3), 20–23.

Chapman, M., Filipenko, M., McTavish, M., & Shapiro, J. (2007). First graders' preferences for narrative and/or information books and perceptions of other boys' and girls' book preferences. *Canadian Journal of Education, 30*(2), 531–553.

Chavkin, N.F. (Ed.). (1993). *Families and schools in a pluralistic society.* Albany, NY: SUNY Press.

Christakis, D.A., Zimmerman, F.J., DiGiuseppe, D.L., & McCarty, C.A. (2004). Early television viewing and subsequent attentional problems in children. *Pediatrics, 113*(4), 708–713. doi:10.1542/peds.113.4.708

Christenson, S.L., & Conoley, J.C. (Eds.). (1992). *Home-school collaboration: Enhancing children's academic and social competence.* Silver Spring, MD: National Association of School Psychologists.

Cipielewski, J., & Stanovich, K.E. (1992). Predicting growth in reading ability from children's exposure to print. *Journal of Experimental Child Psychology, 54*(1), 74–89. doi:10.1016/0022-0965(92)90018-2

Clark, E.V. (1993). *The lexicon in acquisition.* Cambridge, England: Cambridge University Press.

Clark, M.M. (1984). Literacy at home and at school: Insights from a study of young fluent readers. In H. Goelman, A. Ober, & F. Smith (Eds.), *Awakening to literacy* (pp. 122–130). Portsmouth, NH: Heinemann.

Cohen, M.R. (1997). Individual and sex differences in speed of handwriting among high school students. *Perceptual and Motor Skills, 84*(3), 1428–1430.

Cole, D.A., Martin, J.M., Peeke, L.A., Seroczynski, A.D., & Fier, J. (1999). Children's over- and underestimation of academic competence: A longitudinal study in gender differences, depression, and anxiety. *Child Development, 70*(2), 459–473. doi:10.1111/1467-8624.00033

Cole, M., & Cole, S.R. (1993). *The development of children* (2nd ed.). New York: Scientific American.

Coles, M., & Hall, C. (2002). Gendered readings: learning from children's reading choices. *Journal of Research in Reading, 25*(1), 96–108. doi:10.1111/1467-9817.00161

Coley, R.J. (2001). *Differences in the gender gap: Comparisons across racial/ethnic groups in education and work.* Princeton, NJ: Educational Testing Service.

Coley, R.J. (2002). *An uneven start: Indicators of inequality in school readiness.* Princeton, NJ: Educational Testing Service.

Collins-Standley, T., Gan, S.-L., Yu, H.-J., & Zillmann, D. (1996). Choice of romantic, violent, and scary fairy-tale books by preschool girls and boys. *Child Study Journal, 26*(4), 279–302.

Combs, M. (2002). *Readers and writers in primary grades: A balanced and integrated approach* (2nd ed.). Upper Saddle River, NJ: Merrill/Prentice Hall.

Cone-Wesson, B., & Ramirez, G. (1997). Hearing sensitivity in newborns estimated from ABRs to bone-conducted sounds. *Journal of the American Academy of Audiology, 8*(5), 299–307.

Constantino, R. (2005). Print environments between high and low socioeconomic status (SES) communities. *Teacher Librarian, 32*(3), 22–25.

Cooksey, E.C., & Fondell, M.M. (1996). Spending time with his kids: Effects of family structure on fathers' and children's lives. *Journal of Marriage and the Family, 58*(3), 693–707. doi:10.2307/353729

Cooper, J.D., Chard, D.J., & Kiger, N.D. (2006). *The struggling reader: Interventions that work.* New York: Scholastic.

Corbett, H.D., & Wilson, R.L. (1995). Make a difference with, not for, students: A plea for researchers and reformers. *Educational Researcher, 24*(5), 12–17.

Cummins, J. (2001). Magic bullets and the grade 4 slump: Solutions from technology? *NABE News, 25*(1), 4–6.

Davenport, S.V., Arnold, M., & Lassman, M. (2004). The impact of cross-age tutoring on reading attitudes and reading achievement. *Reading Improvement, 41*(1), 3–12.

Davies, B. (1997). Constructing and deconstructing masculinities through critical literacy. *Gender and Education, 9*(1), 9–30. doi:10.1080/09540259721420

Dodd, B., & Bradford, A. (2000). A comparison of three therapy methods for children with different types of developmental phonological disorder. *International Journal of Language & Communication Disorders, 35*(2), 189–209. doi:10.1080/136828200247142

Doiron, R. (2003). Boy books, girl books: Should we re-organize our school library collections? *Teacher Librarian, 30*(3), 14–16.

Donahue, P., Daane, M., & Grigg, W. (2003). *The nation's report card: Reading highlights 2003.* Washington, DC: National Center for Education Statistics.

Duke, N.K. (2000). 3.6 minutes per day: The scarcity of informational texts in first grade. *Reading Research Quarterly, 35*(2), 202–224. doi:10.1598/RRQ.35.2.1

Dweck, C.S. (1999, Spring). Caution—Praise can be dangerous. *American Educator,* 1–5.

Edmunds, K.M., & Bauserman, K.L. (2006). What teachers can learn about reading motivation through conversations with children. *The Reading Teacher, 59*(5), 414–424. doi:10.1598/RT.59.5.1

Eichstedt, J.A., Serbin, L.A., Poulin-Dubois, D., & Sen, M.G. (2002). Of bears and men: Infants' knowledge of conventional and metaphorical gender types. *Infant Behavior and Development, 25*(3), 296–310. doi:10.1016/S0163-6383(02)00081-4

Eisenberg, N. (1996). Gender development and gender effects. In D.C. Berliner & R.C. Calfee (Eds.), *Handbook of educational psychology* (pp. 358–396). New York: Macmillan.

Evans, J. (1998). *What's in the picture: Responding to illustrations in picture books.* London: Paul Chapman.

Fagan, J., & Palm, G. (2003). *Fathers and early childhood programs.* Clifton Park, NY: Delmar Cengage Learning.

Falk, L. (2005). Paintings and stories: Making connections. *Arizona Reading Journal, 31*(2), 19–21.

Farrer, F. (2000). *The quiet revolution: Encouraging positive values in our children.* London: Rider.

Fein, G.G. (1986). Pretend play: Creativity and consciousness. In D. Gorlitz & J.F. Wohlwill (Eds.), *Curiosity, imagination, and play: On the development of spontaneous cognitive and motivational processes* (pp. 281–304). Hillsdale, NJ: Erlbaum.

Fields, J. (2001). Living arrangements of children: Fall 1996. Current Population Reports, P70–P74. Washington, DC: U.S. Census Bureau.

Fletcher, R. (2006). *Boy writers: Reclaiming their voices.* Portland, ME: Stenhouse.

Flippo, R.F. (2003). *Assessing readers: Qualitative diagnosis and instruction* (2nd ed.). Portsmouth, NH: Heinemann.

Freberg, L.S. (2005). *Discovering biological psychology.* New York: Houghton Mifflin.

Frieman, B.B., & Berkeley, T.R. (2002). Encouraging fathers to participate in the school experiences of young children: The teacher's role. *Early Childhood Education Journal, 29*(3), 209–213. doi:10.1023/A:1014544927667

Fryer, R.G., & Levitt, S.D. (2002). *Understanding the black-white test score gap in the first two years of school.* (Working Paper No. 8975). Cambridge, MA: National Bureau of Economic Research.

Fuoco, L.W. (2007, August 29). Theories abound on boys' slow reading. *Pittsburgh Post-Gazette.* Retrieved from www.post-gazette.com/pg/07241/812969-44.stm

Furstenberg, F.F., Jr., & Cherlin, A.J. (1991). *Divided families: What happens to children when parents part.* Cambridge, MA: Harvard University Press.

Gambrell, L.B. (1996). Creating classroom cultures that foster reading motivation. *The Reading Teacher, 50*(1), 14–25.

Gambrell, L.B., Morrow, L.M., & Pressley, M. (Eds.). (2007). *Best practices in literacy instruction* (3rd ed.). New York: Guilford.

Gambrell, L.B., Palmer, B.M., Codling, R.M., & Mazzoni, S.A. (1996). Assessing motivation to read. *The Reading Teacher, 49*(7), 518–533. doi:10.1598/RT.49.7.2

Gambell, T.J., & Hunter, D.M. (1999). Rethinking gender differences in literacy. *Canadian Journal of Education, 24*(1), 1–16. doi:10.2307/1585767

Gans, H.J. (1995). *The war against the poor: The underclass and antipoverty policy.* New York: Basic.

Garvey, C. (1990). *Play* (Enlarged ed.). Cambridge, MA: Harvard University Press.

Gates, A. (1961). Sex differences in reading ability. *The Elementary School Journal, 61*(8), 431–434. doi:10.1086/459919

Gee, J.P. (1992). *The social mind: Language, ideology, and social practice.* New York: Bergin & Garvey.

Gee, J.P. (1996). *Social linguistics and literacies: Ideology in discourses* (2nd ed.). London: Taylor & Francis.

Geraci, P.M. (2003). Promoting positive reading discourse and self-exploration through a multi-cultural book club. *Journal of Correctional Education, 54*(2), 54–59.

Geschwind, N. (1965). Disconnexion syndromes in animals and man. *Brain, 88*(2), 237–294. doi:10.1093/brain/88.2.237

Gilliam, W.S., & Shahar, G. (2006). Prekindergarten expulsion and suspension: Rates and predictors in one state. *Infants and Young Children, 19*(3), 228–245.

Gonzalez, K.P., Field, T.M., Lasko, D., Harding, J., Yando, R., & Bendell, D. (1995). Adolescents from divorced and intact families. *Journal of Divorce & Remarriage, 23*(3/4), 165–176. doi:10.1300/J087v23n03_10

Gopnik, A., Meltzoff, A.N., & Kuhl, P.K. (2001). *The scientist in the crib: What early learning tells us about the mind.* New York: Perennial.

Gorski, P.C. (2003). Privilege and repression in the digital era: Rethinking the sociopolitics of the digital divide. *Race, Gender & Class, 10*(4), 145–176.

Gorski, P.C. (2008). The myth of the "culture of poverty." *Educational Leadership, 65*(7), 32–36.

Goswami, U. (1999). The relationship between phonological awareness and orthographic representation in different orthographies. In M. Harris & G. Hatano (Eds.), *Learning to read and write: A cross-linguistic perspective* (pp. 134–156). Cambridge, England: Cambridge University Press.

Gould, R. (2006). *Father and son read-aloud stories.* Carlsbad, CA: Big Guy.

Greig, A.D., Taylor, J., & MacKay, T. (2007). *Doing research with children* (2nd ed.). London: Sage.

Grigg, W., Daane, M., Jin, Y., & Campbell, J. (2003). *The nation's report card: Reading 2003, National Assessment of Educational Progress*. Washington, DC: National Center for Education Statistics.

Gurian, M., & Ballew, A.C. (2003). *The boys and girls learn differently action guide for teachers*. San Francisco: Jossey-Bass.

Gurian, M., & Stevens, K. (2005). *The minds of boys: Saving our sons from falling behind in school and life*. San Francisco: Jossey-Bass.

Guthrie, J.T., & Humenick, N.M. (2004). Motivating students to read: Evidence for classroom practices that increase reading motivation and achievement. In P. McCardle & V. Chhabra (Eds.), *The voice of evidence in reading research* (pp. 329–354). Baltimore: Paul H. Brookes.

Guthrie, J.T., Schafer, W.D., Von Secker, C., & Alban, T. (2000). Contribution of reading instruction and text resources to achievement and engagement in a statewide school improvement program. *The Journal of Educational Research, 93*(4), 211–225.

Guthrie, J.T., & Wigfield, A. (2000). Engagement and motivation in reading. In M.L. Kamil, P.B. Mosenthal, P.D. Pearson, & R. Barr (Eds.), *Handbook of reading research* (Vol. 3, pp. 403–422). Mahwah, NJ: Erlbaum.

Guthrie, J.T., Wigfield, A., Metsala, J., & Cox, K. (1999). Motivational and cognitive predictors of text comprehension and reading amount. *Scientific Studies of Reading, 3*(3), 231–256. doi:10.1207/s1532799xssr0303_3

Hadadian, A., & Merbler, J. (1995). Parents of infants and toddlers with special needs: Sharing views of desired services. *Infant-Toddler Intervention, 5*(41), 141–152.

Halpern, D.F. (2000). *Sex differences in cognitive abilities* (3rd ed.). Mahwah, NJ: Erlbaum.

Halpern, D.F. (2004). A cognitive-process taxonomy for sex differences in cognitive abilities. *Current Directions in Psychological Science, 13*(4), 135–139. doi:10.1111/j.0963-7214.2004.00292.x

Hammond, C., Linton, D., Smink, J., & Drew, S. (2007). *Dropout risk factors and exemplary programs*. Clemson, SC: National Dropout Prevention Center, Communities in Schools, Inc.

Harasty, J., Double, K.L., Halliday, G.M., Kril, J.J., & McRitchie, D.A. (1997). Language-associated cortical regions are proportionally larger in the female brain. *Archives of Neurology, 54*(2), 171–176.

Hart, B., & Risley, T. (1995). *Meaningful differences in the everyday experience of young American children*. Baltimore, MD: Paul H. Brookes.

Hedges, L.V., & Nowell, A. (1995). Sex differences in mental test scores, variability, and numbers of high-scoring individuals. *Science, 269*(5220), 41–45. doi:10.1126/science.7604277

Henderson, A., & Berla, N. (Eds.). (1994). *A new generation of evidence: The family is critical to student achievement*. Washington, DC: National Committee for Citizens in Education.

Herman, M. (1975). *Male-female learning achievement in eight learning areas: A compilation of selected assessment results*. Denver, CO: Education Commission of the States.

Heshusius, L. (1995). Listening to children: "What could we possibly have in common?" From concerns with self to participatory consciousness. *Theory Into Practice, 34*(2), 117–123.

Hoffman, M.L. (1991). Empathy, social cognition, and moral action. In W.M. Kurtines, J. Gewirtz, & J.L. Lamb (Eds.), *Handbook of moral behavior and development: Volume 1, Theory* (pp. 275–299). Hillsdale, NJ: Erlbaum.

Hofstetter, C.R., Sticht, T., & Hofstetter, C.H. (1999). Knowledge, literacy and power. *Communication Research, 26*(1), 58–80. doi:10.1177/009365099026001004

Holbrook, H.T. (1988). Sex differences in reading: Nature or nurture? *Journal of Reading, 31*(6), 574–576.

Horvath, T.L., & Wikler, K.C. (1999). Aromatase in developing sensory systems of the rat brain. *Journal of Neuroendocrinology, 11*(2), 77–84. doi:10.1046/j.1365-2826.1999.00285.x

Hull, G., & Schultz, K. (2002). *School's out! Bridging out-of-school literacies with classroom practice.* New York: Teachers College Press.

Huston, A.C., & Wright, J.C. (1998). Mass media and children's development. In W. Damon (Series Ed.), I.E. Sigel, & K.A. Renninger (Vol. Eds.), *Handbook of child psychology: Vol. 4. Child psychology in practice* (5th ed., pp. 999–1058). New York: Wiley.

Hyde, J.S. (2004). *Half the human experience: The psychology of women* (6th ed.). New York: Houghton Mifflin.

Iijima, M., Arisaka, O., Minamoto, F., & Arai, Y. (2001). Sex differences in children's free drawings: A study on girls with congenital adrenal hyperplasia. *Hormones and Behavior, 40*(2), 99–104. doi:10.1006/hbeh.2001.1670

International Reading Association. (2002). *Family-school partnerships: Essential elements of literacy instruction in the United States* (Position statement). Newark, DE: Author.

Jacklin, C.N., & Martin, I. (1999). Effects of gender on behavior and development, In M.D. Levine, W.B. Carey, & A.C. Crocker (Eds.), *Development-behavioral pediatrics* (3rd ed., pp. 100–106). Philadelphia: W.B. Saunders.

Jaeger, L., & Demetriadis, S.N. (2002). Book club on a budget. *School Library Journal, 48*(3), 47.

James, A.N. (2007). *Teaching the male brain: How boys think, feel, and learn in school* (3rd ed.). Thousand Oaks, CA: Corwin.

Jensen, E. (2006). *Enriching the brain: How to maximize every learner's potential.* San Francisco: Jossey-Bass.

Jimerson, S.R. (2001). Meta-analysis of grade retention research: Implications for practice in the 21st century. *School Psychology Review, 30*(3), 313–330.

Johns, J.L., & Lenski, S.D. (2005). *Improving reading: Strategies and resources* (4th ed.). Dubuque, IA: Kendall/Hunt.

Johnson, R. (2006). *Better dads, stronger sons: How fathers can guide boys to become men of character.* Grand Rapids, MI: Gleming H. Revell.

Jones, P., Gorman, M., & Suellentrop, T. (2004). *Connecting young adults and libraries: A how-to-do-it manual for librarians.* New York: Neal-Schuman.

Jusczyk, P.W. (2000). *The discovery of spoken language.* Cambridge, MA: MIT Press.

Karoly, L.A. (2001). Investing in the future: Reducing poverty through human capital investments. In S. Danzinger & R. Haveman (Eds.), *Understanding poverty* (pp. 314–356). New York: Russell Sage Foundation.

Karr-Morse, R., & Wiley, M.S. (1997). *Ghosts from the nursery: Tracing the roots of violence.* New York: Atlantic Monthly.

Keene, E.O., & Zimmermann, S. (1997). *Mosaic of thought: Teaching comprehension in a reader's workshop.* Portsmouth, NH: Heinemann.

Kidder, R.M. (1994). *Shared values for a troubled world: Conversations with men and women of conscience.* San Francisco: Jossey-Bass.

Kids and family reading report. (2008). New York: Scholastic. Retrieved May 17, 2008, from www.scholastic.com/aboutscholastic/news/kfrr08web.pdf

Kids Count. (2004). *2004 Kids Count data book : Moving youth from risk to opportunity .* Retrieved January 6, 2005, from www.aecf.org/upload/publicationfiles/da0000k218.pdf

Kimura, D. (1992). Sex differences in the brain. *Scientific American, 267*(3), 118–125.

Kindlon, D., & Thompson, M. (2000). *Raising Cain: Protecting the emotional life of boys.* New York: Ballantine.

Kipnis, A. (1999). *Angry young men: How parents, teachers, and counselors can help "bad boys" become good men.* San Francisco, CA: Jossey-Bass.

Kolb, B., Gibb, R., & Robinson, T.E. (2003). Brain plasticity and behavior. *Current Directions in Psychological Science, 12*(1), 1–5. doi:10.1111/1467-8721.01210

Kong, A., & Fitch, E. (2002). Using Book Club to engage culturally and linguistically diverse learners in reading, writing, and talking about books. *The Reading Teacher, 56*(4), 352–362.

Kragler, S., & Nolley, C. (1996). Student choices: Book selection strategies of fourth graders. *Reading Horizons, 36*(4), 354–365.

Krampe, E.M., & Fairweather, P.D. (1993). Father presence and family formation: A theoretical reformulation. *Journal of Family Issues, 14*(4), 572–591. doi:10.1177/019251393014004006

Kuhl, P.K., Stevens, E., Hayashi, A., Deguchi, T., Kiritani, S., & Iverson, P. (2006). Infants show a facilitation for native language phonetic perception between 6 and 12 months. *Developmental Science, 9*(2), F13–F21. doi:10.1111/j.1467-7687.2006.00468.x

Lamb, M.E. (1994). How fathers care for the next generation: A four-decade study. *Human Development, 37*(6), 385–387.

LeDoux, J. (1996). *The emotional brain: The mysterious underpinnings of emotional life.* New York: Simon & Schuster.

Lee, P.W. (1999). In their own voices: An ethnographic study of low-achieving students within the context of school reform. *Urban Education, 34*(2), 214–244. doi:10.1177/0042085999342005

Leventhal, T., & Brooks-Gunn, J. (2004). A randomized study of neighborhood effects on low-income children's educational outcomes. *Developmental Psychology, 40*(4), 488–507. doi:10.1037/0012-1649.40.4.488

Lewis, M. (1993). Self-conscious emotions: Embarrassment, pride, shame, and guilt. In M. Lewis & J. Haviland (Eds.), *The handbook of emotions* (pp. 563–573). New York: Guilford.

Livingstone, S. (2002). *Young people and new media: Childhood and the changing media environment.* Thousand Oaks, CA: Sage.

Lonsdale, M. (2003). *Impact of school libraries on reading achievement: A review of the research.* Melbourne, VIC: Australian Council for Educational Research.

Maccoby, E.E. (1998). *The two sexes: Growing up apart, coming together.* Cambridge, MA: Belknap.

Males, M. (2001). Debunking the 10 worst myths about America's teens. *Teacher Librarian, 28*(4), 300–310.

Marachi, R., Friedel, J., & Midgley, C. (2001, April). *"I sometimes annoy my teacher during math": Relations between student perceptions of the teacher and disruptive behavior in the classroom.* Paper presented at the annual meeting of the American Educational Research Association, Seattle, WA.

Martin, A.J. (2003). Boys and motivation. *The Australian Educational Researcher, 30*(3), 43–65.

Martin, C.L., & Halverson, C.F. (1987). The roles of cognition in sex role acquisition. In D.B. Carter (Ed.), *Current conceptions of sex roles and sex typing: Theory and research* (pp. 123–137). New York: Praeger.

Martinez, M., Roser, N.L., & Strecker, S. (1999). "I never thought I could be a star": A readers theatre ticket to fluency. *The Reading Teacher, 52*(4), 326–334.

McDevitt, T.M., & Ormrod, J.E. (2007). *Child development and education* (3rd ed.). Upper Saddle River, NJ: Pearson.

McFadden, D. (1998). Sex differences in the auditory system. *Developmental Neuropsychology, 14*(2/3), 261–298.

McGowan, M. (2008, March 10). Children's literature conference focuses on what boys like to read, books for boys. Retrieved May 15, 2008, from www.niu.edu/northerntoday/2008/march10/litconf.shtml

McQuillan, J., & Au, J. (2001). The effect of print access on reading frequency. *Reading Psychology, 22*(3), 225–248. doi:10.1080/027027101753170638

Millard, E. (1997). *Differently literate: Boys, girls, and the schooling of literacy.* London: Falmer.

Morisset, C.E., Barnard, K.E., & Booth, C.L. (1995). Toddlers' language development: Sex differences within social risk. *Developmental Psychology, 31*(5), 851–865. doi:10.1037/0012-1649.31.5.851

Morrow, L.M. (1992). The impact of a literature-based program on literacy achievement, use of literature and attitudes of children from minority backgrounds. *Reading Research Quarterly, 27*(3), 250–275. doi:10.2307/747794

Mullis, I.V.S., Martin, M.O., Gonzalez, E.J., & Kennedy, A.M. (2003). *PIRLS 2001 international report: IEA's study of reading literacy achievement in primary schools in 35 countries.* Chestnut Hill, MA: Boston College.

Mullis, I.V.S., Martin, M.O., Kennedy, A., & Foy, P. (2007). *PIRLS 2006 international report: IEA's progress in international reading literacy study in primary schools in 40 countries.* Chestnut Hill, MA: Boston College.

National Assessment of Educational Progress. (2004). *Long term trend assessment in reading and writing, 2004: Major results.* Retrieved July 29, 2006, from nces.ed.gov/nationsreportcard

National Assessment of Educational Progress. (2005). *The nation's report card.* Washington, DC: Author. Retrieved May 15, 2008, from nationsreportcard.gov/reading_math_2005/

National Center for Education Statistics. (2000). *Trends in educational equality of girls and women.* Washington, DC: U.S. Department of Education.

National Center for Education Statistics. (2001). *Entering kindergarten: Findings from the condition of education 2000.* Washington, DC: U.S. Department of Education Office of Educational Research and Improvement.

National Institute of Child Health and Human Development. (2000). *Report of the National Reading Panel. Teaching children to read: An evidence-based assessment of the scientific research literature on reading and its implications for reading instruction* (NIH Publication No. 00-4769). Washington, DC: U.S. Government Printing Office.

Nettles, S.M., Caughy, M.O., & O'Campo, P.J. (2008). School adjustment in the early grades: Toward an integrated model of neighborhood, parental, and child processes. *Review of Educational Research, 78*(1), 3–32. doi:10.3102/0034654307309917

Newkirk, T. (2002). *Misreading masculinity: Boys, literacy, and popular culture.* New York: Heinemann.

Opitz, M.F., & Rasinski, T.V. (2008). *Good-bye round robin: Twenty-five effective oral reading strategies.* Portsmouth, NH: Heinemann.

Organisation for Economic Co-operation and Development. (2001). *Knowledge and skills for life: First results from PISA 2000.* Paris: Author.

Owens, R.E. (2005). *Language development: An introduction* (6th ed.). Boston: Allyn & Bacon.

Perry, B.D., & Szalavitz, M. (2007). *The boy who was raised as a dog: And other stories from a child psychiatrist's notebook—What traumatized children can teach us about loss, love, and healing.* New York: Basic.

Peterson, K. (2002, January/February). Creating home-school partnerships. *Early Childhood News, 14*(4), 39–45.

Piaget, J., & Inhelder, B. (2000). *The psychology of the child.* New York: Basic.

Pintrich, P.R., & Schunk, D.H. (2002). *Motivation in education* (2nd ed.). Upper Saddle River, NJ: Pearson Education.

Pipher, M. (1996). *The shelter of each other: Rebuilding our families.* New York: Putnam.

Poest, C.A., Williams, J.R., Witt, D., & Atwood, M.E. (1989). Physical activity patterns of preschool children. *Early Childhood Research Quarterly, 4*(3), 367–376. doi:10.1016/0885-2006(89)90021-5

Pollack, W. (with Shuster, T.) (2000). *Real boys' voices.* New York: Random House.

Porpora, D.V. (2001). *Landscapes of the soul: The loss of moral meaning in American life.* New York: Oxford University Press.

Posner, M.I., & Petersen, S.E. (1990). The attention system of the human brain. *Annual Review of Neuroscience, 13*, 25–42. doi:10.1146/annurev.ne.13.030190.000325

Pottorff, D.D., Phelps-Zientarski, D., & Skovera, M.E. (1996). Gender perceptions of elementary and middle school students about literacy at home and school. *Journal of Research and Development in Education, 29*(4), 203–211.

Prensky, M. (2001a). Digital natives, digital immigrants part 1. *On the Horizon, 9*(5), 1–6. doi:10.1108/10748120110424816

Prensky, M. (2001b). Digital natives, digital immigrants part 2: Do they really think differently? *On the Horizon, 9*(6), 1–6. doi:10.1108/10748120110424843

Prince, J.M. (2008, May/June). Where the boys are. *Society of Children's Books Writers and Illustrators Bulletin, 9.*

Prior, J., & Gerard, M. (2007). *Family involvement in early childhood education: Research into practice.* Clifton Park, NY: Delmar Cengage Learning.

Pruett, K.D. (2000). *Fatherneed: Why father care is essential as mother care for your child.* New York: Free Press.

Ramey, C.T., & Ramey, S.L. (1998). Early prevention and early experience. *American Psychologist, 53*(2), 109–120. doi:10.1037/0003-066X.53.2.109

Ramey, C.T., & Ramey, S.L. (1999). *Right from birth: Building your child's foundation for life—Birth to 18 months.* New York: Goddard.

RAND Reading Study Group. (2002). *Reading for understanding: Toward an R&D program in reading comprehension.* Santa Monica, CA: Author.

Raphael, T.E., Florio-Ruane, S., & George, M. (2001). Book club plus: A conceptual framework to organize literacy instruction. *Language Arts, 79*(2), 159–169.

Rasinski, T.V. (2003). *The fluent reader: Oral reading strategies for building word recognition, fluency, and comprehension.* New York: Scholastic.

Ready, D., LoGerfo, L., Burkham, D., & Lee, V. (2005). Explaining girls' advantage in kindergarten literacy learning: Do classroom behaviors make a difference? *The Elementary School Journal, 106*(1), 21–38. doi:10.1086/496905

Renold, E. (2004). "Other" boys: Negotiating non-hegemonic masculinities in primary school. *Gender and Education, 16*(2), 247–266. doi:10.1080/09540250310001690609

Rideout, V.J., Vandewater, E.A., & Wartella, E.A. (2003). *Zero to six: Electronic media in the lives of infants, toddlers, and preschoolers.* The Henry J. Kaiser Family Foundation. Retrieved May 5, 2008, from www.kff.org/entmedia/upload/Zero-to-Six-Electronic-Media-in-the-Lives-of-Infants-Toddlers-and-Preschoolers-PDF.pdf

Roberts, D.F., Foehr, U.G., Rideout, V.., & Brodie, M. (1999). *Kids & media @ the new millennium.* Menlo Park, CA: Kaiser Family Foundation.

Roberts, L.C., & Blanton, P.W. (2001). "I always knew mom and dad loved me best": Experiences of only children. *Journal of Individual Psychology, 57*(2), 125–140.

Rosenblatt, L.M. (1978). *The reader, the text, the poem: The transactional theory of the literary work.* Carbondale: Southern Illinois University Press.

Rothenberger, A., & Banaschewski, T. (2004). Informing the ADHD debate. *Scientific American Mind, 14*(5), 50–55.

Rothstein, R. (2008). Whose problem is poverty? *Educational Leadership, 65*(7), 8–13.

Rowe, M.B. (1987). Wait-time: Slowing down may be a way of speeding up. *American Educator, 11*(1), 38–43, 47.

Rubin, K., Bukowski, W., & Parker, J.G. (1998). Peer interactions, relationships, and groups. In Damon, W. (Series Ed.), and N. Eisenberg (Ed.), *Handbook of child psychology: Vol. 3. Social, emotional, and personality development* (5th ed., pp. 619–700). New York: Wiley.

Rutter, M., Caspi, A., Fergusson, D., Horwood, L.J., Goodman, R., Maughan, B., et al. (2004). Sex differences in developmental reading disability: New findings from four epidemiological studies. *Journal of the American Medical Association, 291*(16), 2007–2012. doi:10.1001/jama.291.16.2007

Sadoski, M., & Paivio, A. (2000). *Imagery and text: A dual coding theory of reading and writing.* Mahwah, NJ: Erlbaum.

Samuels, F. (1943, April). Sex differences in reading achievement. *The Journal of Educational Research, 36*, 594–603.

Santrock, J.W. (2008). *Life-span development* (11th ed.). Boston: McGraw-Hill.

Sax, L. (2005). *Why gender matters: What parents and teachers need to know about the emerging science of sex differences.* New York: Doubleday.

Sax, L. (2007). *Boys adrift: The five factors driving the growing epidemic of unmotivated boys and underachieving young men.* New York: Basic.

Schank, R.C. (1995). *Tell me a story: Narrative and intelligence.* Evanston, IL: Northwestern University Press.

Schwarzchild, M. (2000). Alienated youth: Help from families and schools. *Professional Psychology, Research and Practice, 31*(1), 95–96. doi:10.1037/0735-7028.31.1.95

Scieszka, J. (2003). Guys and reading. *Teacher Librarian, 30*(3), 17–18.

Shaywitz, S.E. (2003). *Overcoming dyslexia: A new and complete science-based program for reading problems at any level.* New York: Knopf.

Shaywitz, S.E., Shaywitz, B.A., Fletcher, J.M., & Escobar, M.D. (1990). Prevalence of reading disability in boys and girls: Results of the Connecticut longitudinal study. *Journal of the American Medical Association, 264*(8), 998–1002. doi:10.1001/jama.264.8.998

Sherif, C.W. (1982). Needed concepts in the study of gender identity. *Psychology of Women Quarterly, 6*(4), 375–398. doi:10.1111/j.1471-6402.1982.tb01067.x

Shucard, J.L., & Shucard, D.W. (1990). Auditory evoked potentials and hand preference in 6-month-old infants: Possible gender-related differences in cerebral organization. *Developmental Psychology, 26*(6), 923–930. doi:10.1037/0012-1649.26.6.923

Sininger, Y.S., Cone-Wesson, B., & Abdala, C. (1998). Gender distinctions and lateral asymmetry in the low-level auditory brainstem response of the human neonate. *Hearing Research, 126*(1–2), 58–66. doi:10.1016/S0378-5955(98)00152-X

Sipe, L.R. (2001). Picturebooks as aesthetic objects. *Literacy Teaching and Learning, 6*(1), 23–42.

Skidmore, C. (2008). *Boys: A school report.* London: The Bow Group.

Smith, M.W., & Wilhelm, J.D. (2002). *"Reading don't fix no Chevys": Literacy in the lives of young men.* Portsmouth, NH: Heinemann.

Smith, M.W., & Wilhelm, J.D. (2006). *Going with the flow: How to engage boys (and girls) in their literacy learning.* Portsmouth, NH: Heinemann.

Smith, S. (2006). The reading behaviours of young successful boy readers in the classroom. *Journal of Reading and Writing, 1*(1), 65–82.

Sommers, C.H. (2000). *The war against boys: How misguided feminism is harming our young men.* New York: Simon & Schuster.

Stamm, J. (with Spencer, P.). (2007). *Bright from the start: The simple, science-backed way to nurture your child's developing mind from birth to age 3.* New York: Gotham.

Stanovich, K.E. (1986). Matthew effects in reading: Some consequences of individual differences in the acquisition of literacy. *Reading Research Quarterly, 21*(4), 360–407. doi:10.1598/RRQ.21.4.1

Stanovich, K.E. (2000). *Progress in understanding reading: Scientific foundations and new frontiers.* New York: Guilford.

Stanovich, K.E., & Cunningham, A.E. (1992). Studying the consequences of literacy within a literate society: The cognitive correlates of print exposure. *Memory & Cognition, 20*(1), 51–68.

Steen, F., & Owens, S.A. (2000, March). *Implicit pedagogy: From chase play to collaborative world-making.* Paper presented at the Evolution and Social Mind Speakers Series, University of California at Santa Barbara.

Stipek, D.J. (1993). *Motivation to learn: From theory to practice* (2nd ed.). Boston: Allyn & Bacon.

Stipek, D.J. (2002). *Motivation to learn: Integrating theory and practice* (4th ed.). Boston: Allyn & Bacon.

Stipek, D.J., & Seal, K. (2001). *Motivate minds: Raising children to love learning.* New York: Henry Holt.

Sullivan, M. (2003). *Connecting boys with books: What libraries can do.* New York: American Library Association.

Sum, A., Khatiwada, I., McLaughlin, J., & Tobar, P. (2007, March). *The educational attainment of the nation's young black men and their recent labor market experiences: What can be done to improve their future labor market and educational prospects.* Boston: Center for Labor Market Studies, Northeastern University.

Swick, K. (2003). Communication concepts for strengthening family-school-community partnerships. *Early Childhood Education Journal, 30*(4), 275–280. doi:10.1023/A: 1023399910668

Tallal, P. (2003). Language learning disabilities: Integrating research approaches. *Current Directions in Psychological Science, 12*(6), 206–211. doi:10.1046/j.0963-7214 .2003.01263.x

Taylor, B.M., Frye, B.J., & Maruyama, G.M. (1990). Time spent reading and reading growth. *American Educational Research Journal, 27*(2), 351–362.

Thompson, R.H., McKerchar, P.M., & Dancho, K.A. (2004). The effects of delayed physical prompts and reinforcement on infant sign language acquisition. *Journal of Applied Behavior Analysis, 37*(3), 379–383. doi:10.1901/jaba.2004.37-379

Tompkins, G.E. (2005). *Literacy for the 21st century: A balanced approach* (4th ed.). Upper Saddle River, NJ: Merrill Prentice Hall.

Tompkins, G.E., & McGee, L.M. (1986). Visually impaired and sighted children's emerging concepts about written language. In D.B. Yaden, Jr., & S. Templeton (Eds.), *Metalinguistic awareness and beginning literacy: Conceptualizing what it means to read and write* (pp. 259–275). Portsmouth, NH: Heinemann.

Topping, K., & Ehly, S. (Eds.) (1998). *Peer assisted learning.* Mahwah, NJ: Erlbaum.

Trelease, J. (2006). *The read-aloud handbook* (6th ed.). New York: Penguin.

Troia, G.A., Roth, F.P., & Graham, S. (1998). An educator's guide to phonological awareness: Assessment measures and interaction activities for children. *Focus on Exceptional Children, 31*(3), 1–12.

Tuman, D. (1999). Sing a song of sixpence: An examination of sex differences in the subject preference of children's drawings. *Visual Arts Research, 25*(49), 51–62.

Turbiville, V., & Marquis, J. (2001). Father participation in early childhood education programs. *Topics in Early Childhood Special Education, 21*(4), 223–241. doi:10.1177/ 027112140102100403

Turner, J. (1995). The influence of classroom contexts on young children's motivation for literacy. *Reading Research Quarterly, 30*(3), 410–441. doi:10.2307/747624

Tyre, P. (with Murr, A., Juarez, V., Underwood, A., Springen, K., & Wingert, P.). (2006, January 30). The trouble with boys. *Newsweek,* 44–52.

U.S. Chamber of Commerce, Center for Workforce Preparation. (2004). *A chamber guide to improving workplace literacy: Higher skills, bottom-line results.* Washington, DC: Author. Retrieved April 3, 2008, from www.uschamber.com/icw/publications/reports/training.htm

U.S. Department of Education. (1994). *Strong families, strong schools: Building community partnerships for learning.* Washington, DC: Author. (ERIC Document Reproduction Service No. ED 371909)

Viadero, D. (2006). Concern over gender gap shifting to boys. *Education Week, 25*(27), 1, 16–17.

Vygotsky, L. (1978). *Mind in society: The development of higher psychological processes* (M. Cole, V. John-Steiner, S. Scribner, & E. Souberman, Eds. & Trans.). Cambridge, MA: Harvard University Press.

Wasley, P.A., Hampel, R.L., & Clark, R.W. (1997). *Kids and school reform.* San Francisco: Jossey-Bass.

Weaver-Hightower, M. (2003). The "boy turn" in research on gender and education. *Review of Educational Research, 73*(4), 471–498. doi:10.3102/00346543073004471

Wenger, E. (1998). *Communities of practice: Learning, meaning, and identity.* Cambridge, MA: Cambridge University Press.

West, J.M. (2000). *Increasing parent involvement for student motivation.* Armidale, NSW, Australia: University of New England. (ERIC Document Reproduction Service No. ED 448411)

Wigfield, A., Eccles, J.S., Yoon, K.S., Harold, R.D., Arbreton, A., Freedman-Doan, K., et al. (1997). Change in children's competence beliefs and subjective task values across the elementary school years: A 3-year study. *Journal of Educational Psychology, 89*(3), 451–469. doi:10.1037/0022-0663.89.3.451

Wigfield, A., & Guthrie, J.T. (1997). Relations of children's motivation for reading to the amount and breadth of their reading. *Journal of Educational Psychology, 89*(3), 420–432. doi:10.1037/0022-0663.89.3.420

Willis, J. (2007). The gully in the "brain glitch" theory. *Educational Leadership, 64*(5), 68–73.

Wolf, M. (2007). *Proust and the squid: The story and science of the reading brain.* New York: HarperCollins.

Woodard, E. H., & Gridina, N. (2000). *Media in the home 2000: The fifth annual survey of parents and children.* Philadelphia: Annenberg Public Policy Center of the University of Pennsylvania.

Woolfolk, A.E. (2006). *Educational psychology* (10th ed.). Boston: Allyn & Bacon.

Worthy, J. (1998). "On every page someone gets killed!" Book conversations you don't hear in school. *Journal of Adolescent & Adult Literacy, 41*(7), 508–517.

Worthy, J., Moorman, M., & Turner, M. (1999). What Johnny likes to read is hard to find in school. *Reading Research Quarterly, 34*(1), 12–27. doi:10.1598/RRQ.34.1.2

Yopp, H.K., & Yopp, R.H. (2000). Supporting phonemic awareness in the classroom. *The Reading Teacher, 54*(2), 130–143. doi:10.1598/RT.54.2.2

Young, J.P., & Brozo, W.G. (2001). Conversations: Boys will be boys, or will they? Literacy and masculinities. *Reading Research Quarterly, 36*(3), 316–325. doi:10.1598/RRQ.36.3.4

Zambo, D. (2006). Using thought-bubble pictures to assess students' feelings about reading. *The Reading Teacher, 59*(8), 798–803. doi:10.1598/RT.59.8.7

Zambo, D. (2007). Using picture books to provide archetypes to young boys: Extending the ideas of William Brozo. *The Reading Teacher, 61*(2), 124–131. doi:10.1598/RT.61.2.2

Zambo, D., & Brem, S.K. (2004). Emotion and cognition in students who struggle to read: New insights and ideas. *Reading Psychology, 25*(3), 189–204. doi:10.1080/02702710490489881

Zirkel, S. (2002). Is there a place for me? Role models and academic identity among white students and students of color. *Teachers College Record, 104*(2), 357–376. doi:10.1111/1467-9620.00166

LITERATURE CITED

Aretha, D. (2005). *Steroids and other performance-enhancing drugs.* Berkeley Heights, NJ: Myreportlinks.com.

Barrett, J. (1982). *Cloudy with a chance of meatballs.* New York: Aladdin.

Braulick, C.A. (2005). *Blue Angels.* Mankato, MN: Coughlin Publishing.

Browne, A. (1995). *Willy the wimp.* New York: Walker.

Browne, A. (1996). *Willy the wizard.* New York: Knopf.

Childress, A. (1973). *A Hero Ain't Nothing but a Sandwich.* New York: Putnam.

Cline-Ransome, L. (2003). *Satchel Paige.* New York: Aladdin.

Dupre, R. (1993). *The wishing chair.* Minneapolis, MN: Lerner.

Henkes, K. (1993). *Owen.* New York: Greenwillow.

Henkes, K. (1996). *Lilly's purple plastic purse.* New York: Greenwillow.

Kellogg, S. (1992). *Mike Fink.* New York: Morrow Junior.

London, J. (1993). *The eyes of gray wolf.* San Francisco: Chronicle.

Long, M. (2003). *How I became a pirate.* San Diego, CA: Harcourt.

Martin, P.A.F. (2003). *Gray wolves.* New York: Children's Press.

McGowen, T. (1999). *African-Americans in the old west.* New York: Scholastic.

Pinkney, A.D. (1999) *Bill Pickett: Rodeo-ridin' cowboy.* New York: Voyager.

Polacco, P. (1995). *My ol' man.* New York: Philomel.

Roza, G. (2004). *The incredible story of aircraft carriers.* New York: PowerKids Press.

Savage, J. (2005). *Sammy Sosa.* New York: First Avenue Editions.

Scieszka, J. (1992). *The stinky cheese man.* New York: Viking.

Scieszka, J. (1995). *Math curse.* New York: Viking.

Scieszka, J. (1996). *The true story of the three little pigs.* New York: Puffin.

Scieszka, J., Shannon, D., Long, L., & Gordon, D. (2008). *Smash! Crash!* New York: Simon & Schuster.

Stewart, M. (2006). *Chicago Cubs.* Bel Air, CA: Norwood House.

Stone, L.M. (2003). *Gray wolves.* Minneapolis, MN: Lerner.